Global Marxism

Manchester University Press

Global Marxism

Decolonisation and revolutionary politics

Simin Fadaee

Manchester University Press

Published by Manchester University Press
Oxford Road, Manchester, M13 9PL

www.manchesteruniversitypress.co.uk

British Library Cataloguing-in-Publication Data
A catalogue record for this book is available from the British Library

ISBN 978 1 5261 7797 1   hardback
ISBN 978 1 5261 7798 8   paperback

First published 2024

The publisher has no responsibility for the persistence or accuracy of URLs for any external or third-party internet websites referred to in this book, and does not guarantee that any content on such websites is, or will remain, accurate or appropriate.

Typeset in Minion by R. J. Footring Ltd, Derby, UK
Printed in Great Britain
by TJ Books Ltd, Padstow

Contents

Introduction: rethinking Marxism's revolutionary potential

Karl Marx's global impact has been exceptional. In the words of the historian Eric Hobsbawm, Marxism is 'the most practically influential (and practically rooted) school of theory in the history of the modern world'.[1] The sociologist Göran Therborn sees Marxism as a perspective that has been 'surpassed in social significance – in terms of numbers of adherents – only by the great world religions'.[2] In particular, Marx's influence on decolonisation and revolutionary politics – a politics that raises hope supported by ideologies and utopian imaginaries and is carried out by groups that represent a political project – has been outstanding.[3] For much of the twentieth century, Marx's ideas not only inspired anti-colonialism but also provided the backbone of other movements for social justice around the world.[4] Although Marx did not theorise revolution in non-European contexts, the application of his methods within the social experience of the global South led to the development of Marxist revolutionary theory beyond Europe. These endeavours extended and indigenised Marxism – defined not as a sequence of fixed suppositions applied to differing realities irrespective of their specific content, but as 'a guide to action in a specific system of social relations which takes into account the always changing relationship of forces in an always changing world situation'.[5]

In the global South, Marxist revolutionary groups have toppled states and reordered social life by forming governments after successful revolutions or national liberation struggles. In other instances, Marxism has significantly influenced Southern countries' political and intellectual history. The Russian 1917 October Revolution was the first revolution driven by Marxism. It became a model for many anti-colonial struggles, and the post-revolutionary government supported these struggles actively.[6] During the Cold War, a large number of governments in the global South adhered to Marxist ideas, and a number of revolutionary movements that came to power had Marxist orientations. Today, Marxism inspires the Chinese Communist Party and the Maoist Naxalite movement in India, while in Nepal the Maoist party is the largest political party. In Latin America Marx has inspired contemporary policies of many countries, such as Cuba, Venezuela, Peru, Colombia and Bolivia, to name but a few. These examples show that Marx and Marxism have proved to be resilient in the global South, regardless of the circumstances, even during the long period marked by the widespread establishment of the neoliberal agenda.

On the global level, each new crisis that has exposed humans' vulnerability to capitalism – defined not as a system that originated in the global North and expanded to the periphery with the exact same characteristics but as a global set of relations that change in each specific context – has brought back Marx's name and his analysis of the destructive forces of the capitalist system. Most recently, Marxism experienced a renaissance as a result of the 2008 global financial crisis and an unprecedented climate crisis (alongside other crises, in health and food) that have brought humanity to a tipping point.

After the collapse of the Soviet Union, many rushed to dismiss Marxist thought as dead and irrelevant to the post-Cold War world, yet what we see today, more than 200 years after Marx's birth, is that his theory still provides the most 'compelling account of capitalism, outlining possible challenges to capitalism and envisioning alternatives to capitalism'.[7] This is 'the magic of Marxism', which combines diagnosing capitalism as the problem with providing in-depth knowledge about its flaws, as well as daring to propose an alternative to it, knowing that capitalism as a system constantly forecloses such possibility.[8] More than anything, the appeal of Marxism in the third decade of the twenty-first century must be understood as emerging from a context in which we are faced with the fundamental question of what would happen to humanity in the absence of an alternative to global capitalism.

Yet, Marx has been repeatedly accused of Eurocentrism, and some have referred to Marxism as a specifically white European model for social transformation and emancipation that does not resonate with the majority world outside of Europe and North America. The literary critic and political activist Edward Said even went so far as to criticise Marx's work as both racist and Orientalist.[9] Such criticisms, which mainly come from postcolonial approaches, have remained influential despite a large body of scholarship that has responded to such allegations.[10] The collapse of the Soviet Union, the cultural turn of the late twentieth century, and disenchantment with the trajectories of the postcolonial world after independence played an important role in the further development of such criticism against Marxist thought.

As an alternative approach, some postcolonial scholars have suggested a recovery of subaltern knowledges and ways of being. They have also emphasised aspects of the colonial legacy that go beyond economic analysis. These are all very valuable efforts. However, postcolonial scholars have also consistently referred to Marx's analysis of colonialism, his notion of the Asiatic mode of production and his theory of social transformation as serious drawbacks of his theory. With regard to colonialism, most critiques refer to the passage in *The Communist Manifesto* – first published in 1848 – where Marx and Engels declare their optimism that pre-capitalist societies such as China, which they describe as backward, would be forcibly modernised. Thus, it is not so difficult to see how their understanding of modernisation could be interpreted as the equivalent of Westernisation or Europeanisation. Moreover, in his 1853 essays to the *New York Daily Tribune* Marx optimistically praised the 'progressive' role of British colonialism in India. He predicted that in spite of the violence that would be involved in the process, the transformation to industrial capitalism would lead to the disappearance of colonial cruelties and pave the way for historical changes. He also described the pre-capitalist order of India within the framework of what he called the 'Asiatic mode of production', which was distinguished by the lack of private land ownership, the isolation of village communal living from urban areas, a unity between agriculture and manufacturing that hindered the development of production, and urban centres ruled by despots who controlled the villages and exploited the peasantry.

At first glance, these criticisms of Marx seem fair. However, a more accurate appraisal of Marx's thinking reveals that he reconsidered many of these aspects of his original analysis. Marx's perspective on the progressiveness of capitalism and colonialism had shifted by 1853, and by 1856–1857 he had become a critic of colonialism.[11] For example, when Indian people rose up against the British East Indian Company in 1857, Marx's support was unconditional. Similarly, he supported the millenarian Taiping Revolution (1850–1864) in China. Marx interpreted both of these as uprisings of 'great Asiatic nations' against British colonial rule.[12] Moreover, it was during this period that he started to sketch out – and partly incorporate in the *Grundrisse* – a multilinear theory of history. He demonstrated that Asian societies developed along pathways that were different from the successive mode of production he attributed to Western Europe. Furthermore, he included a comparison of communal social production in India with early Roman society and, in contrast to his earlier arguments regarding the despotic character of the Asiatic mode of production, he highlighted that they could be either despotic or democratic.[13]

Marx's later work on Ireland and the Civil War in the United States was complemented by his fascination with Russia and its revolutionary movements and rural communal life, which encouraged him to start learning Russian and engage with the debates surrounding the publication of *Capital* in Russia towards the end of his life. These developments in Marx's thinking and work are all indicators of the dynamism of his approach and the development of his ideas about colonialism, slavery, the peasantry, class and emancipation. For example, Marx showed how British colonialism in Ireland had led to that country's underdevelopment and uneven integration into the world market, resulting in famines and massive migration. Marx also concluded that the communal property forms he had regarded as despotic in the 1850s could in fact serve as points of resistance.[14] Regarding slavery, Marx not only referred to it as an important moment of primitive accumulation, but, in Chapter 6 of *Capital, Volume 1*, he occasionally referred to (in his phrase) 'wage slavery', which demonstrated that 'the (colonial) ghost of slavery continued … to haunt "free" wage labour'.[15] At the moment of its decline, slavery was paving the way for the organisation of wage labour and the emergence of working-class politics.[16] In fact, in 1890 Engels wrote that it had become apparent to both himself and

Marx that their initial materialist conceptualisation of history needed to be extended to studying the whole of history anew, which meant the history of the world beyond Europe.[17]

Any overall assessment of Marx therefore needs to take into consideration the entire scope of his work and not just a certain period or piece of writing.[18] It is also indispensable to admit that at the time of his death in 1883, Marx was still developing his theories. Travel was generally slow and difficult, which hindered him from going to the places he was writing about, and hence he could not observe their realities at first hand. In fact, it was only in 1882, towards the very end of his life, that he travelled to Algeria, a country under colonial rule. Thus, his work, similarly to any other intellectual, should be read and assessed in relation to the specific experiences of the social, cultural, historical and epistemological realities within which he lived.[19]

In the early 1850s, Marx drew most of his knowledge of colonialism from sources contained in the British Library. These were immensely Eurocentric and included British travel writing, parliamentary reports and theoretical treatises. Put simply, in this period Marx lacked access to sources that would have helped him develop a nuanced understanding of non-European and non-capitalist societies. By the 1860s he had produced a more accurate analysis. In Chapter 31 of *Capital, Volume 1*, 'The genesis of the industrial capitalist', Marx was clear that it is absolutely necessary to consider colonial relations as a fundamental aspect of capitalist relations. He referred to the discovery of gold and silver in the Americas and to the enslavement and extirpation of the Indigenous population of the continent as precursors of the 'plunder of India' and 'the conversion of Africa into a preserve for the commercial hunting of blackskins', which all, according to him, marked the beginning of the era of primitive accumulation and capitalist production.[20] Therefore, as the sociologist John Bellamy Foster and his colleagues have demonstrated, for Marx it was 'the plunder of the entire world, outside of Europe' that provided the 'chief moments of primary expropriation and the genesis of the industrial capitalist'.[21] In fact, Marx's analysis of colonialism and Indigenous populations became much more sophisticated than those of his contemporaries, and included gender relations, language and material culture in addition to analysis of various forms and relations of property, production and exchange.[22]

In addition, Marx's revision between 1872 and 1875 of the first volume of *Capital* for the French translation, as well as clarifications he made regarding the relevance of some of his arguments to Europe alone and not all countries, constitute an important effort to show that he did not regard Western European history as a universal model for development.[23]

Finally, the political economist Lucia Pradella has argued that a close reading of Marx's notebooks demonstrates that, from the very beginning of his economic studies, Marx was concerned with the relationship between capitalism, colonialism and world history, which proved to be essential for developing his labour theory of value and providing an analysis that incorporated interconnected global development trajectories.[24] That explains why, in his critique of political economy in *Capital*, he regarded the accumulation of capital as a globalising system that incorporates diverse forms of exploitation and oppression and is dependent on a global working class.[25] This expansive understanding of the roots of capital provided a platform for international solidarity and reveals a 'civilizational alternative' beyond Eurocentrism.[26] According to Pradella, this global outlook not only made Marx's critique of political economy very dynamic but also enabled him to show a clear relationship between capitalism and imperialism, particularly with regard to the latter's implications for capitalism as an international system.[27] Moreover, Marx's analysis of the world market and his emphasis on the position of England in it paved the way for the extension of debates on imperialism by Marxists such as Rosa Luxemburg and Vladimir Lenin.[28]

In spite of the complexity of Marx's analysis of capitalism, postcolonial theory has remained critical, even dismissive of Marxism. This is because most proponents of the theory reject all narratives that are the result of the post-Enlightenment European history and so they naturally reject Marxism's theory of capitalism and social transformation.[29] There is no doubt that Europe needs to be decentred and provincialised,[30] but postcolonial theorists' tendency to deny that capitalism is the basis of European power, hegemony and global expansion reveals a serious flaw of culturalism in postcolonial arguments.

In fact, refusing the fundamental role of capital in structuring our societies and lives 'renders impossible the cognitive mapping that must be the point of departure for any practice of resistance', as the historian Arif Dirlik has argued.[31] This has had serious implications for understanding the actual nature of anti-colonial struggles, leading some postcolonial theorists to repudiate any Marxist inspiration or socialist goals altogether.[32] At the same time, it seems that more recent postcolonial thinkers have forgotten that theory should be a guide to action and, following Lenin, that, more than anything, it needs to tell us 'what is to be done'.[33] For these theorists, anti-colonial, anti-racism or anti-inequality movements are to be understood as a response to questions of identity, and they ignore the fundamental interrelations that exist between capitalism, colonialism and racism.

In his *Postcolonial Theory and the Specter of Capital*, the sociologist Vivek Chibber has provided one of the most powerful criticisms of postcolonial theory's approach to capitalism.[34] Postcolonial theorists and particularly those of the Subaltern Studies Collective have argued that there is a fundamental difference between the global North and the South and that these differences lie in the nature of bourgeoisie, in the power relations produced by capitalism and in the nature of political actors and their psychology. Chibber offers a deep analysis of these claims and argues that although differences exist between the trajectories of capitalist development in the North and the South, they are not fundamental and, therefore,

> we are permitted to consider the possibility that the theories emerging from the European experience might well be up to the task of capturing the basic structure of Eastern development in the modern epoch. Instead of being entirely different forms of society, the West and the non-West would, according to this perspective, turn out to be variants of the same species. Further, if they are indeed variations of the same basic form, the theories generated by the European experience would not have to be overhauled or jettisoned, but simply modified.[35]

Chibber shows that, in order to avoid economic reductionism, postcolonial theorists have fallen into the trap of eliminating economic analysis from the picture they provide. As he puts it, 'it is surely problematic to see capital lurking behind every social phenomenon, but it is no less objectionable to deny its salience where it is in fact a relevant causal agent'.[36] In contrast to what has been argued by postcolonial theory, Chibber shows that capitalism is not only compatible with social difference but also actually systematically (re)produces it.[37] Hence the arguments about the homogenising tendencies of Marxian analysis raised by postcolonial theory are not valid. Chibber suggests that the project of provincialising Europe[38] should focus on demonstrating how the universal logic of capital and social agents' universal interest in well-being (which drives them to resist capital's expansion) have 'different intensities' and 'different registers' in various parts of the world.[39]

It is in fact Marx's analysis of the universal logic of capital and the universal interest of social agents in well-being (and therefore resistance to capital) that can help explain why Marxism has been embraced by revolutionaries in such diverse places as China, Iran, Cuba and Ghana. In fact, Marxism is the only theory that has systematically and over a long period inspired revolutionary thought throughout the global South. Lenin's development of Marxism at the dawn of the October Revolution later provided a much-needed theoretical tool for Southern revolutionaries, who on many occasions were materially supported by the Communist International (Comintern).[40] It is fair to say that the October Revolution significantly contributed to the transformation of European Marxism into global Marxism.[41] Lenin, in his speech at the Second Congress of the Comintern, referred to it as a 'World Congress', due to the presence of representatives of revolutionaries from around the world.[42]

In *Imperialism, the Highest Stage of Capitalism*, first published in 1917, Lenin argued that capitalism in Europe had reached its limits, and in order to expand it needed to gain access to new sources of raw materials and cheap labour as well as new markets and sources of investment. This would be possible only through colonisation and he therefore concluded that colonisation was integral to the process of capitalist expansion. The profit extracted from the colonies by Europe improved the living standard of the European working class and therefore hindered the revolution that Marx and Engels had predicted. Any uprising in the colonies that impeded the flow of profit to Europe would, according to Lenin, revolutionise the European working class. This would assist the world revolutionary struggle and ultimately lead to the end of the exploitative imperialist international economic system. Until the end of his life Lenin constantly repeated the significance of the alliance between the national liberation movements and the European working-class movement for the success of world revolution.[43] Lenin's analysis had a far-reaching impact on anti-colonial struggles. As the academic Nick Knight explains, it promoted an understanding of anti-colonial struggles as part of a world revolution instead of as localised and disparate national struggles.[44] Interestingly, even anti-colonial leaders who did not agree with the Soviet leadership found Lenin's theory of imperialism to be 'a powerful intellectual weapon with which to attack colonial rule'.[45] However, being part of the world revolution was only one aspect of revolutionary politics in the ex-colonies; modifying Marxism so that it could grapple with the specificity of their particular context was just as important. This latter effort led to the rise of numerous revolutionary thinkers and practitioners in the global South, a selection of whom are discussed in this book.

Marxism helped Jawaharlal Nehru combine nationalism and socialism and reconstruct nationalist thought by situating it within the framework of an ideology. During the struggle for Indian independence, he focused his efforts on moving the ideology of the Indian National Congress (INC) towards socialism. After independence, his attempts to combine Marxism and nationalism remained confined to policy reforms.

In stark contrast, his Vietnamese counterpart Hồ Chí Minh introduced a revolutionary path for his people that followed a Leninist two-stage revolutionary process. He also emphasised the significance of national independence and coalition building; he asserted that peasants were fundamental to the Vietnamese context and argued that revolutionary processes needed a clear ideology, organisation and future vision.

China's Mao Zedong intervened in Marxist revolutionary theory by centring the peasantry as the main drivers of the revolution and asserting the significance of ideology in defining class instead of defining it solely in relation to the means of production. Moreover, he extended the issue of revolutionary consciousness to cultural matters and defined contradiction as an essential element of all societies, which helped him justify the idea of permanent revolution.

Kwame Nkrumah tried to develop Lenin's analysis of imperialism to a new level by incorporating it into the context of neo-colonial Africa (focusing on Ghana). Nkrumah's approach to socialism was associated with 'conscience', which, more than anything, is about the reconstruction of social cohesion. His socialist pan-Africanism became inseparable from the spirit of care and solidarity that traditionally existed in Africa.

Amílcar Cabral led Guinea-Bissau and Cape Verde to independence by emphasising the significance of the mode of production as the motive force of history. He demonstrated that national liberation required a change in both the mode of production and neo-colonial structures. Cabral saw the role of the national petite bourgeoisie as central to this transformation, and he consistently asserted the importance of culture and its relation to national liberation struggle.

Frantz Fanon developed a dialectical analysis of the colonial subject's psychological condition in relation to colonialism and the culture of empire. Based on his experience within the Algerian national liberation movement, Fanon's primary concern was the interconnection of racism, colonialism and capitalism, and manifestations of these intersections. For Fanon, it was the broad category of 'the wretched of the earth' who would ultimately bring down the capitalist system.

Ernesto 'Che' Guevara developed his theory of *foco*, a revolutionary situation that can be created in rural areas with highly trained guerrilla fighters, as a revolutionary strategy for armed movements in the global South. In addition, he focused on the political economy of the transition to socialism in Cuba and the significance of the emergence of the 'new man' (*hombre nuevo*) that each human being would become in the development of socialism.

In Iran, Ali Shariati became preoccupied with the Islamisation of Marxism and the Marxification of Islam. He reconstructed the entire history of Islam and demonstrated that social justice and equality were inherent values in Shia Islam. His 'red Shiism' spread awareness of multiple levels of exploitation and injustice in Iranian society.

Rafael Sebastián Guillén Vicente, who is widely known by his *nom de guerre* Subcomandante Insurgente Marcos (often shortened to Subcomandante Marcos), revitalised the Marxist political language in the post-Soviet era in an innovative way that merged with the literary traditions of Latin Americans and the political reality of Indigenous people. His encounter with the Indigenous Mayans and the subsequent rise of the Zapatista Army of National Liberation in southern Mexico led to the emergence of one of the most inspiring anti-capitalist social movements of the late twentieth century. This movement is ongoing and, unlike the other figures in the book, Marcos is still alive.

The twentieth-century history of Marxism has shown that, rather than being a rigid set of propositions, it has been situated in ways that reflect local conditions and contexts of mobilisation. As Marx himself noted, people make their own history under the circumstances they encounter and inherit from the past. These political, social, economic and cultural conditions determine how a theoretical tradition can be indigenised. The objective of this book is primarily, but not exclusively, to make available to a large community of readers, the lives, ideas and legacies of a selection of revolutionary figures from the global South who have played an exceptional role in contributing to counter-hegemonic change. For these thinkers and practitioners of revolutionary politics, Marxism provided a guide to action. They all played a significant role in the revolutionary politics of at least one specific country in the global South in the twentieth century and advanced Marxist theory in one way or another. Their ideas and visions certainly were not born in isolation but benefited from their experiences and life trajectories as well as the broader economic, social and political contexts (both national and international) in which they lived. Importantly, not all of these revolutionaries identified as Marxists, but Marxism did provide a methodology and a framework for developing their revolutionary politics.

Although these revolutionaries have been the subjects of numerous books, there is no single book that discusses all of them together. In this volume I focus on the impact of Marxism on their thought processes and ideologies, and show how each of them had a unique encounter with Marx. In some instances, their political innovations have generated a distinctive ideology, such as Maoism or Nkrumahism. However, these ideologies or bodies of revolutionary thought are not rigid and inflexible but have been subject to constant revision. Above all, these political innovations should be seen as diverse examples of the global South's contribution to revolutionary theory.

The book traces the history of each revolutionary and the movements with which they are associated. I begin each chapter by presenting their life trajectory and how they came to Marxism. I then analyse those aspects of Marxism that each thinker adapted before situating them in their social, political and historical contexts to demonstrate how local particularities led to their unique approaches to adapting and innovating

Marxist ideas. Some of the contexts will already be familiar, but others are unknown or less well known to the broad range of readers I hope this book will reach. At the end of each chapter, I discuss the legacies of each revolutionary, alongside their ideas and their impact beyond their historical and local contexts. The chapters are not long and do not presuppose any specialist knowledge. They connect the personal, historical and ideological characteristics that made these revolutionaries influential figures of twentieth-century decolonisation and revolutionary politics, and they show how their victories and failures have shaped the world of the twenty-first century in profound ways. The chapters appear in chronological order, based on the birth date of the revolutionary, to reflect the particular local and global challenges they had to respond to with specific forms of political engagement. I believe this way of encountering history and theory resonates more with individuals' experiences and lives, and makes history and theory accessible.

The figures presented in this book provide exemplary cases of how the conditions and historical circumstances in which one lives can determine one's path. Moreover, bringing together the biographical sketches of these figures allows one to see more clearly the intersections and convergences between them. For example, Mao Zedong and Hồ Chí Minh were both revolutionary leaders from Asia who were convinced of the revolutionary potential of the peasantry, yet neither denied the significant role of the urban proletariat. Mao was a prolific writer who wrote about a number of philosophical issues. In contrast, Hồ's writings are narrower and focus on the anti-colonial struggle in Vietnam. This is mostly because he was acting in an actual colonial situation, but Mao's context also allowed him to exercise a broad criticism of the West and its attempt to expand its political and economic hegemony over China. Moreover, Hồ needed to address a French-speaking audience, the citizens of the metropole responsible for the colonisation of his homeland. Both Mao Zedong and Hồ Chí Minh sought broad-based support, but while Mao focused more on class interest, nationalism played a very important role for Hồ in seeking such support. Hồ remained in close contact with the Comintern throughout his life but Mao's context allowed him to act independently whenever he felt it was necessary.[46]

The individuals discussed in the book remain embedded in their own context. While some were inspired or influenced by their predecessors, they remained explicitly engaged with Marxism as a metanarrative and a methodology. It was, in fact, not their concern to remain in close conversation with previous modifications of Marxism by their revolutionary counterparts. This is because each of them experienced a different social reality, albeit with some similarities. For example, both Che Guevara and Ali Shariati took great interest in Fanon. However, not much systematic engagement with Fanon is to be found in their revolutionary theories. In 1963, when Amílcar Cabral and his comrades began their armed struggle, they were not particularly familiar with the writings of Che Guevara or Mao Zedong. According to Cabral, such knowledge would be of only secondary importance anyway because the success of the struggle against the Portuguese in Guinea could only emerge from the distinct context of the country, including its people and history. Moreover, he argued that each liberation movement must function in harmony with the specific stage reached by the society within which it arises.[47]

Edward Said showed how theory travels in time and space,[48] and the travelling tendencies of Marxist theory among Southern revolutionaries provides an outstanding example. Examining the transnational travel and translation of Marxism in different times and spaces, the book engages in what the academic Fadi A. Bardawil calls 'fieldwork in theory',[49] that is, looking 'into the different social lives of theory'. It asks not only how Marxism helps us understand decolonisation and revolutionary politics but also how it has attracted revolutionaries and engendered political practice and future visions. The data collected for the book consists of primary and secondary materials. The primary materials include revolutionary figures' major speeches and writings. The reader will realise that in some chapters I frequently draw on direct quotations from such texts. This is to provide a more nuanced sense of the discussions at hand. The secondary materials consist of studies by scholars on these revolutionaries.

Although the protagonists of this book are all male, this does not mean that women played no role in the production, circulation and practice of the ideas discussed here. Therefore, I have made a conscious attempt to highlight the role of women wherever they emerge in the course of the stories. Some important female historical figures I came across in the course of my research certainly warrant great attention in future. In contrast to their male revolutionary counterparts, these women never became particularly visible in the transformation of the societies within which they lived and worked, and, thus, it is a much more challenging task to assemble a meaningful and representative sample. That task is especially difficult given that many women had to disguise their identities to be heard or remain safe within the dominant patriarchal revolutionary culture.

Moving forwards

The great Marxist debate that enriched many social scientific disciplines in the 1960s had completely vanished by the turn of the twenty-first century. Although academia has seen a small revival of Marxism since the 2008 financial crisis,[50] much social scientific work has remained steadfastly focused on narrow and empirical questions. While there is definitely merit in analysis of any aspect of social life, it is very problematic for social sciences to ignore the big-picture questions of our time. One of the most distressing examples of such ignorance can be seen in the decolonial turn in social sciences in recent years. A topic which more than anything needs to be driven by the big-picture questions has fallen into the trap of 'metaphorisation',[51] using decolonisation as an 'empty signifier' for many things.[52] Decolonial perspectives need to systematically engage with global Marxism and its relationship to anti-colonial movements and revolutionary struggles. This new way of thinking about decolonisation would not only challenge problematic and homogenising definitions of decolonisation in academia but would help us envision a world beyond colonialism. As the historian C. L. R. James writes in his seminal work *Nkrumah and the Ghana Revolution*, 'colonialism is alive and will continue to be alive until another *positive doctrine* takes its place'.[53]

Most critiques concerned with decolonisation debates have rightly emphasised the Eurocentric history and development of social sciences, and the consequent neglect of the history and intellectual traditions of the global South. Numerous solutions have been proposed to overcome this problem: some scholars have argued that social sciences need to rethink their origins and go beyond Eurocentric accounts of modernity and history,[54] while others argue that Southern theory and traditions should be introduced into social scientific textbooks and discussions.[55] In both *Epistemologies of the South* and *The End of the Cognitive Empire*, the sociologist Boaventura de Sousa Santos has argued that a focus on the sociology of absence, that is, the experience and resistance of various groups against capitalism, colonialism and patriarchy, is necessary in social sciences' decolonisation efforts.[56]

Although these approaches provide some useful insights for a decolonial turn, Priyamvada Gopal's and Mahvish Ahmad's recent interventions provide convincing reasoning that what actually is missing from the decolonisation debates is a close engagement with questions and issues that arise from anti-colonial movements and *actual* political struggles against colonialism. The academic Gopal draws on her seminal book *Insurgent Empire*[57] and criticises (in a later article) the correspondence of decolonisation debates with 'any form of critical engagement with race and representation, or indeed, the mildest of curricular reforms'.[58] She instead advocates 'reframing discussions of decolonisation in the light of anticolonial thought – as the theory and practice of anticolonialism', which not only 'gives grounding, heft and direction' to the discussions but also enables 'rich questions to be posed and answered towards the wider horizon of making another world possible'.[59] Gopal goes so far as to say that the insurgency of the colonised in their liberation struggles and the formal ending of empire as well as the vast literature of anti-colonial thought threaten 'to overwhelm "decolonisation's" current academic currency as shorthand for reforms'.[60]

The sociologist Ahmad draws attention to the point that, although someone like Fanon, who was actually engaged in anti-colonial movements, belonged to the first wave of critiques of colonialism, the later wave of criticism, that is, the postcolonial turn, 'turned its back on the connections forged by anti-colonial thinkers'.[61] Ahmad is sympathetic to Santos's approach to the sociology of absence and his dialogue with other decolonial thinkers such as María Lugones and Anibal Quijano in giving voice to and legitimising knowledge from movements and struggles from the global South.[62] However, she criticises Santos's conceptualisation of the global South as an epistemological entity and not a geographical one that has in one way or another experienced colonial and imperial rule.[63] Ahmad argues that 'the Global South as geography is a direct product of empire',[64] but in fact some forms of hierarchies and associated struggles against them have their origins in the pre-colonial era (e.g. caste and anti-caste struggles), even though they might have been exacerbated through the encounter with the West. Therefore, although these issues are definitely related to social justice, Ahmad insists that discussions on decolonisation need to remain focused on those struggles in the geographical South that were and have been counter-hegemonic and directly opposed to colonial and imperial rule. She condemns putting together everything possible in the name of decolonisation. Building on both Gopal's and Ahmad's points, I argue that, as the contributions of the individuals in this book show, Marxism is inseparable from anti-colonial thought and practice, and therefore the rejoining of Marxism and debates on decolonisation is imperative.

In his recent interventions, the sociologist Michael Burawoy has suggested an initial reconstruction of the sociological canon by introducing the life and work of W. E. B. Du Bois (1868–1963), a Marxist and an African-American scholar.[65] The author of numerous masterpieces on race and the slave trade, such as *The Philadelphia Negro* (1899) and *Black Reconstruction in America* (1935), Du Bois's fierce anti-colonialism made him a leader in all five Pan-African Congresses from 1900 to 1945. These engagements led to the publication of his 1947 treatise *The World and Africa*.[66] According to Burawoy,[67] Marx and Du Bois, as well as Max Weber and Émile Durkheim, all reflected on various dimensions of raw capitalism – the main force behind the creation of empires – and as we are returning to a similar era of raw capitalism,[68] Burawoy suggests that incorporating Du Bois within the canon will forge: (1) a global and historical perspective on capitalism centred around race, the slave trade, colonialism and imperialism; (2) a moral science, centred around the 'changing limits of the possible'; (3) a reflexive science that situates social scientists within the world and their fields of study; (4) an interdisciplinary science that recognises the importance of blending social sciences with history and humanities; and (5) a public engagement that pushes social scientists to leave their 'academic cocoon' and engage with the world.[69]

Such historical engagement with Du Bois has many advantages for contemporary discussions on capitalism and decolonisation. However, the most interesting aspect of such an encounter with his Marxist writings on issues of his time (the end of the nineteenth century and beginning of the twentieth century) is that it would provide an excellent example of what Burawoy calls 'living Marxism'.[70] Marxism 'remains a living tradition' which 'revitalizes itself through taking on the new challenges that history throws up, challenges that are deliberately chosen'.[71] Marxism as a tradition resembles

> a tree with roots, trunk, branches, twigs, and foliage. Its growth has an 'internal logic' of its own founded in the roots, the 'fundamental' writings of Marx and Engels. But it also possesses an 'external' logic responsive to the climate and winds of the time.[72]

In other words, context impacts the way we embrace Marxism, but it also inspires new questions that need to be answered to tackle today's problems as well as those of the future.

My hope is that the knowledge presented in this book can revive something of the past in the imagination of contemporary revolutionary thinkers. Indeed, the issues addressed by the revolutionaries in this book remain extremely relevant today – combating imperialism, inequality, poverty, hunger and injustice. Moreover, through their views and work emerged a noble vision for the future of different nations and regions, a vision that is still cherished by many and has laid the foundations on which present politics and struggle have acted. This point is very significant in that it addresses the most challenging question of our time, of how to create a viable alternative to capitalism. This does not mean that the works and ideas presented here can immediately provide an answer to that question, but they can inspire and energise those of us in search of an alternative vision. More concretely, in this moment of crises and retrogression, we should ask what we can learn from the creative use of Marxian categories. As Hobsbawm wrote, 'each generation discovers not only Marx but its own Marx'.[73] So, the question is: what does the Marx of our generation and time look like?

I began this introduction by writing about the success and resilience of Marxism in the global South in the twentieth century and beyond. I now end by reiterating this point. Adam Mayer, an academic and the author of *Naija Marxisms*, an excellent book on the immense role of Marxism in Nigeria and West Africa from the late 1940s to the present, has argued that, given the constant presence of Marx and Marxism in the global South for the past decades, it is Eurocentric to think that Marxism is dead.[74] I would like to complement this argument by saying that it is in fact Eurocentric to claim that Marxism is Eurocentric, because this entails dismissing the cornerstone of some of the most transformative movements and revolutionary projects of recent human history. Instead of making such sweeping claims, a more fruitful engagement with history would instead urge us to learn from the experiences of the global South with Marxism, and ask what we can learn from Marxism's global relevance. This book adds to the growing call to reconnect with Marxism as a framework for analysing global capitalism's multiple crises and the prospects for revolutionary change but also as the basis for reimagining a world beyond capitalism. I hope it will familiarise more people – whether students, academics or activists – with the important ideas developed by the Southern revolutionaries discussed here, address the vital questions of our time and encourage further attempts to rethink contemporary revolutionary politics.

Chapter 1

Jawaharlal Nehru: a living force in the tremulous world

Jawaharlal Nehru (1889–1964) was a leader of India's independence movement and subsequently served as its first prime minister after India's independence from the British Raj (1858–1947) until his death. Many consider him the founder of the modern Indian state. He influenced India's progressive thinkers for years and inspired generations of nationalists in Asia and Africa. He has been referred to as a Marxist, a socialist who was committed to civil liberties and a radical who followed a path of non-violence.[1] In 1927, while in Europe, Nehru proclaimed himself a socialist. From then onwards, Marxism was the constitutive element in Nehru's thought, which he tried to adapt to the Indian condition throughout his political career. He made an earnest attempt to define socialism as widely as possible, to make it acceptable to Indian politicians as well as the masses. With the help of Marxism, Nehru combined nationalism and socialism. In fact, he reconstructed nationalism by reformulating it within the framework of an ideology. During the struggle for independence, his efforts focused on moving the ideology of the Indian National Congress, the party that he led, from a prevailing nationalism towards socialism; after independence, his efforts to combine Marxism and nationalism remained confined to policy reforms.

What held Nehru's thought together was a set of humanist values aimed at improving the welfare of his people.[2] The three basic doctrines of his politics remained socialism, democracy and secularism.[3] At the same time, he kept an internationalist outlook. Nehru was one of the most prominent spokes-people for socialist ideas in India, although he never became a member of any socialist organisation. He made socialism a respectable doctrine among middle-class nationalist intellectuals.[4] However, according to many, Nehru remained half-Marxist and half-liberal throughout his political career. He once stated that it was challenging to impose socialism in India 'because most Indians were not socialists'.[5] What is significant, though, is his 'appropriation of Marxism in the service of a nationalism that was not Marxist'.[6]

Revolutionary pathways[7]

Nehru was born on 14 November 1889 in Allahabad, a city in the now north Indian state of Uttar Pradesh. His father was a successful and affluent barrister who was himself twice the President of the Indian National Congress (henceforth Congress). Nehru grew up in a privileged atmosphere with private tutors as his educators. In his autobiography he wrote that the Russo-Japanese War and Japan's victories made him enthusiastic about nationalistic ideas: 'I mused of Indian freedom and Asiatic freedom from the thraldom of Europe'.[8] In 1905, he began studying at a prestigious school in England, where he was introduced to the thought of the Italian revolutionary Giuseppe Garibaldi, whom he began to admire. Although belonging to a different context and time, he found Garibaldi's ideas suitable for India. In his autobiography he wrote that 'visions of similar deeds in India came before me, of a gallant fight for freedom, and in my mind India and Italy got strangely mixed together'.[9] Nehru graduated from the University of Cambridge in natural sciences in 1910 and moved to London to study law afterwards. During these years, he educated himself in politics, economics and history, and thus began his intellectual attachment to socialism. He became particularly interested in learning about the Fabian Society – a British socialist organisation that advocates principles of democratic socialism – and the scholars associated with it.

Nehru returned to India in 1912 and spent a few years in Allahabad practising law. In 1916 he married Kamala Kaul, a Kashmiri and the mother of Indira Gandhi, the future prime minister. Kamala was a political activist and remained Nehru's close companion until her death. Although she died at a young age – in 1936 due to tuberculosis – she participated in numerous phases and campaigns of the independence movement, particularly focusing on organising women. Due to her popularity (among women in particular), she was arrested a few times by the British. In the same year that Nehru married Kamala, he became involved in the Indian Home Rule movement, which played a significant role in the path towards Indian independence. That movement had many similarities to other home rule movements of the time, which advocated that citizens of a colony should govern themselves. In 1920, Nehru joined the non-cooperation movement and led it in his own province. Non-cooperation had been launched by the anti-colonial activist Mahatma Gandhi (no relation to Indira), who sought to persuade all Indians to withdraw their labours from any activity that benefited the British government and economy. Around the same time, the Congress, with which Nehru had a close association at this time, withdrew its support for British reforms following the Rowlatt Act – a piece of legislation passed by the Imperial Legislative

Council in Delhi which gave the Council inordinate power to detain and incarcerate Indian people. This was the start of Nehru's involvement in national politics. Influenced by and following Gandhi's emphasis on the Indian peasantry, Nehru's leading role in the non-cooperation movement in his province brought him into direct contact with rural India. His visits to villages where he observed the misery of the peasantry in rural India (whom he described as the 'naked hungry mass') during this time not only opened his eyes to the plight of the majority of his people but also made him aware of the enormous ignorance that existed among the Indian elite about the country they were attempting to liberate. These visits to villages were a principal source of Nehru's interest in socialism and nationalism in later years.

Nehru attended meetings of the Congress for the first time in 1912, but it was only after the entry of Mahatma Gandhi into Indian politics, following his return from South Africa in 1915, that he became active in the party.[10] In 1924, Nehru began to play a key role in the Congress as its principal spokesman on nationalism and internationalism. He travelled extensively to various countries to seek allies. During his travels in Europe, Nehru enthusiastically visited trade unions and labour organisations, mines and factories. He witnessed strikes, class injustices and violations of workers' rights. The hardships of the striking miners he visited in 1926 in Derbyshire in England particularly influenced him.

In February 1927, Nehru was invited to attend the Congress of the League against Imperialism and Colonial Oppression in Brussels and represented the Indian National Congress in this meeting. It was here that he started to think more broadly about the significance of the Indian independence struggle for the world and realised that their local struggle could only make sense if seen in the broader context of dependency and colonialism. He also started to recognise that political independence without social and economic emancipation would be meaningless, not only for India but for any other country under the colonial rule. The League against Imperialism and Colonial Oppression, a transnational anti-imperialist organisation that had representatives from anti-colonial, anti-imperialist and communist struggles from all over the world, was initiated by communists in Germany and was supported by the Comintern in Moscow. Participation in subsequent meetings of the League and its leftist politics made Nehru more curious about the dynamics of the Second and the Third Internationals and provided him with the foundations of Marxist and socialist thought and practice. These anti-imperialist, anti-capitalist and anti-fascist institutions and networks helped Nehru navigate between communism, socialism and nationalism.[11]

In his autobiography, originally published in 1936, he wrote:

> I turned inevitably with goodwill towards communism, for whatever its faults, it was at least not hypocritical and not imperialistic. It was not a doctrinal adherence, as I did not know much about the fine points of communism, my acquaintance being limited at the time to its broad features. These attracted me, as also the tremendous changes taking place in Russia.[12]

In October 1927, Nehru attended the tenth anniversary celebrations of the October Revolution; he was deeply impressed and developed an appreciation for many of the Soviets' achievements. He wrote several articles on the Soviet Union after returning to India and continued to improve his knowledge of Marxism. Above all, he started to push the Congress to the left in terms of the party's domestic politics as well as its foreign relations.

During the 1920s, Mahatma Gandhi's interpretation of 'Swaraj' (self-rule), which focused on internal transformation as much as political transformation, had started to become popular among many Indians, but for Nehru economic and social Swaraj had become the idea's most significant aspects, and he constantly argued they should be put at the centre of the overall demand for Swaraj.[13] In other words, for Nehru the struggle for national independence could not be separated from the struggle for social and economic transformation, and therefore he started to place an enormous emphasis on socialism. As the academic Sanjay Seth has argued, it was this 'Nehruvian socialism' that provided a unique touch to the nationalist patterns of India in the late 1920s and early 1930s.[14] Because of the particular historical moment within which Nehru was living, he had no choice but to swing between socialism and nationalism. Moreover, Nehru started to consistently challenge both fascism and British imperialism, which he considered two manifestations of rotten capitalism, which had different formats in different places, but were both representative of the same forces.[15] Due to his anti-fascist standpoints, Nehru declined invitations to visit Italy and Germany under fascist rule.

In 1929 he was elected President of the Congress, and in his first presidential address, in Lahore, he stated: 'I must frankly confess that I am a socialist and a republican'. The 1929 Lahore Congress is famous because it was the first time Congress (under Nehru's influence) declared its goal as 'Purna Swaraj' (complete self-rule or independence) as opposed to dominion status (a form of autonomy, supposedly equal in status, within the British Empire). In 1936, when Nehru again became the party's President, he repeated this commitment:

I am convinced that the only key to the solution of the world's problem and of India's problem lies in socialism and when I use this word I do so not in a vague, humanitarian way but in the scientific, economic sense. I see no way of ending poverty, the vast unemployment, the degradation and subjection of the Indian people except through socialism. That involves vast revolutionary changes in the social structure, the ending of vested interest in land and industry, as well as the feudal and autocratic Indian States system.[16]

Nehru became the President of the Congress again in 1937 and 1946. He played an important role in negotiations with the British over independence and in 1946 he formed the Interim Government of India. From 1947 until his death in 1964 he served as the Prime Minister of India. Nehru was imprisoned a few times in the course of his life and it was during these periods that he wrote his three major works: *Glimpses of World History* (written between 1930 and 1933 and published in 1934), *An Autobiography* (written while he was in prison from June 1934 to February 1935 and published in 1936) and *The Discovery of India* (written between 1942 and 1945 and published in 1946).

Jawaharlal Nehru's Marxism

The notions of history and historical progress were central to Nehru's thought, and Marxism provided a framework and an outlook for his understanding of history and historical developments. In his autobiography Nehru wrote:

> The theory and philosophy of Marxism lightened up many a dark corner of my mind. History came to have a new meaning for me. The Marxist interpretation threw a flood of light on it and it became an unfolding drama with some order and purpose, however unconscious, behind it.... The great world crisis and slump seemed to justify the Marxist analysis. While other systems and theories were groping about in the dark, Marxism alone explained it more or less satisfactorily and offered a real solution.[17]

In his 1936 Congress presidential address, he urged his audience to develop a historic sense and to put current events in a broader perspective. In his writings on history – *Glimpses of World History* and *The Discovery of India* – Nehru constantly emphasised the role of economic factors, particularly modes of economic production and organisation in analysis of historical developments. He accepted the materialist conception of history, which was the basis of Marxist theory of historical materialism, a theory that argues that history and historical change should be viewed in relation to the economic development of societies, rise of classes and struggles of these classes. Nehru believed historical materialism provided a scientific method for understanding history. He wrote:

> He [Marx] seems to me to have possessed quite an extraordinary degree of insight into social phenomena, and this insight was apparently due to the scientific method he adopted. This method, applied to past history as well as current events, helps us in understanding them far more than any other method of approach, and it is because of this that the most revealing and keen analysis of the changes that are taking place in the world today come from Marxist writers…. But the whole value of Marxism seems to me to lie in its absence of dogmatism, in its stress on a certain outlook and mode of approach, and in its attitude to action. That outlook helps us in understanding the social phenomena of our own times, and points out the way of action and escape.[18]

It was this outlook that gave Nehru the means through which he could not only understand India's problems but also their solutions, which he saw as being all economic. For example, he connected the existence of communalism in India to the elites pursuing their economic interests by manipulating the religious feelings of the masses, a manipulation that was possible only because of the economic inequalities that existed between different communities. He constantly insisted that the

Congress should link its nationalist demands to the economic and social demands of the peasantry and the proletariat. Nehru argued that nationalism, although inevitable under the given conditions of India, could not offer any solutions to the economic problems of the country, while socialism in fact directly tackled them all.[19]

However, his attachment to Marxism went through some changes over time. During his first encounters with it, Nehru accepted the Marxist method of thinking and analysis, and most of its premises. Later on, although still very much attached to Marxism, he concluded that, because of its emphasis on the economy, it was not broad enough to explain all aspects of social life.[20]

Nehru believed in the existence of class conflict based on economic interests. However, he did not believe in the revolutionary overthrow of any particular class as the only path to social transformation. For India, he chose to tackle the issue of class and economic inequality through socialist policies. According to the academic Paul Power, for Nehru, revolution was synonymous with cultural and social change, which would lead to the abolishment of injustice and ignorance.[21] Nehru believed that such revolutionary change could be achieved through the reform of economic institutions. Marxism would allow him and his followers to implement such reforms and build a democratic collectivism in India in a scientific manner. Nehru's commitment to science was absolutely crucial in terms of how he imagined development, and particularly the possibility of revolutionary change that was *non-violent*. It was science and technology that promised the radical transformation of society, culture and the economy in postcolonial India.[22]

Moreover, Marxism helped Nehru's nationalism to become rationalist and build a foundation on socialist and internationalist ideas. Division of nations between the oppressor and the oppressed gave credit to certain nationalisms, while allowing for criticism of nationalism in general. Hence, international cooperation, economic equality and social justice became the cornerstones of Nehru's thought regarding India's progress.[23] Marxian principles allowed Nehru to break away from other Congress leaders who only concentrated on India and the imperial question. He linked ideas of self-determination with Marxist analysis and the upheavals of European countries in the period 1927–1938, which coincided with the rise of fascism. For Nehru, the rise of fascism was completely explicable with Marxian doctrines. He claimed that the only legitimate Indian nationalism would be one that supported the internationalist fight against fascism and imperialism.[24]

Nehru was heavily influenced by Soviet Marxism and the Soviet model, which at the time was using the resources of the state to build a self-sufficient economy, maintain the state's autonomy and provide the platform for its economic development and political influence. This model of 'building socialism' was based on building heavy industry and technological advancements in farming. Nehru found this model attractive and implemented state-directed planning with strict regulations imposed on imports and exports.[25] He constantly expressed his admiration for the Soviets' achievements, pointing to the significance of the Soviet Union for the future of nations in terms of their peaceful coexistence with the Soviet Union and the alternative vision it offered for the divided world of the Cold War era.

In spite of his optimism about the Soviet Union, he was clearly aware that Marxism as a theory was separate from its various manifestations. For example, in his autobiography he emphasised that 'the success or failure of the Russian social experiments do not directly affect the validity of the Marxian theory'.[26] In 'The basic approach', an essay first published in 1958, he was more critical of Soviet communism and criticised its suppression of individual freedom. Moreover, he raised his concerns about increasing association of communism with violence, and highlighted the significance of a Gandhian non-violent path towards social transformation.[27] He viewed himself as a scientific socialist, but he criticised Indian communists for their rigid understanding of Marxism and their failure to move beyond nineteenth-century Marxism.[28] This disparity got to the point where he did not hesitate to use state violence against Indian communists in suppressing the Telangana uprising.[29]

According to Nehru, adapting Marxism to the Indian condition was inevitable. He held that socialism was the only solution to India's problems, but he did not believe socialism should be imposed on India. In addition, he was not convinced by the Marxist revolutionary method. In fact, he was much more inspired by Ghandi's non-violent strategy as the most suitable for India because it had unified different segments and groups in spite of various disagreements among them. The historian Sarvepalli Gopal has classified Nehru as a 'libertarian Marxist' who believed in democratic socialism and regarded civil liberties as an inseparable aspect of any socialist society.[30] He envisioned a socialist society in which economic and social obstacles are removed to pave the way for individual freedom.

Marxism and socialist ideas strongly influenced Nehru, but he constantly emphasised that Marxism 'had to be suited to circumstances'. This suitability needed to go hand in hand with developing an 'organic sense of social life'.[31] Hence, for him, socialism was a growing and dynamic concept which must evolve according to the changing conditions of society in the country where it is implemented.[32] It seems that 'socialism to Nehru was an evolving idea acquiring, like a pearl, layer over layer of meaning'.[33] He once said in Parliament:

> Marx was a great man and everybody could profit by his teachings and thinking. But am I to be told that what he said about England 100 or 150 years ago is going to be applied to India or in any other country? It is fantastic, it is completely unjust to Marx if to nobody else.[34]

The fact is that Nehru's efforts in implementing Marxism and socialism largely took place within the framework of the Congress. Nehru was particularly interested in the encounter between Asia and the West as two separate worlds with their own unique economic and social organisations and value systems.[35] Hence, he was keen on thinking specifically about the condition and particularities of his country at the time. Embedding his thinking in India's circumstances meant that, as Prime Minister, Nehru had to overcome poverty, industrialise the country, and eliminate any kind of feudal relations, caste relations, communalism and regionalism.[36]

Moreover, Nehru considered socialism a component of his nationalism and regarded the two as interconnected. According to the political scientist and anthropologist Partha Chatterjee, Marxism's emphasis on economic factors as the driver of social development and its scientific outlook provided Nehru with a useful framework through which he could embrace nationalism.[37] Therefore, the formation of an independent Indian nation-state was not only desirable because of questions of sovereignty and self-rule, but Nehru also advocated for an independent state that was seen as the instrument for a modernising India, which would be founded on ideals of equality and social justice. This meant adopting a transformative stance towards the Indian state, which was not only nationalist and progressive but also internationalist.[38]

In 1920, Lenin highlighted that in oppressed and dependent nations nationalism was historically inevitable and moreover was a progressive project. This was a call to communists to support national liberation movements in the global South. This endorsement of nationalism in the global South, as well as Marxism's representation of Enlightenment rationalism, facilitated Nehruvian socialism. Nehru continuously advised the Congress to define its position on independence more clearly, as well as its stance on what kind of social and economic transformation the country needed. This brought him into conflict with some of the more conservative members of the Congress, but Nehru never gave up his socialist and nationalist position in an organisation which was nationalist but extremely heterogeneous and largely non-socialist.[39]

Although Nehru believed it was possible to overthrow a system through revolution, he argued this might not lead to the intended outcome and could be rather disruptive. Therefore, he maintained that, if democracy was to some extent functioning and there were some peaceful methods of transformation available, violence should be avoided. That is why during the struggle for independence Nehru fully supported Gandhi's non-violent strategy and why, in post-independent India as Prime Minister, he proposed the introduction of an 'evolutionary socialism' through a number of measures.[40]

Nehru believed the petite bourgeoisie, which was the class most represented by the Congress, was an important class and he encouraged them to take on the leadership of the large, economically impoverished classes. According to him, this would advance democracy and socialism and would make a peaceful transition to an independent India more feasible. The socialist programme which Nehru proposed to the Congress included nationalisation of large-scale industry, expansion of the public sector and an emphasis on cooperatives, which was meant to stoke the revolutionary passion of the class which was most heavily represented in the Congress as well as ensure that the Congress remained on the side of the majority of the Indian population.[41]

The partition of India in 1947, which divided British India into the two independent dominions of India and Pakistan, led to the division of two provinces, Bengal and Punjab. This was the result of the collapse of discussions over the status of religious minorities, particularly Muslims, in an independent Indian state with a majority Hindu population, and affirmed the Muslim League's claim to self-determination for Indian Muslims. After partition, Nehru realised that India was not a society to be simply divided into Marxist categories such as labourers, landlords and peasants but, rather, a composite of numerous 'small pre-capitalist societies divided further by various forms of tribal and other totems and taboos, extremely conscious of their separateness, and only very loosely linked together by economic and other interests'.[42] This realisation convinced him even more that the path to socialism in India was not through violence or any revolutionary turmoil; rather, the solution was to promote social mobility through economic development and the creation of new social relations in the process, which would eventually transform the old system and replace it with something new.[43] Therefore, Nehru constantly emphasised that what was actually done was more important than any particular definition of socialism. In 1949 he stated, 'Our problem today is to raise the standard of the masses, supply them with their needs, give them the wherewithal to lead a decent life.... I do not care what "ism" it is that helps me to set them on that road, provided I do it'.[44]

Nehru spread his socialist ideas on numerous platforms, among youth, trade unions, peasants and meetings organised by the Congress. Also, in many of his writings, especially in the series of newspaper articles published in 1933 under the title 'Whither India?' and in his autobiography (written in the mid-1930s), he repeatedly emphasised the significance of socialism for India's future. Above all, Nehru introduced socialism to the Indian Congress and thereby facilitated its radicalisation. It was Nehru's reappointment as the President of the Congress in 1936 that marked the party's sharp shift towards socialist orientations.

Nehru's socialism was to a large extent focused on state planning, which for him meant a movement from the political to the social and economic, a movement that entailed a number of objectives. The first was the establishment of a socialist state which was democratic and secular. Second, he aimed to make the state an instrument in the service of the production and equitable distribution of wealth and income. His third objective was to persuade people and gain consensus on his ideas about planning.[45] He had done a lot of work to advocate for the idea of economic planning since the late 1920s. For example, he was instrumental in the Karachi Resolution of 1931, which, as the academic K. V. Viswanathaiah has put it, was 'the first official pledge of the Congress party in favour of socialism'.[46] For the first time in the history of the Congress, Nehru presented a resolution on 'fundamental rights and economic changes', arguing that these were particularly important matters that the nation should focus on when educating the masses.[47] In 1938, he led the Congress to form a National Planning Committee. After he became Prime Minister, he introduced his ideas about planning for welfare and established a Planning Commission in 1950. His planned economic development was more pragmatic than doctrinaire socialist, and he became 'a liaison between the planners and the people'.[48]

Nehru incorporated a clear economic policy based on the premise of a mixed economy in the Industrial Policy

Resolution of the Government of India 1948. According to Viswanathaiah, this resolution 'was the most concrete expression of Nehru's means for achieving socialism in India'.[49] Indian industry would be divided into three categories: first, industries owned and managed by the state; second, industries in which the state and the private sector coexist; and third, industries which were in the private sector but nevertheless subject to state control. Nehru assumed an important role for the private sector in developing the national plan, but at the same time he emphasised the significance of the cooperative method of organisation, particularly in agriculture, small-scale industry and the retail trade. He also advocated a major role for the workers in the management of an industry. Finally, for Nehru, socialism was not only about a transformation in economic relations but also involved changes in the social structure, where caste and class inequalities would have to be eliminated.[50] His vision for India was of a prosperous and free nation where the entire population could live life fully. His planned economic growth was supposed to meet this social end.[51] It is important to note that the above-mentioned visions and policies were crucial components of the constitution of India, which declared the Indian state to be socialist. Nehru played a seminal role in drafting the constitution but this was not his accomplishment alone (it was a collective endeavour). It was in fact the jurist and activist B. R. Ambedkar who headed the committee drafting the constitution.

In 1951, Nehru persuaded the Congress to declare its aim to be 'the establishment of a cooperative commonwealth, based on equality of opportunity and of political, economic and social rights and aiming at world peace and fellowship'.[52] Nehru was fully aware that India needed some time before it could embrace socialism. In 1954, at his address of the National Development Council, he argued that India should still follow a 'socialist pattern of society' which was 'classless and casteless'.[53]

This was followed by the Congress's well-known resolution in 1955 declaring that planning should be directed towards the establishment of a socialist pattern of society, with social ownership and control of the means of production.[54] Nehru did not give a comprehensive definition of the term 'socialist pattern of society', but in 1956, at his address to a conference of the All India Manufacturers' Organisation, he indicated that 'a socialistic pattern of society is socialism. Some people seem to make fine distinctions among socialistic pattern, socialist pattern and socialism. They are all exactly the same thing without the slightest difference.'[55] However, in practice, the idea was that in a socialist pattern of society the basic aspects of socialism would be adopted but other things would depend on the condition of the country. Therefore, the socialist pattern of society was used to point the country in the right direction rather than being a rigid doctrine. The main objectives were social or state ownership of the means of production, progressive acceleration of production and just distribution of national wealth in order to raise the standard of living, achieve full employment, use all resources for social purposes and control industrial development. In 1955, the Congress adopted a resolution stating that a socialist pattern of society had become its objective for policy-making and emphasising that the principal means of production would be under social ownership or control, that national wealth needed to be distributed equitably and that the state would play a vital role in planning and development.[56]

Nehru was an admirer of democracy and believed that any plan for economic growth and increased opportunities for individuals should be articulated within the framework of political democracy. In its 1964 session, the Congress made it clear that democratic socialism was the party's goal.[57] However, Nehru emphasised that political democracy cannot lead to real democracy unless society has become classless.[58] As Nehru wrote in his autobiography, 'Our final aim can only be a classless society with equal economic justice and opportunity for all'.[59] He believed parliamentary democracy could be meaningful only if it could provide for economic democracy.[60] He did not see any contradiction between socialism and democracy and assumed that democracy without socialism was meaningless. Therefore, his main objective in defending democracy entailed prioritising the impoverished masses in economic planning, arguing that democracy could not last long in the middle of poverty and inequality.[61]

Jawaharlal Nehru's legacy

Nehru was a significant figure in the struggle for India's independence, and along with Mahatma Gandhi he developed effective strategies for the liberation struggle. Also, he played a major role in shaping the ideology of the Indian National Congress and in moving it towards a more socialist politics. Moreover, he takes centre stage in the realm of modern political thought in India, and indeed provided a 'very particular, Indianised version of democracy and modernity',[62] which was inspired by Enlightenment rationalism but was also an endeavour to develop a radical critique of it by combining Marxism and nationalism.[63]

Nehru served as the Prime Minister of independent India for almost two decades, which allowed him to put into practice many of his social, economic and political aspirations. During this time, he highlighted commonality among Indians and promoted ideas which could be identified as socialist, nationalist as well as internationalist. He tried to transform the Indian state into a modern republic and promoted a modernisation programme, which for him was a national philosophy with a number of objectives, including socialism, national unity, parliamentary democracy and non-alignment. Nehru pushed for a mixed economy with a strong government-controlled public sector in key industries and a private sector which was subject to state control. He led a successful land reform that included the abolition of large holdings. Moreover, his government established numerous institutions of higher education and guaranteed free and compulsory primary education for everyone.

Reflecting on the developments of the 1970s, it was argued that Nehru 'grafted socialism onto Indian vocabulary and Indian consciousness…. Nehru laid the foundations, but he left the word socialism to acquire further connotation and denotation with the passage of time'. Because Nehru was not rigid or dogmatic about the meaning of the word, 'socialism would emerge constantly, acquiring new dimensions suited to each generation according to evolving contemporary demands'.[64] Although India has gone through profound trans-formations since Nehru and, in particular, its economy has shifted to a neoliberal model, his legacy still affects India's politics today. He might not have succeeded in achieving all his objectives, but his contributions were fundamental in transforming India into a secular, democratic country with a 'socialistic common sense'.[65]

Nehru's optimism towards the state and his Indianised understanding of democracy and modernity, which was merged with ideals of social justice, led him set up public institutions that would help him modernise India. Many of those institutions still exist.[66] Nehru championed a welfare state whose objectives were to improve the welfare of the impoverished segments of society and to tackle inequality.

Most governments after him, willingly or unwillingly, had to take into account the significance of battling poverty and inequality in India in their own policies, although some of these policies became controversial at the time. Today, the language and framework of rights enables the poor to fight for some basic rights, for example to land, to food and to education, pushing the government to provide them with better conditions. It is worth mentioning that much of this language is drawn from the constitution and therefore, as mentioned above, it should also be understood as part of Ambedkar's legacy.

In addition, Nehru institutionalised the significance of decision-making processes in Parliament and trust in the constitution. His programme for universal primary education still provides the poorest segments of society with free education and, more generally, his emphasis on the importance of education has resulted in the development of excellent educational and scientific institutions, such as the Indian Institute of Technology and All India Institute of Medical Sciences.

Various institutions and places across India are devoted to Nehru. For example, Jawaharlal Nehru University in Delhi is one of the most prestigious institutions of higher education in the country, and a large port near the metropolitan city of Mumbai is named after him. Nehru's birthday, 14 November, is celebrated in India as Children's Day, in recognition of his work for the development of children, and his pictures and statues can still be seen in many places across India. He also remains a significant figure in popular culture. A number of films and documentaries have been devoted to his life and legacy, and his writings are popular not only among activists and intellectuals but also among the broader Indian population, in spite of the fact that the nationalist Hindu government of Narendra Modi has continuously demonised Nehru's character and legacy. Finally, Nehru remains an important symbol for the Indian National Congress, and his legacy continues to shape the party's policy and philosophy in spite of the ongoing debates and disagreements about the past and the future of the party. It is commonly believed that his daughter's rise to the leadership of the Congress was because of his legacy. Indeed, the party, apart from one brief period, has remained in the leadership of his family.

Outside of India, Nehru is known and remembered as one of the main architects of the Non-Aligned Movement and the key organiser of the Bandung Conference in 1955, which for the first time brought together numerous newly independent Asian and African states. He became a leading figure for the ongoing anti-colonial struggles of the time and openly supported many liberation struggles; he inspired generations in Asia and Africa.[67] Also, his policy of non-alignment helped establish a joint front, independent of either of the two world powers, against colonialism and imperialism. Hence, India under Nehru became a significant actor in the newly independent world but also, as one of the founding members of the United Nations, played an important role in pushing the UN to incorporate the concerns of the newly independent nations in its agenda. Nehru has been commemorated in different countries in a variety of different ways, such as busts and status as well as appearances on stamps in the case of the Soviet Union. Martin Luther King, the prominent leader of the Civil Rights Movement in the United States, was deeply inspired by Nehru and the non-violent strategy of the Indian independence movement. He visited Nehru and India in 1959 and returned to the United States deeply transformed. In *The Legacy of Nehru: A Memorial Tribute*, which was published one year after Nehru's death, King stated:

In all of these struggles of mankind to rise to a true state of civilization, the towering figure of Nehru sits unseen but felt at all council tables. He is missed by the world, and because he is so wanted, he is a living force in the tremulous world of today.[68]

Chapter 2

Hồ Chí Minh: always truly uncle

Hồ Chí Minh (1890–1969) led the Vietnamese independence movement, and under his leadership French colonial rule in Indochina came to an end after three-quarters of a century. For many years he had to tolerate a difficult life far from his home and in numerous countries. In his struggle for Vietnam's independence and unity, Hồ became a prominent member of the international communist movement and shaped its strategy and tactics for half a century.[1] He introduced a revolutionary path for his people that followed a Leninist approach of a two-stage revolutionary process, but in addition he emphasised the significance of national independence and coalition building. He asserted that the role of the peasants was fundamental in the Vietnamese context and that a revolutionary process needed a clear ideology, organisation and future vision. He founded the Communist Party of Vietnam and established the Democratic Republic of Vietnam, where he served as the President until his death. Moreover, he played a significant role in the People's Army of Vietnam and the Việt Cộng (the National Liberation Front of Southern Vietnam) during the Vietnam War, which started in 1955 and lasted 20 years. The victory of Vietnam in the war against the US military forces led to the unification of Vietnam under communist rule. Hồ's resistance against the Americans and eventual unification of Vietnam was a turning point in the Cold War and dramatically impacted both American and Vietnamese societies.

Throughout his life Hồ's goal was to bring an 'end to the global system of capitalist exploitation and create a new revolutionary world characterized by the utopian vision of Karl Marx'.[2] More than many other anti-colonial revolutionaries of the time, Hồ understood that Vietnam's situation should be seen in the context of the world capitalist and colonial system. He was a dynamic leader, strategist and writer whose struggles and ideas transcended the fate of his country. Without him, not only would Southeast Asia have been a different region, but the fates of many Asian people would have been far different.

Revolutionary pathways[3]

Hồ Chí Minh was born in 1890.[4] Both sides of his family were subsistence farmers. In 1887, French Indochina had been formed from Cambodia and Vietnam, and the French had divided Vietnam into three protectorates: Tonkin (north), Annam (middle) and the colony of Cochinchina (south). Annam, the protectorate Hồ was from, was known as a hotbed of nationalistic ideas, and under French rule it developed into a region recognised for persistent resistance against the colonisers. His father, Nguyen Sinh Sac, was a Confucian scholar who trained him in Confucian values, although the level of traditional Confucian education he received in childhood has been disputed.[5] Nguyen Sinh Sac was also the village teacher and later studied for a doctorate, passed the civil service examination and took a government job. In his position as vice magistrate, he became known as a supporter of the weak and the oppressed and as a staunch opponent of French officials. Hồ's father enrolled him in a Franco-Vietnamese school, which he believed was necessary to prepare his son for their new reality of French colonialism and domination. According to his teachers, Hồ was interested in French Enlightenment thinkers such as Descartes, Diderot, Rousseau and Montesquieu, revealing an emphasis on post-Revolution secular thought and anti-colonialism. In 1910, he was expelled from school because of his revolutionary activities, which consisted mostly of involvement in peasant protests against French tax policies and forced labour. In 1911, Hồ started to work as a cook's assistance on a steamship, which departed from Saigon for French ports. Economic necessity, his frustration with French colonial rule and his interest in discovering the world outside of Vietnam compelled him to leave.

Hồ spent two years at sea and observed the life of people in different ports from Bordeaux to Lisbon, Tunis, Dakar and the ports of East Africa. He also visited the United States, Mexico and South America before stopping in London for a longer period. During these two years, his understanding of the colonial oppression and the misery of people throughout the world deepened. In many places he visited, he observed conditions similar to those in Vietnam. In the United States, he became aware of the actual conditions of people of colour, who were subjected to constant humiliation. This period of travel abroad influenced him very much and laid the foundations for his revolutionary worldview.

Upon arrival in London in 1913, Hồ first washed dishes and shovelled snow before becoming a chef at a renowned hotel. He joined a clandestine organisation of expatriates called the Overseas Workers Association. This was the first political group he joined as an adult. Also during this time, he became interested in the Irish uprising and socialised with people from the Fabian Society. Hồ arrived in England shortly before the First World War started. At that time, manual workers in London had begun to demand better conditions and England's labour unions were involved in debates about their future and the possibility of adopting communist methods: to what extent should they support the Bolsheviks or think about a similar revolutionary stance for their own country? Some of Hồ's biographers refer to this time as what prompted his interest in Marxism.

Hồ arrived in Paris between 1917 and 1919 (the sources give different dates). There were political reasons for his move. If it was towards the latter part of that time span, then the Paris Peace Conference – which was held from January 1919 to January 1920 – would have been a strong draw. The Conference was supposed to be a yearlong summit meeting of world leaders to decide what the post-war world would look like. Hence, it offered colonies an opportunity to make a case for independence or improved conditions. In addition, Paris was the capital of French colonialism, and Hồ believed a better understanding of this oppressive system from its centre would benefit resistance against it. From the moment he entered France, he became involved in politics and claimed that his goal was the liberation of people affected by colonial relations. Shortly after his arrival, he joined the French Socialist Party, as well as a group of anti-colonialist resistance workers, and founded a Vietnamese network, the Association of Annamite Patriots (the French called all Vietnamese 'Annamites'). Hồ and his colleagues in the Association of Annamite Patriots took advantage of the situation created by the Paris Peace Conference and drafted an eight-point petition entitled 'Demands of the Annamite People', which called for political autonomy, equality and democratic freedoms for Vietnam.

The petition did not receive any official response from the French authorities.

Even after the Bolsheviks' victory in the October Revolution in 1917 and the founding of the Third International, social democracy failed to adequately address imperialist and colonial atrocities. Hồ was already unhappy with the French Socialist Party because it was largely ignoring the issue of colonial oppression, and he started to lean towards the politics of the Third International. Lenin's 'Theses on the national and colonial questions', which was written for the 1920 Third International meeting, addressed colonialism as a great injustice and considered the national liberation movements of Asia and Africa to be allies of the communists in their fight against imperialism. After reading Lenin's theses, Hồ stated: 'Though sitting alone in my room, I shouted aloud as if addressing large crowds: Dead martyrs, compatriots! This is what we need, this is the path to our liberation.'[6] Lenin was opening up a new horizon for revolutionary strategy as opposed to the reforms advocated by many social democrats of the time. In addition, Hồ was aware that his people in Vietnam had no urban, industrial background and therefore could not manifest proletarian solidarity. However, Lenin's revision of Marx clearly suggested that the peasantry, including colonial peasants, could play a role in the revolutionary process.

In December 1920, during the Eighteenth Congress of the French Socialist Party, Hồ argued that the party needed to join the Third International and place the liberation of colonised people on its agenda. A delegate from the party voted for adherence to the Third International, which led to the founding of the French Communist Party. Hồ first participated in the French Communist Party's colonial commission and then founded the political group Intercolonial Union in 1921 to represent colonial subjects living in France.

The Intercolonial Union published a weekly journal called *Le Paria* ('The Pariah') and Ho regularly contributed to it with his writings, drawings and caricatures. He also continued writing for *L'Humanité* ('Humanity') – the newspaper of the French Socialist Party and, later, the French Communist Party – and started another publication, *VietNam Hon* ('Soul of Vietnam'), which targeted people living outside France.[7] Inside France, his writings in *L'Humanité* were focused on philosophical ideas and Marxist doctrine, while in *Le Paria* he provided a detailed account of French violence and colonial affairs..

In the summer of 1923, Hồ finally decided to move to Moscow, because he thought people there could understand what was going on in Asia and Africa better than those in Paris, and because he hoped to meet Lenin. He also believed going to Moscow would make it easier for him to return to Vietnam. In Moscow, he studied at the Communist University of the Toilers of the East. Unfortunately, he did not meet Lenin because Lenin was ill when he arrived and, much to Hồ's disappointment, Lenin died in the winter of 1924. Shortly after Lenin's death, Hồ praised him in a widely published essay: '[Lenin] was our father, teacher, comrade and advisor. Nowadays, he is the bright star showing us the way to the socialist revolution. Eternal Lenin will live for ever in our work.'[8]

During his time in Moscow, Hồ studied at the University, actively participated in Comintern and constantly emphasised the importance of the colonial question. He gradually started to be considered a specialist on colonial issues as well as on Asia more broadly. Apart from regularly contributing to the journal of the Comintern, he also continued to write for *L'Humanite* and *Le Paria*. One of his most important pieces of writing during his stay in Moscow was 'Le procès de la colonisation française' ('French colonialism on trial'), which was a demonstration of the colonial condition throughout the world and ended with a call to Indochinese youth to rise up against the colonisers.

In 1924, Hồ joined the Soviet mission in Canton (present-day Guangzhou), China, and in 1925 he started organising the Marxist-Leninist Revolutionary Youth League, founded on the two pillars of nationalism and social revolution. In linking these two issues, Hồ followed the Leninist model that had been approved by the Comintern. Through the activities of the League, he was able to spread Marxist-Leninist ideas in the region and also recruited a number of young Vietnamese to come to Canton to receive training. After returning to Vietnam, these trainees would spread the revolutionary doctrine and find new recruits to send to Canton. Formation of the League was Hồ's first concrete step towards the Vietnamese Revolution. Apart from constructing the backbone of the revolution in Vietnam he also cooperated with Chinese revolutionaries in mobilising Chinese peasants and collaborated with the Peasant Movement Training Institute, which was one of the outcomes of the alliance between the Nationalist Party and the Chinese Communist Party in China at the time.

In 1927, after the Nationalist Party's coup against the Communist Party in South China, the Revolutionary Youth League was dissolved, and Hồ fled Canton back to Moscow. In the coming years he travelled to various places in Europe and Asia. In 1930, he brought together various communist groups with roots in the Revolutionary Youth League and other national liberation groups and formed the Communist Party of Vietnam, a united communist organisation. From then on, he focused on advancing the work of the party, but from 1938 to 1941 he also collaborated with the Chinese Communist Party before returning to Vietnam. He translated *The History of the Bolshevik Communist Party of the USSR* into Vietnamese and wrote *Guerrilla Tactics* and *The Instruction of Military Cadres*. After his return to Vietnam in 1941, Hồ established a military-political front known as the League for the Independence of Vietnam, commonly referred to as the Việt Minh. The Việt Minh included various groups seeking independence for Vietnam. It became the most important force against the Japanese occupation and rapidly rose to popularity. In August 1945, Hồ and the Việt Minh launched a revolution against both the Japanese and French colonial rule, and on 2 September 1945 the Democratic Republic of Vietnam was established. Hồ served as its President until his death on 2 September 1969, the twenty-fourth anniversary of Vietnamese national independence.

Hồ Chí Minh's Marxism

According to his biographer Duiker, Hồ's interest in socialism 'can be seen as a natural consequence of his dislike of capitalism and imperialism'.[9] For him, Marxism functioned as 'a basic plan for revolutionary action'.[10] Similar to many in Asia, Hồ's first encounter with capitalism was through the exploitation of his country by the colonial powers. However, his understanding of capitalism, imperialism and colonialism was strengthened during the years he spent at sea, visiting different parts of the world.[11] Moreover, for many Asian intellectuals, particularly those, like Hồ, who were familiar with Confucian rhetoric, socialism's stress on community and equality had strong overlaps with Confucian tradition.[12] Confucianism underlined that human beings are 'brothers across the four oceans' and that social order should be ensured through a just distribution of the means of production.[13] Therefore, for Hồ, the 'philosophical transition' from Confucius to Marx was not difficult.[14] The relationship between Confucianism and Hồ Chí

Minh is, however, a contested issue among scholars and will be discussed in the following pages.

Hồ became fascinated with and supported the October Revolution 'instinctively'.[15] At the time of the establishment of the Third International by Lenin, there were heated debates around the nature of the Second and Third Internationals and whether the French Socialist Party should remain in one or the other. On this, Hồ expressed his incomprehension: 'Why were the discussions so heated? … What I wanted most to know – and this precisely was not debated in the meetings – was: Which International sides with the people of colonial countries?'[16] Describing his fascination with Lenin and his work, Hồ writes that after reading Lenin's 'Theses on the national and colonial questions', he had

> entire confidence in Lenin, in the Third International…. At first, patriotism, not yet Communism, led me to have confidence in Lenin, in the Third International. Step by step, along the struggle, by studying Marxism-Leninism parallel with participation in practical activities, I gradually came upon the fact that only Socialism and Communism can liberate the oppressed nations and the working people throughout the world from slavery.[17]

Lenin had clearly stated that the workers of the industrial world needed to understand and assist liberation movements in the colonies.[18] This made Lenin 'the embodiment of universal Brotherhood' in the eyes of the masses in the colonial world.[19] Also, although Marx had predicted that the first communist revolution would happen in a highly industrialised country, the triumph of the revolution in Russia led to Lenin's formula about the importance of the peasantry alongside the industrial working class. This was very attractive to Hồ, who was interested in the liberation of Vietnam, which had a large peasant population. According to Hồ, 'Lenin brought scientific socialism to a new stage' and developed Marxism by arguing for the importance of a workers and peasants alliance, bringing together the national and international questions while building a new type of political party based on the power of the working class.[20]

Hồ Chí Minh constantly referred to the guidance Lenin provided to the 'revolutionaries in the East', where he urged them to 'rely on the theory and common practice of communism and apply them to specific conditions which do not exist in Europe'. That is why many in the colonies regarded Lenin 'as a symbol of faith and a torchlight of hope'.[21] Moreover, thanks to Lenin's view of imperialism, Hồ embedded the struggle against French colonialism in Vietnam within an international context and as complementary to other anti-colonial movements of the time.[22] In short, Hồ's admiration for Lenin was based on the way the latter brought together nationalism, internationalism and (localised) communism.

In the early 1920s, Hồ constantly tried to convince his European comrades that communism could be applied in Asia. In one of his articles, he pointed to Japan, the first country in Asia which had become capitalist and had just seen the formation of a socialist party. Moreover, he drew attention to China, where a new revolutionary government led by Sun Yat-sen was giving birth to 'a proletarianized China'.[23] In a report which clearly demonstrates his vision regarding the revolution and social transformation, he emphasises that 'Europe is not all of humanity' and argues that social scientists need to 'revise Marxism, down to its historical foundations, by strengthening it with Oriental ethnology'.[24] Moreover, he underlined that the main objective of the revolution in the colonies was their liberation from the coloniser.[25]

Hồ Chí Minh was truly a Marxist-Leninist, although, given the circumstances of his struggle, nationalism was also a strong driving force for him. Hence, most of his efforts were devoted to liberating Vietnam from colonialism and imperialism. Although in comparison with some of the other revolutionaries discussed in this book, for example, his Chinese counterpart Mao, Hồ was less attracted to the theoretical aspects of Marxism-Leninism, and thus his efforts were more focused on adapting and applying Marxist-Leninist principles to the Vietnamese situation. In addition, he believed the conditions in Vietnam had to be understood as a manifestation of an international imperialist and capitalist system explained by Lenin and based on Marx's analysis of capitalism.[26]

Hồ believed in the Marxist conception of class. In 1941 (after returning to Vietnam) he formed the Việt Minh, through which he successfully brought together various groups and classes, from peasants to the middle classes, intellectuals and nationalist organisations. Creating such a coalition reflected Lenin's view that social classes and groups in the colonies were impacted differently by colonial relations and that most groups would support the nationalist cause.[27] In line with Lenin's concept of a two-stage revolution, in his 'Theses on the national and colonial question', Hồ assumed national independence would come first and the socialist revolution and 'Communist Utopia' would follow. In other words, he supposed nationalism would eventually be transformed into internationalism.[28]

The Fifth Congress of the Comintern, held in the summer of 1924, provided Hồ with an opportunity to express his views within the organisation. Although a special appeal to colonial people was already part of the agenda, Hồ asked that the address include the words 'to the colonial peoples'.[29] The Fifth Comintern Congress symbolised the beginning of Hồ Chí Minh's emergence as a renowned Asian leader in the world communist movement. He was recognised as the spokesperson for the Eastern question and for emphasising the significance of the peasantry. Both issues had of course been highlighted by Lenin but were still ignored by many in Moscow.[30] After these achievements, Hồ decided to return to Asia and build a revolutionary movement in Indochina. He was very well aware that not many people in the colonies, including Vietnam, understood what communism was about and those who did were mostly from the native bourgeoisie. The implication was that the Vietnamese people needed to understand the importance of a revolution for their context. They also needed to become familiar with Marx and Lenin, but the initial emphasis had to be on national independence.[31] It was this context that had led to the establishment of the Marxist-Leninist Revolutionary Youth League, as it would provide a thorough training in the ideology and organising methods of Marxism-Leninism.[32]

Although Hồ Chí Minh was a very good writer and his writings and speeches comprise thousands of pages, he is not known as someone who showed much interest in theory and, therefore, he is rarely discussed as an original theoretician alongside revolutionary thinkers such as Lenin or Mao. However, in one of his seminal writings, he attempted to localise Marxism and apply it to the Vietnamese context. At the time, there was no writing about Marxism-Leninism in Vietnamese. Hồ's response to this deficiency was the preparation of a short pamphlet in 1926 or early 1927 called 'The revolutionary path' ('Duong Kach Menh' in Vietnamese), which was an introduction to Marxism-Leninism and its relevance to Vietnam. This pamphlet could be regarded as the first written ideological work in the history of the Vietnamese communist movement. It educated the first generation of Vietnamese Marxist-Leninist revolutionaries and played a significant role in the unfolding of the Vietnamese Revolution.

Ho prepared this pamphlet while serving Comintern in Canton. However, during this period he was also building the Revolutionary Youth League, the first Marxist organisation in Vietnam. Students in Canton took some copies of the pamphlet, while other copies were sent to Vietnam for distribution.[33]

The word 'revolution' (*kach menh*) had been introduced to the Vietnamese language only in the early twentieth century and was the Vietnamese equivalent of the Chinese word for revolution (*ge ming*), which means 'to change the mandate'. The pamphlet began with defining revolution. For Hồ Chí Minh, revolution meant 'to destroy the old and build the new, or to destroy the bad and construct the good'.[34] In addition, he referred to a list of ethical principles for revolutionary behaviour. Some of these principles, such as the emphasis on duty, dedication and self-sacrifice, were standard principles of Marxist-Leninist organisations. Other principles, such as the need for prudence, thrift and honesty, were drawn from Confucianism.[35] The relationship between Confucianism and Hồ Chí Minh is, however, a contested issue among scholars. Some renowned scholars and activists, such as Paul Mus, Nguyen Khac Vien and Dao Phan, have claimed that Hồ utilised Confucian practices and rhetoric to attract the peasantry.[36] According to his biographer Brocheux, for Hồ Chí Minh, 'Karl Marx represented the realization of Confucian ideals in a modern historical context'.[37] However, the historian Robert Brigham emphasises that the peasants were more attracted to Hồ's use of the concept of 'proletarian virtue' and joined the Communist Party of Vietnam because of its land-to-tiller programme and because they believed that Ho and his revolutionary followers could replace a corrupt and outdated social system with a better one.[38] Brigham concludes his argument by writing that 'Hồ never promoted himself as a Confucian. Instead, he made appeals to proletarian virtue and land reform, two aspects of the revolution that resonated loudly with Vietnam's peasants.'[39]

In the pamphlet, Hồ presented a two-stage revolutionary process for his people: after a successful first stage of national liberation, a world revolution would follow. In other words, Vietnam would first liberate itself from French colonial rule and afterwards would enter the second transformative stage by joining the world socialist revolutionary movement.[40] Although Hồ followed Lenin's lead in underlining the need for leadership, particularly during the second stage of the revolutionary process, throughout the whole pamphlet he reinforces the position he had taken in Moscow regarding the significance of the peasants for the revolution. Also, he did not explicitly attribute a leading role to the working classes, and that is why some have referred to it as one of the first examples of 'peasant communism', which at the time felt like an unorthodox approach to Marxist-Leninist revolutionary strategy.[41]

In reading and analysing the pamphlet we must understand that Hồ's main objective was to popularise Marxism in a very rural society and among people who did not know anything about Marxism.[42] There are a number of interesting points to be observed in the pamphlet. First, Hồ emphasises national independence, which was strongly advocated by Lenin as a tactic against feudal and imperialist rule. However, in the pamphlet Hồ attributes a rather subjective value to the issue and characterises it as the product of the alliance of several classes to end foreign domination. Unlike the Leninist interpretation of nationalism, which was considered a revolutionary stage which would then lead to the socialist revolution, for Hồ the issue of national independence was on its own a very significant issue, although he had also declared that the national stage of the revolution would be followed by the second stage, based on class struggle. However, Hồ was not clear about the timing and the conditions under which the second stage would materialise.

Second, Hồ emphasised that the national revolution would include a coalition of classes and that the second stage of revolution, that is, the international socialist revolution, would be led by the working class. Third, Hồ followed Lenin's analysis of the question of revolutionary alliance. Lenin had developed the concept of a four-class alliance for revolution in pre-industrial societies. He had argued that the indigenous proletariat was too weak in these societies and needed to cooperate with other progressive classes, such as the peasants and the petite and national bourgeoisies. After the completion of the first stage of the revolution, the communists would take over and, under the leadership of the proletariat, complete the second stage of the revolution. Hồ followed Lenin's lead regarding a united front of progressive classes, but he differed from Lenin in the crucial role he attributed to the peasants in the revolutionary process, as well as his demonstration of the lack of a close alliance between town and country as a serious problem for the victory of the revolutionary process.

Finally, Hồ placed enormous importance on ideology and organisation and emphasised that a revolution needed a clear vision for the future and a revolutionary party which would bring together numerous committed individuals who could unite the oppressed masses under the umbrella of a clear ideology. In other words, he put providing a vision for Vietnam's post-independence future at the centre of the national liberation struggle.[43] It is worth noting that, although Hồ Chí Minh was to some extent influenced by the events taking place in South China at the time (see the previous section), his ideas on the significance of national independence and the role of the peasantry in the revolution predated his time in China. However, he gained substantial practical experience while he was in China, which may have affected his work with the Revolutionary Youth League.[44]

In 1941, Hồ set up the Việt Minh, which was the continuation of the Revolutionary Youth League in many senses but more advanced. Its two pillars were national independence and social justice. Hồ had anticipated that these issues would appeal to all progressive groups and forces across the country. With this strategic move, he managed to reach out widely, beyond what would be considered the traditional constituency of a communist party, to include various voices in what would soon be Vietnamese nationalism.[45] There has been some debate among Hồ Chí Minh scholars questioning if he was more of a nationalist or a communist. This question does not seem to be correct, however, as Hồ was a nationalist and a communist at the same time. One biographer, William Duiker, has put it nicely: this 'is more a question of his tactics. Hồ Chí Minh was a believer in the art of the possible, of adjusting his ideals to the conditions of the moment.'[46] Hồ believed that the transition to a socialist society was necessary but that it should come gradually and after winning broad popular support.

Vietnamese independence was declared on 2 September 1945. The Democratic Republic of Vietnam (DRV) was established by Hồ Chí Minh with himself as its President. Throughout his post-independence address, Hồ emphasised Vietnamese rights to freedom and independence and announced that the national symbols and metaphors were back in Vietnam. He referred to himself as Uncle Hồ, which implied kinship and solidarity. After independence, he announced that the first stage of the revolution was over[47] and went on to restructure Vietnam along socialist lines. The most important example of such restructuring was the land reform and rural collectivisation programme.

In 1956, in a letter to the peasants and cadres he wrote:

Two years have passed since the victorious end of the Resistance. The northern end of our country has been completely liberated from the colonialists' shackles; now the peasants in the North are also freed from the yoke of the feudal landlords. Nearly 10 million peasants have received land, tens of thousands of new cadres have been trained in the countryside. The organization of the Party, administration, and peasants' associations in the communes has been readjusted. This is a great victory, which opens the way for our peasants to build a life with enough food and clothing, and brings a valuable contribution to economic rehabilitation and development and to the consolidation of the North into a solid base for the struggle to reunify our country.... Land reform is a class struggle against the feudalists; an earth-shaking, fierce, and hard revolution.[48]

France's refusal to accept Vietnam's independence led to the First Indochina War, in which the French were eventually defeated. The 1954 Geneva Conference that ended French colonialism in Vietnam temporarily divided it into North and South with an anticipated reunification after general elections. However, with the interference of the United States, these elections were never held and instead lead to the Second Indochina War, which did not end until 1975, with the defeat of United States. By the end of 1959, North Vietnam had gone through a socialist transformation in both rural and urban areas, including the implementation of a Soviet-style five-year plan of socialist industrialisation.[49]

Unfortunately, Hồ did not live long enough to see a reunited Vietnam. In his final testament, which was first drafted in 1965 and amended in 1968 and 1969, he repeated the importance of nationalism and socialism. He stated that the immediate objective had to be improving the lives of the Vietnamese people. He asked that after the end of the conflict agricultural taxes be cancelled for one year to reduce the hardships imposed on the people during the war and to show the Party's appreciation for their sacrifices. In addition, he requested the unity of the world communist movement.[50]

Hồ Chí Minh's legacy

'Hồ was always intimate, always accessible, always truly uncle'.[51] These are the words of Charles Fenn, one of Hồ Chí Minh's numerous biographers. Years after his death, 'Uncle Hồ', as he is most commonly referred to in Vietnam, remains a major figure in that country and beyond. His legacy is, more than anything, intertwined with the issues that marked an eventful era of national liberation and revolution. Under his leadership, an army of mostly peasants defeated French colonialism (1954) and American imperialism (1975). From a poor country subordinated by various imperialist powers, Vietnam is today an independent nation which has made significant progress in public health, education and industrialisation.

Saigon, the former capital of South Vietnam, was renamed Hồ Chí Minh City in his honour after its seizure by North Vietnamese forces in 1975. In Vietnam, Hồ Chí Minh's image can be found everywhere, from classrooms to banknotes and town centres. Also, there are statues immortalising him all over the country, and his mummified body is exhibited at the centre of the capital. A number of museums are devoted to celebrating his life, ideas and words, such as his famous slogan 'Nothing is more precious than independence and freedom', and they appear in public speeches and on billboards.[52]

Above all, Hồ's life, ideas and personality are celebrated by the Communist Party of Vietnam, which he founded and which is still in power in the country. Instead of calling its doctrine Marxist-Leninist, the Party refers to the theories and policies implemented by Hồ during the anti-colonial struggle and his later development of a socialist system in Vietnam as 'Hồ Chí Minh thought'. This localised Marxist-Leninist ideology has been taught officially in schools since 1997,[53] and continues to shape the Party's agenda, albeit not always in a coherent and profound manner.[54]

Two ideals that Hồ Chí Minh represented, namely national independence and social and economic justice, have transcended the borders of his home country. Hồ's message has been communicated to the oppressed and the colonised beyond Vietnam. He was a prolific writer, and his various writings, from pamphlets to articles and letters, appear in the numerous languages he mastered in addition to Vietnamese. These include English, French, Chinese and Russian. Being such a creative and multifaceted personality made it rather natural for Hồ to take a place 'in the pantheon of revolutionary heroes who have struggled mightily to give the pariahs of the world their true voice'.[55] In fact, before Mao, Gandhi or Nehru had become revolutionary figures famous outside of their countries, Hồ Chí Minh had become known to a broad European circle and peoples of the global South, particularly among Asians living in Asia and in diaspora.[56] As such, he inspired many people and leaders during the national and independence struggles of the twentieth century.

Also, Hồ Chí Minh significantly contributed to the cause of the world communist movement. His work with the Comintern enriched its agenda and made it more appealing to the colonised world. He should be credited for (co-)founding numerous communist parties apart from the Communist Party of Vietnam, including the French Communist Party and the Indochinese Communist Party. Moreover, his leadership was fundamental to defeating the Americans and driving them out from South Vietnam. The victory of North Vietnam against the Americans was not only significant for the unification of Vietnam but also symbolised the Cold War conflict between capitalism and communism. As time passed, the role of the Communist Party of Vietnam in the world communist movement became more apparent, and it played an important role in defending the unity of the world socialist movement. Moreover, it significantly contributed to the development and consolidation of the anti-imperialist front. Hồ Chí Minh himself remained a loyal and militant comrade of the Comintern until the end of his life.[57] As Duiker has noted, the cause Hồ Chí Minh promoted

> provided a defining moment of the twentieth century, representing both the culmination of an era of national liberation in the Third World and the first clear recognition of the limits of the U.S. policy of containment of communism. After Vietnam, the world would never be the same.[58]

Various places around the world are named after him, including in countries where he used to live, such as France, Britain and Thailand, as well as past and present socialist and communist states like Russia, China and the state of Kolkata in India. He has also been celebrated in folk and revolutionary songs and music worldwide, as well as in cultural and diplomatic conferences, events, journals and magazines – in addition to academia and scholarship. For example, a seminar entitled 'Hồ Chí Minh's Legacy and Vietnam-France Cooperation' was held in Paris in 2011 to celebrate the one-hundredth anniversary of Hồ Chí Minh's first arrival in France (in Marseille, when he was working on the French steamer) and the sixty-fifth anniversary of his visit to France as an official guest of the French government.[59] In September 2019, for the fiftieth anniversary of Hồ 's passing, the French newspaper and the organ of the Communist Party *L'Humanité* – to which Hồ had been a prolific contributor himself – published a series of articles and praised his legacy.

After Hồ Chí Minh's death, thousands of messages from over 120 countries, many from the global South, were sent to Vietnam. Numerous countries held memorial services, and an official statement from Moscow praised him as 'an outstanding leader of the international Communist and national liberation movement'.[60] As cited in *Time Magazine*, he once told a French acquaintance:

> I am a professional revolutionary. I am always on strict orders. My itinerary is always carefully prescribed – and you can't deviate from the route, can you?[61]

Chapter 3

Mao Zedong: a virtual god

Mao Zedong (1893–1976) was the founder of the People's Republic of China. He established and led the Chinese Communist Party (CCP) for over three decades until his death. He unified China by fighting against imperialist forces and transformed the country into a world power. Mao contributed to revolutionary theory by centring his work around the role of the peasantry as the main drivers of the revolution, the significance of ideology in defining classes, extending the issue of consciousness to cultural matters and defining contradictions as essential to all societies, thereby justifying the idea of permanent revolution. One biographer, Ross Terrill, praised Mao for his contribution to the success of the Chinese Revolution, and argued that although without Mao a strong communist movement probably still would have existed in China, the CCP would not have gained power (as it did in 1949) without his leadership.[1] Understanding Mao and his thought is relevant for learning not only about China's past and present but also about the history of socialism in the latter half of the twentieth century. This is because Mao's ideas also challenged the hegemony of Soviet Union and the Soviet interpretation of Marxism; this challenge led to various splits in communist and socialist political parties and organised groups around the globe during the Cold War and beyond.

Mao's ideology continues to resonate in contemporary struggles and movements from the global South in various ways. As Dirlik has argued, Mao stood at the intersection of two histories.[2] On the one hand, in the late nineteenth century, interactions with the outside world exposed China to global realities, which impacted the Chinese people's consciousness about their position in the world. On the other hand, China began to reconsider questions of autonomy as it faced the increasing threat of subordination and marginalisation. Hence, a 'Third-World revolutionary consciousness' lay at the heart of Mao's revolutionary thinking, which has since inspired a large body of revolutionary thought and numerous social movements.[3]

Revolutionary pathways[4]

Mao Zedong was born in 1893, in a village in Hunan Province. His father had previously been a poor peasant, but by the time Mao was ten he had raised the family to a middle level of the peasantry. Mao grew up in rural Hunan and learned Confucian classics at primary school. He did not become interested in revolutionary ideas because of his parents or the immediate conditions of the village where he grew up but rather due to the broader conditions in China that he witnessed and experienced.

In 1911, he went to Changsha – the capital and most populous city of Hunan Province – for further education. This marked an important stage in his political and intellectual life. He started reading newspapers for the first time and gradually became familiar with anti-monarchic revolutionary politics advocated by republicans such as Sun Yat-sen. Shortly after arriving there, he experienced the outbreak of the 1911 Xinhai Revolution in Changsha, which overthrew the Qing Dynasty.

Mao joined the rebel army to help advance the revolution but did not actually get involved in any fighting. However, he stayed in the army for six months and this helped him develop his political education. It was around this time that he first discovered socialism, from a newspaper article. He also read pamphlets distributed by a student who had come back from Japan and had founded a Chinese socialist party in November 1911. Inspired by all these developments, he discussed socialism and social reformism with other soldiers and corresponded on the subject with some of his student friends. These were Mao's first encounters with radical ideas. Thereafter, he spent much of his time reading and studying independently. This was when he first read important works of the Western tradition such as Adam Smith's *The Wealth of Nations* as well as major works by Darwin, J. S. Mill, Rousseau and Spencer. He also studied history and geography. At school, Mao was a student of Yang Changji – a well-known educator, philosopher and writer – who guided him further towards radical ideas and revolutionary groups.

While at school, Mao remained profoundly immersed in the peasant environment within which he had spent most of his childhood. At the end of 1917, he played an important role in the development of the New People's Study Society, which was one of the most radical student societies in China at the time – all its members eventually joined the CCP. The group was formally established in the spring of 1918.

Although it was the Bolshevik victory in the October Revolution in 1917 that marked the systematic introduction of Marxism to China as a revolutionary theory, Marxism was not completely new there. For example, a fragment of *The Communist Manifesto* had already been translated into Chinese. However, the influence of Marxism on China's political and intellectual life grew very rapidly thereafter and altered the debates over China's future. Although Mao was at first more sympathetic to anarchism, during the winter of 1919 he rapidly shifted his sympathies towards Marxism. It was during the meetings of Li Ta-chao's Marxist Study Society that Mao started to attract the attention of others with his clear efforts to combine what he had learned about socialism with his knowledge of ancient Chinese traditions and philosophy. It is important to note that these developments took place during the years 1919–1920, when the May Fourth Movement – an anti-imperialist cultural and political movement led by students – was changing the social, political and cultural landscape of China.

Mao spent some time in Beijing, but when he returned to Changsha he played an active role in spreading the twin messages of the May Fourth Movement – new culture and anti-imperialism – through the creation of and participation in related associations and organisations, as well as by publishing his writings in different periodicals, which increased his fame among the activists and intellectuals of the day. By the winter of 1920, Mao had become heavily influenced by Marxist theory and the history of the Russian Revolution. He claimed that three books in particular impacted him and helped him become interested in Marxism: *The Communist Manifesto* by Marx and Engels, *Class Struggle* by Kautsky and a *History of Socialism* by Kirkup. By the summer of 1920, Mao had declared himself a Marxist. His activities from then on were more systematically inspired by Marxism. Shortly after this, he started building a branch of the Socialist Youth Corps, which was finally established in December 1920; during the autumn of that year Mao had been informed that a communist group had been established in Beijing. He got involved in organising labour unions, and his activities were closely connected with establishment of the CCP. The first Congress of the

CCP was held in July 1921, with delegates, including Mao, representing a few cities. He continued working as the Party secretary for Hunan Province while also maintaining involvement in labour unions and cultural activities. For example, he set up the Self-Study University, which had the objective of providing students with an opportunity to study and learn independently.

It was only in early 1925 that Mao started to understand the peasantry's revolutionary force. He had gone back to his village, where he recognised the significant changes that the peasantry had undergone. The countryside had become a restless place, with peasants increasingly developing an interest in politics. The Peasant Movement Training Institute – which was one of the outcomes of the alliance between the Nationalist Party (Kuomintang, or KMT) and the CCP – presented Mao with the opportunity to train cadre for militant activities and to teach the peasants some of the principles of Marxism and left-wing politics. He then briefly became the Director of the Peasant Department of the CCP. In April 1927, Mao joined the KMT's five-member Central Land Committee, where he led different peasant activities and groups. For example, he encouraged peasants not to pay rent and worked towards a resolution on the ownership and redistribution of land.

In 1927, the KMT and the CCP started fighting a civil war – although they temporarily allied during the second Sino-Japanese War (1937–1945) – that led the latter to create the Party's armed forces, the Chinese Peasants' and Workers' Red Army. Mao was appointed commander-in-chief of the Red Army and led four regiments in what is known as the Autumn Harvest Uprising. This led to the establishment of the short-lived Hunan Soviet, which was meant to spark a peasant uprising across Hunan Province but was defeated shortly after its formation. This was the beginning of a series of military attacks and uprisings which led to the establishment of the Jiangxi Soviet Republic of China (1929–1934) and the Long March of 1934–1935. The Long March was a military retreat of the main group of the Red Army to evade the KMT. It is worth mentioning that, although we speak of it as a single march, it actually consisted of a series of marches that were undertaken by various groups. The most famous of these went from Jiangxi Province to Shaanxi Province and lasted from October 1934 to October 1935. The Long March marked the beginning of Mao's rise to power because of his successful leadership of it. In November 1935, Mao was appointed Chairman of the Military Commission, and he became Chairman of the CCP itself in 1943. The civil war between the nationalists and the communists finally ended in 1949. Mao declared the founding of the People's Republic of China on 1 October 1949 and led the CCP until his death in 1976.

Mao Zedong's Marxism

'The Bolshevik success got to his gut', Mao's biographer Ross Terrill writes,[5] explaining that the success of the October Revolution was an inspiration for Mao, who had gradually begun to find his way in the world of revolutionary politics. For Mao, theory and practice were inseparable, and his thought developed in a 'dialectical interaction of theory and practice',[6] which allowed him to create 'a new system of practical thought'.[7] Marxism provided Mao with a theory of social dynamics that included a strong practical component. The theory of class struggle and the significance of the party remained the most important aspects of his Marxist politics. It was obvious in Mao's 1926 articles on the peasant classes that he had adopted a Marxian class analysis for classifying the conditions of different social groups and their revolutionary potentials. This showed Mao's interest in 'class struggle rather than the relationships of production'.[8] When he was asked what lessons he learned from *The Communist Manifesto* – which he apparently read more than 100 times – he responded, 'class struggle, class struggle, class struggle'.[9] Mao was aware that Marx's analysis of class conflict was rooted in an analysis of inequalities in the economy, but he used the concept to explain more broadly the 'struggle between oppressor and oppressed as the motive force of history'.[10]

Unlike what a number of scholars and political opponents of Mao have argued, Mao did not reject the importance of the working class as a revolutionary force. Rather, following Marx, Mao believed that it was the working class and not the peasants who would assume a leadership role in the class struggle, although he had to involve the peasantry in his strategy for China, given the country's strong rural base. However, from the early 1920s to the mid-1940s he repeatedly argued that the organisational skills and historical vision of the working class would qualify them as the leaders of the Chinese Revolution. Also for Mao, urban areas and struggles played a central role in the revolution, and he believed that the separation of the urban and the rural (and their revolutionary potentials) from each other was negatively impacting the capacity and success of the CCP.

After 1927, Mao articulated a revolutionary strategy based on mass peasant participation. He argued that the peasantry could organise and lead a revolution in a rural context, but because of the circumstances of their lives, the peasants were not quite suitable for the kind of industrialised and modern socialist society Mao envisioned for China. It was clear to Mao that the economic and sociological characteristics of the working class would make such a future possible. Thus, he promoted the leadership of workers within the party in order to encourage labour unions and urban areas to participate in the revolution.[11]

Like Marx, Mao considered the forces and relations of production to be the determining factors in history, although he viewed politics, ideology and culture as important elements of social change.[12] In the 1950s and 1960s, Mao continued to argue that the forces of production were the most significant factors in the development of societies. While the forces of production comprise people as well as the means and objects of labour, Mao claimed that people were the most important force. In 1956 Mao argued that the development of productive forces would lead to a revolution. Furthermore, he suggested there is always an imbalance between the forces of production, the relations of production and the superstructure, which would eventually lead to a major contradiction.[13] In terms of relations of production, he adopted the orthodox Marxist understanding of the five main types of relations of production – primitive communal, slave, feudal, capitalist and socialist.[14] For Mao, Marx's dialectical materialism had two exceptional characteristics. The first was its focus on class, and the second was its practicality. The following passage shows his emphasis on the latter:

> … it [dialectical materialism] emphasizes the dependence of theory on practice, emphasizes that theory is based on practice and in turn serves practice. The truth of any knowledge or theory is determined not by subjective feelings, but by objective results in social practice. Only social practice can be the criterion of truth. The standpoint of practice is the primary and basic standpoint in the dialectical materialist theory of knowledge.[15]

Mao developed his ideas about the party on the basis of his admiration for the October Revolution and Leninist strategy, although it can be argued that he understood the party to have a greater degree of interdependence with the masses.[16] Also, Mao's perspectives regarding the importance of the peasantry were inspired by Lenin's theory that a vanguard of revolutionary intellectuals should make alliances with the peasantry.[17] In 1920, when Mao had recently adopted Marxism and still was not familiar with Leninist strategy, he introduced ideas about the importance of organisation in the labour movement. He argued that labour unions should have democratically formed executive organs with full powers, because any division in authority would inhibit satisfactory results. These ideas were very similar to the Leninist conception of democratic centralism. Ultimately, however, during the two decades from 1920 to 1940 Mao thoroughly embraced Marxist-Leninist analysis.[18]

Finally, Mao's conceptualisation of the future was based on an orthodox understanding of Marx which argued that humans' temporal development is accomplished through a dialectical social process in which the existing configurations of production and social relations are confronted by the arrival of new forces of production and their consequent class structures. This leads to the replacement of one mode of production by a more advanced form. This advancement occurs dialectically until the extremely developed forces of production generated by industrialisation and capitalist relations will be abolished and replaced by communism, a classless and stateless society based on the values of equality and freedom and free from all forms of exploitation and oppression.[19] However, we cannot reduce Mao's vision of a new China to an expression of his orthodox Marxism because a deep understanding of China's needs was inherent in Mao's Marxism.[20] Moreover, the goals of the Chinese Revolution were not only to overthrow capitalism and imperialism and establish a socialist nation but to create a kind of harmony similar to the traditional ideal of the Great Harmony in

Confucian philosophy, which emphasises education and self-cultivation as the key to social harmony.[21]

Mao tried to write works that would establish him as a Marxist philosopher and political thinker. In July and August 1937, he delivered two speeches which were published for general distribution, titled 'On practice' and 'On contradiction'. In the early 1940s, he produced another theoretical piece, titled 'On dialectical materialism', much of which appears to have been copied from translations of Soviet writings. Mao decided to stop its publication shortly after it had appeared.[22]

During his lifetime Mao certainly established himself as a Marxist philosopher and political thinker. However, he also had a number of disagreements with orthodox interpretations of Marx and Marxism. Marx gave significant weight to the realm of the economy, referring to it as a 'base' and to politics and ideology as superstructural elements. Hence, many orthodox Marxists promoted a mechanistic understanding of the base–superstructure dynamic in society, which resulted in the spread of economic determinism. However, Mao diverged from this orthodox understanding of Marxism by emphasising the significance of the superstructure and by ascribing an important capacity to human consciousness.[23] In this sense, in contrast to Marx, Mao gave priority to ideology and defined classes in ideological terms rather than through exclusive reference to economic conditions.

Mao's new post-revolutionary government was based on a coalition of four classes – the proletariat, the peasantry, the petite bourgeoisie and the national bourgeoisie – to reflect a nationalist desire to incorporate most segments of society in his new China but also to demonstrate a different understanding of class, based on people's loyalty to their political system and the ideology it represented.[24] This way of understanding classes made it possible for Mao to emphasise class struggle within an economic class as opposed to struggle only between economic classes. This does not mean that Mao denied the existence of struggle between economic classes but that he always emphasised the importance of ideological definitions of classes.[25] While absorbed in the revolutionary struggle, constant analysis of the effective role of superstructure and ideology remained a core aspect of his task. As the academic Nick Knight writes, 'not only did Mao have to evaluate the strength of the state against which he would pit his revolutionary forces and the consciousness of groups and classes within Chinese society, he also had to determine the level of political influence exercised by other political parties and anticipate their tactics'.[26]

Related to Mao's understanding of classes and their relationship to ideology and the superstructure was his view on consciousness. Unlike Marx, who defined consciousness as being in a dialectical relationship with history, and unlike Marx's association of consciousness with proletarian consciousness as the main form of revolutionary consciousness, Mao believed that consciousness in Chinese society could not be understood only with reference to politics and material conditions but also needed to consider cultural matters. Although revolutionary consciousness was an important factor for revolutionary activity, consciousness 'was not simply a reflection of social reality, but a mode of comprehending and changing it'.[27] It was contradiction and not dialectical integration which could explain revolutionary consciousness in China and, therefore, a 'revolution in consciousness and culture was the precondition to a revolution in material existence'.[28]

Although in the early 1920s it could have been possible to believe in working-class consciousness and uprisings in Chinese cities, after 1927 Mao was convinced that the revolution had to be carried out in rural China, where the most challenging task was to transform peasant grievances into a revolutionary consciousness.[29] This shaped the basis of his rural revolutionary strategy, which espoused an 'egalitarian redistribution of resources, a cadre ethic emphasizing closeness to the masses, and a military-political structure which integrated mass support'.[30]

Moreover, Mao differed from Marx in his analysis of the relationship between contradictions. According to Marx, the contradictions between classes (i.e. the proletariat and the bourgeoisie) would lead to the destruction of the bourgeoisie and eventually the emergence of a harmonious communist society, one without any contradictions. In contrast, Mao believed contradictions were an essential component of societies, and therefore social systems would need to be reformed continuously. He defined this continuous struggle as 'permanent revolution', a perpetual part of communist society and not merely one of the characteristics of the stages leading up to it. Mao saw the world as being in a continual and permanent flux that would never reach a definitive harmony, even under communism. According to this theory, 1949 did not signal the end of the Chinese Revolution but rather the commencement of new contradictions, which would emerge in the post-revolutionary era and require new solutions and struggles. For Mao, permanent revolution helped maintain revolutionary zeal and facilitated the continuation of the revolution into the future. A famous line often attributed to Mao regarding the permanent revolution reads: 'summon up all our energies, advance with all our strength, to build socialism more, faster, better and more economically'.[31] It shows how he believed the idea of progress was embedded in any society that saw itself in a state of a permanent revolution.

Mao developed the theory of permanent revolution in 1958, right before the Great Leap Forward – an economic and social campaign led by the CCP from 1958 to 1962. For Mao, the Great Leap Forward represented one of the many revolutions within the continuous permanent revolution.[32] One of his main objectives after the Chinese Revolution was to push China towards modernisation and industrial development. According to him, the development of the forces of production was a necessity for moving China's political economy towards industrial socialism. However, he believed these changes would be relatively small, and on the level of industrial advancement that China had already achieved. Therefore, it would be the restructuring of the relations of production and superstructure that would help create conditions for generation of a 'leap forward'. That is why the Great Leap Forward campaign reorganised working conditions through the formation of people's communes and the collectivisation of agriculture, and focused on the ideological transformation of China's huge population, through which the preconditions for the transformation of society to the next stage would be achieved.[33]

Mao believed Marxism provided a methodology which was capable of grasping particular contexts through universal laws. As early as 1938, he emphasised that abstract Marxism was meaningless and that Marxism only made sense when applied to concrete conditions of the society and the struggles embedded in it.[34] In 'On new democracy', published in 1940, Mao stated, 'the universal truth of Marxism must be combined with specific national characteristics and acquire a definite national form if it is to be useful, and in no circumstances can it be applied subjectively as a mere formula'.[35] He further argued that although the Chinese Revolution was pitted against capitalism, it was taking place in a semi-feudal and semi-colonial society, and its goal beyond combating capitalism was also to create a new nation and a new culture.

By the end of the 'rectification campaign' of 1942–1944, which was the first ideological movement initiated by the CCP, Mao had managed to convince his comrades that it was absolutely necessary to see their problems in the Chinese context. Also, it had become clear that he had his own style of leadership, which was independent from Moscow.[36] In March 1959, he famously stated that, although there were things such as trains and planes which did not need to have a national style, other things such as politics were in absolute need of a national style.[37] These developments in his thought process led him to identify himself as a 'native' or 'indigenous' thinker by the mid-1960s.[38] However, according to most Mao scholars, his thought should be perceived as a synthesis of Marxism and traditional Chinese thought. For example, his emphasis on practice is rooted in Confucian philosophy[39] and his interest in morality in politics has parallels with Confucianism as well.[40] Regardless of the exact roots which contributed to Mao's unique interpretation of Marxism, it has been referred to as a Sinified Marxism by numerous scholars.[41]

The most important aspect of Mao's Sinified Marxism was his development of a revolutionary strategy for the Chinese context by attributing to the peasantry a clear conscious- ness of their historical role and capacity to organise and become the main force in the revolutionary process. China had neither a large alienated working class (unlike Europe), nor a feudal economic system (unlike Russia). China's most important problem was 'the demoralization resulting from imperialist subjugation' as well as 'an economic nightmare', as the philosopher John Koller has put it.[42] In spite of his clear embeddedness in the Chinese context, Mao frequently insisted that his Sinified Marxism was not simply a product of national or cultural influence but was simultaneously in close conversation with a universal perspective and had its roots in and was connected to an international body of thought and movements.[43]

Mao constantly used examples from the past to make his revolutionary theories more comprehensible and acceptable to the Chinese masses. He borrowed Lenin's democratic centralism and combined it with moralism for a just cause, which was a common characteristic of the heroes of Mao's favourite novels. Therefore, one can say he did not only produce 'an explicit intellectual synthesis between Marxism and the Chinese tradition', but that he himself was 'a living synthesis' of these traditions.[44] Mao's Sinified Marxism was accessible to the average Chinese person of the time; it is full of colourful proverbs and phrases with some classical quotations to make it all the more interesting.[45]

'On practice' and 'On contradiction', the pre-revolution speeches mentioned earlier, are excellent examples of Mao's Sinified Marxism. In these, Mao not only integrates the laws and principles of Marxism with the experience of the Chinese Revolution but also combines Marxist philosophical concepts and those of traditional Chinese philosophy. For example, in 'On practice', Mao used the traditional Chinese philosophical couplet of knowledge and action (*zhixingguan*) and linked them to the significance of knowledge, theory and practice.

In 'On contradiction', Mao employed the traditional Chinese saying 'Things that oppose each other also complement each other' (*xiangfanxiangcheng*) to explain his ideas about contradiction and the law of the unity of opposites. Additionally, in these texts he developed original ideas. For example, in 'On practice' he developed the idea that knowledge is both subjective and objective, theory and practice at one and the same time, and, therefore, knowledge and action go together. In 'On contradiction', Mao systematically engaged with the concept of contradiction and elaborated the significance of the particularity of contradiction by referring to the complex and particular contradictions of Chinese society.

'On contradiction' was the result of lessons Mao had learned from a decade of revolutionary activity. In this text, he emphasised that conflict between classes was the basic unit of analysis. He argued that classes should not be understood in terms of their relationship to the means of production, but rather in relation to access to power and proximity to the relations of exploitation. This was because of Mao's interest in developing revolutionary consciousness and activity among different segments of Chinese society, particularly the peasantry. He argued that classes have conflicting goals, and these contradictions, which are rooted in the social structure of society, will eventually lead to the overthrow of the existing order. In summary, Mao's analysis of class in 'On contradiction' provided a necessary step in identifying society's conflicts and served as a guide for revolutionary action. According to Dirlik, '"On contradiction" was the ultimate expression of Mao's view of Marxism as a theory of conflict'.[46] Also, practice as 'activity to change the world' was an essential part of Mao's thought about contradictions. He believed changing the world was a process of solving contradictions but that this process constantly leads to new contradictions and therefore to new practices, in an ongoing process.[47]

Mao referred to two types of contradiction: antagonistic contradictions and non-antagonistic contradictions. He argued that non-antagonistic contradictions have the potential to develop into antagonistic ones. In the 1960s, Mao was convinced that the non-antagonistic contradictions in China were becoming antagonistic. In particular, he believed that a large segment of the CCP's leadership was determined to introduce capitalist measures, which would eventually be harmful to society and betray the objectives of the revolution. That is why Mao began to consider possibility of a campaign which would resolve the antagonistic contradictions that emerged following the Great Leap Forward. The Cultural Revolution, which began in 1966, should be understood in this context. With the launch of the Cultural Revolution, Mao indicated he was ready to move away from Leninism by attacking some segments of the CPP and by mobilising some groups outside of the Party to lead this attack. For Lenin, the party was the vanguard of the working class, and it was un-imaginable that this party or any segment of it would become a regressive force. Mao did not assume that the party was barred from the contradictions of society, and therefore he found it completely legitimate to mobilise progressive forces from outside of the party, such as students, youth, the military and some segments of the working class, to address the party and its problems.[48] In other words, Mao's belief in permanent revolution meant that the Cultural Revolution, as an attempt to move 'further along the path of revolution' and 'toward the creation of a revolutionary culture',[49] was not only desirable but in fact indispensable.

In summary, Mao's Marxism should be understood as part of a national project in a country that was engaged in a protracted struggle for national liberation and development. China's struggle against capitalism could not be separated from its struggle against imperialism. Socialism, as Mao understood it, had to take up burdens which were not the concern of socialists in Europe. At the heart of Mao's project was harnessing the power of the state to transform China into a sustainable and economically developed nation to such a degree that it could survive the imperialist hegemony of the United States. Furthermore, his project was directed towards creating a basis for socialism among the Chinese people through different means, such as cultural reconstruction.[50] Mao's Marxism is unique not only because of his making it Chinese (Sinified Marxism), but also because, through his Marxism, China's past and present started to serve 'as the medium for communicating Marxist abstractions'.[51]

Mao Zedong's legacy

The Chinese Revolution and Mao's legacy have become an inseparable part of today's China, and Mao's portraits can still be seen in many households, particularly in rural areas. Much has been written on Mao's style of running the Communist Party. According to one biographer, Terrill, 'many people who met Mao came away deeply impressed by his intellectual reach, originality, style of power-within-simplicity, kindness toward low level staff members, and the aura of respect that surrounded him at the top of Chinese politics'.[52] Decades after his death, today Mao represents different things to different groups and individuals. This is not only because he expressed his ideas in a variety of ways to make himself accessible to different people and groups but also because people connect to him for various reasons and with different motivations.[53] For example, a large majority of rural farmers and urban workers admire Mao and refer to his time as 'the good old days', although some dislike Mao because they see themselves as the victims of his theory and practice.[54]

Some of Mao's policies and practices remain controversial today. The Cultural Revolution is a prime example. For those who were dismissed from their posts and were obliged to work in what was called the May Seventh Cadre School, the experience is referred to as horrific and comparable to a 'detention in a labour camp'. However, for Mao and many others at that time and even today, the objective of the Cultural Revolution was to create new subjectivities by making the urban and social elite experience physical labour to be able to understand the hardships of the majority of people's lives in China. The idea was to create 'a new way of governing and governance' based on this experience.[55] This practice, although not very popular among some groups, facilitated grassroots participation in management, which led to a flourishing of ideas about popular democracy.[56]

In China, for several years after his death in 1976, Mao remained like 'a virtual god'.[57] His political legacy was still a significant factor in Chinese policy making until the main objective of Vice-Premier Deng Xiaoping in 1978 became breaking with that legacy, which had influenced Chinese politics from the victory of the Chinese Revolution until Mao's death.[58] However, according to some scholars, China's reforms during the post-Mao era were the direct and to some extent unintended consequence of Mao's policies, particularly the Cultural Revolution, and argue these reforms should be seen as a 'complex mingling of past legacies with new policy directions'.[59] For example, it was Mao's decision to normalise and improve the relations between the United States and China in the 1970s. This helped create an international environment that led to China's series of market economic reforms, which were implemented during the Deng Xiaoping era (after Mao's death). Also, China's engagement with Africa – which today is extensive – started with Mao's attempt to support the colonised and oppressed countries of the global South and spread his revolutionary vision, which was very compatible with ideas of national liberation and decolonisation.[60] It was, in fact, the Bandung Conference of 1955 which marked the beginning of China's awareness of the crucial role the global South could play in coalition building and mobilisations against common enemies.[61]

By the 1990s, Deng believed he had replaced Mao. However, instead, in response to the failures and disappointments of the Deng era, a grassroots 'Mao fever' emerged. Large segments of Chinese society had started to show renewed interest in Mao and his thought. Mao's pictures and images re-appeared, he figured again in popular arts and numerous books on Mao's life and work were published.[62] Although the Deng era was a reaction to the Mao era, the post-Deng leaders have not defined themselves in opposition to Mao. In fact, after the failures of the reform era, a Maoist revival movement has emerged and become increasingly popular after Xi Jinping took power as the President of the People's Republic of China in 2013. He has introduced a set of policies and ideals which are referred to as 'Socialism with Chinese Characteristics for a New Era'. It was confirmed in the 19th Congress of the CPP in October 2017 that 'ideology' (i.e. Marxism) would guide the Party. This renewed commitment to Marxism as China's state ideology is another attempt by the Party to claim China's success with the doctrinal particularities of Mao's Sinified Marxism, which, according to the academic Brantly Womack:

> broke the bottleneck of modern Chinese history by developing a political program appropriate to Chinese conditions and yet cognizant of the transformative potential evident in the modern West. The foundations for reconstituting China had to be worked out in practice, and Mao's orientation of populist empiricism enabled him to generate many of the policy innovations which later characterized the successful Chinese revolution.[63]

Outside of China, Maoism has for decades provided a revolutionary blueprint across the world and still shapes world politics today. Above all, Maoism cannot be understood apart from its role in guiding struggles against colonialism and the revolutionary surge it created in the global South, from Latin

America to Africa and Asia, where it became an inspiration for numerous oppressed and marginalised groups. In Asia alone, Maoism has guided Marxist revolutionaries in countries such as India, Nepal, Vietnam, the Philippines, Cambodia and Indonesia.[64] In countries such as India and Nepal, Maoism has continued to be an active force in the twenty-first century. Maoists have directed the Naxalites in India since 1967, one of the longest guerrilla insurgencies in the world. Over the years, the Naxalites have attracted the most marginalised segments of Indian society, and Indigenous peasants have supported the armed struggle in spite of extreme state repression.[65] The Maoists in Nepal led several governments, and they are still one of the largest political parties in that country. Also, Mao has inspired various movements, revolutionary parties and groups in the global North. For example, some of the May 1968 protesters in France were inspired by Maoist ideas of rebellion, and the in Denmark the Communist Working Circle, which was a spin-off of the Communist Party of Denmark, disseminated Maoist literature for years while maintaining a close relationship with the CCP.

Given the global prevalence of Mao's ideology in the 1960s and beyond, and bearing in mind the resurgence of socialist ideas in recent years, not only in numerous countries of the global South – particularly in Latin America – but also in countries such as the United States and the United Kingdom, it is not unlikely that new generations of anti-capitalists and socialists will start re-engaging and reinterpreting Mao's legacy and the Chinese experience.[66]

Chapter 4

Kwame Nkrumah: a political prophet ahead of his time

Kwame Nkrumah (1909–1972) was a Ghanaian revolutionary thinker and politician. He led Ghana – then called the Gold Coast – to independence in 1957, making it the first sub-Saharan country to break free of colonial rule. He became the first Prime Minister of the Gold Coast when the country was still under British control and served as the Prime Minister and President of Ghana from 1957 until 1966, when he was overthrown by a coup led by the police and the military. While studying in the United States he became familiar with Marxist ideas and acquainted himself with numerous political organisations. In 1947, while Nkrumah was living and studying in London, he was invited to become the full-time Secretary of the United Gold Coast Convention (UGCC). The party had just been established, by combining Ghana's only two political organisations, Gold Coast People's League and the Gold Coast National Party, were combined. Immediately after taking office he set up branches in various parts of the country and called for demonstrations, strikes and boycotts. However, differences in ideology and strategy with leadership of the party – which was mostly about his fierce rejection of the British timeline for gradual decolonisation and his insistence on immediate self-government –led him to establish his own political party in 1949, the socialist Convention People's Party

(CPP), which played a direct role in Ghana's decolonisation and independence.

Nkrumah tried to develop Lenin's analysis of imperialism to a new level by incorporating it into the African neo-colonial context. His socialism was associated with 'conscience', which, more than anything, was about the reconstruction of social cohesion. It has been argued that Nkrumah's 'consciencism' is an 'epistemological toolkit' that helps people become aware of their conditions and circumstances so that they can react to them politically.[1] After independence, Nkrumah developed socialist policies, including an Accelerated Development Plan for Education and a state-controlled economy that emphasised industrialisation and domestic manufacturing. He also promoted a socialist pan-African policy. Shortly after independence, he organised the First Conference of Independent States, followed by the All-African Peoples' Conference. In addition, he was instrumental in the creation of the Organisation of African Unity in 1963, which was the forerunner of the African Union.

Revolutionary pathways[2]

Kwame Nkrumah was born in September 1909 in a small village in the south-west of contemporary Ghana. His parents were illiterate and rather poor. His father was a goldsmith and his mother a petty trader. However, his mother worked very hard so that Nkrumah could receive an education. In his auto-biography, Nkrumah refers to his mother as the 'most worthy and vigilant protector'.[3] He was sent to a Roman Catholic elementary school where he became a pupil-teacher for one year around the age of seventeen. This was a life-changing year for him because one day the principal of a teacher training college visited the school and observed Nkrumah's teaching.

Impressed by his capabilities, the principal offered Nkrumah a position at the college, which was in Accra. It was there that Nkrumah became acquainted with Dr James Kwegyir Aggrey, the assistant vice principal of the training college, who inspired him in many ways. Aggrey was the first African member of the staff; he spoke at public meetings with large numbers of people in attendance, and he encouraged his students to work hard so that they could one day free Africa. Nkrumah wrote of Aggrey: 'To me he seemed the most remarkable man that I had ever met.... It was through him that my nationalism was first aroused.'[4] S. R. Wood, the Secretary of the National Congress of British West Africa at the time, was another source of inspiration and support for Nkrumah's education abroad. Apart from these individuals, however, it was the early activities of the anti-colonial movements in the Gold Coast that informed Nkrumah's political thought in his early youth.

Nkrumah worked in Ghana for a few years as a primary school teacher and then a head teacher before Aggrey persuaded him to continue his education in the United States, and he applied to Lincoln University in Pennsylvania, which accepted him. In October 1935 Nkrumah travelled to the United States by way of London, where he heard the news of Mussolini's invasion of Ethiopia, which had a profound impact on him. He wrote: 'My nationalism surged to the fore; I was ready and willing to go through hell itself, if need be, in order to achieve my object'.[5] Upon moving to America, besides focusing on his studies, Nkrumah acquainted himself with numerous political organisations, such as the Republicans, the Democrats, the Communists and the Trotskyites. He met C. L. R. James – the Trinidadian Marxist, activist and historian – and through him learned how underground movements worked. He also was brought into contact with organisations focused on Africa, such as the Council on African Affairs, the Committee on Africa and the Committee on African Students. His connections with these organisations were very helpful in teaching Nkrumah important organisational techniques. However, from an early stage, Marxist and communist writers impacted the development of his thoughts tremendously. In his autobiography he states:

> I knew that, whatever the programme for the solution of the colonial question might be, success would depend upon the organization adopted. I concentrated on finding a formula by which the whole colonial question and the problem of imperialism could be solved. I read Hegel, Karl Marx, Engels, Lenin and Mazzini. The writings of these men did much to influence me in my revolutionary ideas and activities, and Karl Marx and Lenin particularly impressed me as I felt sure that their philosophy was capable of solving these problems.[6]

During his time in the United States, Nkrumah studied numerous subjects, such as theology, sociology, education and philosophy. Also, it was in the US that he started to write his first book, *Towards Colonial Freedom*, which he originally referred to as a pamphlet. At Lincoln University, he obtained a bachelor's degree in theology as well as one in economics and sociology. He went to earn a master of science degree in education and a master of arts degree in philosophy at the University of Pennsylvania. He then decided to do a PhD and as he was finalising his doctoral degree in philosophy, he left for London in May 1945. His purported objective was to study law and to complete his thesis, but he ended up spending most of his time engaged in political activism.

Shortly after arriving in London, Nkrumah was appointed the joint Secretary, together with George Padmore (the Trinidadian Marxist and pan-Africanist), of the organising committee of the Fifth Pan-African Congress, which was to be held in Manchester in October that year. Nkrumah described the Congress as 'a tremendous success',[7] which

> was attended by over 200 delegates from all over the world. We listened to reports of conditions in the colonial territories and both capitalist and reformist solutions to the African colonial problems were rejected. Instead the Congress unanimously endorsed the doctrine of African socialism based upon the tactics of positive action without violence. It also endorsed the principles enunciated in the Declaration of Human Rights and advised Africans and those of African descent wherever they might be to organize themselves into political parties, trade unions, co-operative societies and farmers' organizations in support of their struggle for political freedom and economic advancement.[8]

Nkrumah also wrote a 'Declaration to the Colonial Peoples of the World', which was approved by the Congress and insisted that colonial peoples of the world should unite. Shortly after the Manchester Congress, Nkrumah co-initiated the establishment of a West African National Secretariat and became its first Secretary. Moreover, he became the chairman of the vanguard group of the West African National Secretariat called the Circle. The Circle's members were a special group within the Secretariat and were trained to be able to initiate any revolutionary work in any part of Africa. Shortly after the formation of the Circle, in 1947 Nkrumah was invited to return to the Gold Coast to serve as General Secretary of the United Gold Coast Convention, a political party founded in 1947 with the aim of ending British colonial rule. Although Nkrumah was initially hesitant, he eventually decided to accept this invitation and, after twelve years abroad, left England in November 1947.

Upon assuming his appointment, Nkrumah began to establish UGCC branches in towns and villages around the country. Moreover, he linked up with other organised groups, such as trade unions and farmers' organisations, and formed a Committee of Youth Organisations with which he worked closely. However, within a short period he realised that working with the UGCC had its limits because of ideological and strategic differences. In 1949, he formed a new socialist political party, the Convention People's Party (CPP). The CPP was meant to represent the will of the people, and it demanded the British grant self-government immediately. Its motto was 'Forward ever, backward never!' After a challenging period involving protests, boycotts, strikes, leafleting and educational campaigns – examples of his 'tactics of positive action' as quoted above – and imprisonments, the CPP gradually strengthened its position. In 1951, Nkrumah became the Leader of Government Business and the first Prime Minister of the Gold Coast the following year, when the country was still under colonial rule. After the CPP's victory in a number of general elections, Ghana gained its independence in March 1957, becoming the first country in sub-Saharan Africa to break free from European colonial rule. In 1960, Ghana became a republic and Nkrumah was elected its first President.

Nkrumah's main objective was to forge a new pathway for independent Ghana by building a socialist society. In addition, he established the Winneba Ideological Institute – informally known as the Kwame Nkrumah Ideological Institute – which provided Marxist-Leninist education and training to African revolutionaries across the continent. Shortly after Ghana's independence, Nkrumah invited the heads of state of other independent African states – Ethiopia, Libya, Tunisia, Morocco, Egypt, Liberia and Sudan – to a historic meeting in Accra at the 1958 All-African Peoples' Conference. The Conference brought together leaders of liberation movements from all over the continent and led to a series of meetings in the years that followed. These efforts culminated in the birth of the Organisation of African Unity in 1963.

In February 1966, Nkrumah was on a state visit to North Vietnam and China when his government was overthrown in a coup d'état led by the military and police forces and backed by the CIA. Nkrumah was invited to live in exile in Conakry, Guinea, by his close ally and friend President Ahmed Sékou Touré, who also made him honorary co-President of the country. He never got the chance to return to Ghana and died in 1972. He remained active during his exile, and much of his intellectual and revolutionary thought was developed during this period. He is the author of numerous books and pamphlets, such as *Consciencism: Philosophy and Ideology for De-Colonisation* (1964), *Neo-Colonialism: The Last Stage of Imperialism* (1965), *Dark Days in Ghana* (1968), *Handbook of Revolutionary Warfare* (1968), *Class Struggle in Africa* (1970) and *Revolutionary Path* (1973).

Kwame Nkrumah's Marxism

Nkrumah believed in Marxist dialectics and historical materialism. In *Class Struggle in Africa*, originally published in 1970, two years before his death, Nkrumah provided an acute Marxist class analysis of African societies and highlighted the fact that the African revolutionary struggle must be understood as part of the 'world socialist revolution'. He asserted that the 'total liberation and the unification of Africa under an All-African socialist government must be the primary objective of all Black revolutionaries throughout the world'.[9] Such a victory would not only fulfil the aspirations of Africans and people of African descent, but it would work towards the victory of the international socialist revolution and the move towards global communism.[10]

> A fierce class struggle has been raging in Africa. The evidence is all around us. In essence it is, as in the rest of the world,

a struggle between the oppressors and the oppressed. The African Revolution is an integral part of the world socialist revolution, and just as the class struggle is basic to world revolutionary processes, so also is it fundamental to the struggle of the workers and peasants of Africa.[11]

He argued that class, as a social category, is 'the sum total of individuals bound together by certain interests which as a class they try to preserve and protect'.[12] All forms of political power represent an interest of a certain class or classes, and it is the private ownership of the means of production that is responsible for capitalist exploitation.[13]

According to Nkrumah, both peasants and industrial urban workers are crucial for carrying out the African Revolution. Peasants and agricultural labourers comprise the majority of Africans, while the industrial and urban workers come second. However, 'because of the presence of foreigners and foreign interests, class struggle in African society has been blurred'.[14] Nkrumah believed that, in spite of its small size, a 'modern proletariat' existed in Africa and was 'the class base for the building of socialism'. Furthermore, this class 'must be seen in the context of the international working-class movement from which it derives much of its strength'.[15]

Nkrumah asserted that the working class in Africa emerged because of colonialism and the introduction of foreign capital and that the growth of this strong working class in the most developed African economies, such as Egypt and South Africa, paved the way for the establishment of Africa's first communist parties, which consisted of workers, peasants and intellectuals. He also emphasised the connection between the establishment of the French Communist Party in 1920 and the formation of communist parties in Algeria, Morocco and Tunisia.[16] However, in spite of a strong belief in the revolutionary power of the working class, Nkrumah suggested that the African peasantry should be understood as 'the largest contingent of the working class, and potentially the main force for socialist revolution'. However, because it is 'dispersed, unorganised, and for the most part unrevolutionary' it 'must be led by its natural class allies – the proletariat and the revolutionary intelligentsia'.[17] Also, he asserted, under conditions of class struggle, violent revolutionary action is the only solution.[18]

In his autobiography Nkrumah constantly refers to capitalism as the evil force responsible for colonisation and imperialism.[19] He believed that capitalism had disintegrated the homogeneity of Africa and, based on the theory of dialectical materialism, the solution to contradictory situations was conflict. Hence, Nkrumah argued that transformation in Africa would occur through a revolutionary struggle between the African masses and the bourgeois capitalism and neo-colonialism.[20]

Nkrumah was critical of the concept of 'African socialism' and argued that it is a 'myth' which 'is used to deny the class struggle, and to obscure genuine socialist commitment'.[21] Instead, he identified with scientific socialism and promoted the application of the principles of scientific socialism to the African context, emphasising that socialism was in fact a science based on certain principles and that no alternative to scientific socialism could be envisioned.[22] In other words, he treated scientific socialism as a methodology rather than an ideology and thus focused on people's relationship to their material world.[23] Following Nkrumah, a number of African countries later adopted the term 'scientific socialism' in the late 1960s and 1970s, including Congo-Brazzaville, Ethiopia, Angola and Mozambique.[24] Nkrumah was convinced that socialism was the most appropriate path for post-independence Africa and that socialist ideas were historically an integral part of traditional communal African society.[25] He wrote that 'while there is no hard and fast dogma for socialist revolution, and specific circumstances at a definite historical period will determine the precise form it will take, there can be no compromise over socialist goals'.[26]

Although Marxist concepts and ideas had influenced Nkrumah's thinking at a very early stage, it was Marxism-Leninism and Lenin's theory of imperialism that affected his thinking and writing most profoundly in *Towards Colonial Freedom*, which was written during his time in the United States but was first published in 1945, in *Neo-Colonialism: The Last Stage of Imperialism*, published in 1965, and also in his later work.[27] According to the academic Ali Mazrui, Nkrumah 'saw himself quite consciously as an African Lenin.... Hence the term "Nkrumahism" – a name for an ideology that he hoped would assume the same historic and revolutionary status as "Leninism"'. Also, Nkrumah was behind the publication of a Marxist newspaper called *Spark*, which, some argue, was inspired by *Iskra* (Spark), the Marxist paper founded by Lenin in 1901.[28]

Nkrumah focused on those aspects of Lenin's theory which were concerned with monopoly capitalism, the racist relations between the colonisers and the colonised, and the fact that real decolonisation could come about only through the organised and continuous struggle of the masses in the colonies.[29] In *Towards Colonial Freedom*, Nkrumah wrote: 'The basis of colonial territorial dependence is economic, but the basis of the solution of the problem is political'.[30] He also became increasingly preoccupied with the phenomenon of neo-colonialism, which became applicable in Africa after independence and with the continuation of exploitation through different means, such as multinational corporations and foreign aid.[31]

However, Nkrumah was non-dogmatic and flexible in applying his Marxist-Leninist ideas to the African context.

In *Neo-Colonialism: The Last Stage of Imperialism*, which is a conscious echo of Lenin's work *Imperialism: The Highest Stage of Capitalism*, he wrote: '[Neo-colonialism] means power without responsibility and for those who suffer from it, it means exploitation without redress'.[32] Therefore, similar to Lenin, who had tried to advance Marx's analysis of capitalism through his theory of imperialism, Nkrumah tried to develop Lenin's analysis of imperialism to a new level by incorporating it into the African context: in old-style colonialism, a person or an administration could be held accountable, but neo-colonialism was an irresponsible form of imperialism.[33]

As the academic Vincent Dodoo has put it, for Nkrumah,

> socialism is the sure road to Africa's development; neo-colonialism is the number one enemy of Africa's development. Therefore, socialism is an antidote to neo-colonialism and anything that promotes the growth of socialism serves to frustrate neo-colonialism.[34]

Nkrumah emphasised the fact that, prior to colonialism, egalitarian communalism and values which communally structured resources, labour and social relations were an integral part of African societies but were destroyed by colonialism and capitalism – although he was also aware of the social hierarchies that had existed prior to colonisation. Nkrumah wrote:

> at the opening of the colonial period, the peoples of Africa were passing through the higher stage of communalism characterised by the disintegration of tribal democracy and the emergence of feudal relationships, hereditary tribal chieftaincies and monarchical systems. With the impact of imperialism and colonialism, communalist socio-economic patterns began to collapse as a result of the introduction of export crops such as cocoa and coffee. The economies of the colonies became interconnected with world capitalist markets. Capitalism, individualism, and tendencies to private ownership grew.

Gradually, primitive communalism disintegrated and the collective spirit declined.[35]

Therefore, for Nkrumah, Marxism and socialism would reinstate the fundamental principles of lost African communalism. Socialism was 'reflective of traditional values of communal egalitarianism, which would enable a creative transformation of life' and would be achieved through revolution and not reform.[36] As Nkrumah wrote:

> Socialism, therefore, can be and is the defence of the principles of communalism in a modern setting. Socialism is a form of social organisation which, guided by the principles underlying communism, adopts procedures and measures made necessary by demographic and technological developments. These considerations throw light on the bearing of revolution and reform on socialism. The passage from the ancestral line of slavery via feudalism and capitalism to socialism can only lie through revolution: it cannot lie through reform. For in reform, fundamental principles are held constant and the details of their expression modified. In the words of Marx, it leaves the pillars of the building intact.[37]

He also defended materialism and connected it 'with a humanist organization' that 'inspired an egalitarian organization of society' because of 'its being monistic and its referring all natural processes to matter and its laws'.[38] According to Nkrumah, materialism 'will give the firmest conceptual basis to the restitution of Africa's egalitarian and humanist principles'.[39]

Although in *Neo-Colonialism: The Last Stage of Imperialism* (1965) Nkrumah provided a Leninist economic analysis and in *Class Struggle in Africa* (1970) used 'consciousness' in reference to the proletariat class consciousness, in *Consciencism* (1964), the work that is the most representative of Nkrumah's thought, his socialism is not directly synonymous with European socialism but is, rather, associated with 'conscience', which entails the formation of a web of entangled duties and obliga-tions towards others. It is about the reconstruction of social cohesion, which is necessary for building an anti-colonial egalitarianism.[40] He justified philosophical consciencism as an ideology necessary for decolonisation because of the nature of the change colonialism had wrought on African society, but also because he believed ideologies needed to be connected to the reality of the people they aim to serve in order for them to be operational. He wrote:

> In Africa, this kind of emphasis [that which 'a particular society lays on a given means'] must take objective account of our present situation at the return of political independence. From this point of view, there are three broad features to be distinguished here. African society has one segment, which comprises our traditional way of life; it has a second segment which is filled by the presence of the Islamic tradition in Africa; it has a final segment which represents the infiltration of the Euro-Christian tradition and culture of Western Europe into Africa, using colonialism and neo-colonialism as its primary vehicles. These different segments are animated by competing ideologies. But since society implies a certain dynamic unity, there needs to emerge an ideology which, genuinely catering for the needs of all, will take the place of the competing ideol-ogies, and so reflect the dynamic unity of society and be the guide to society's continual progress.[41]

The ideology of consciencism was echoed in the organisa-tion of the CPP and was intended to bring together the class interest of different fragments of society as well as various wings of the party, such as trade unions, farmers' councils, women and youth, for a unified nation-state and a unified Africa.[42] According to Nkrumah, philosophical consciencism would create a 'harmonious' synthesis of various and at times conflicting cultures in Africa which would work together towards 'the original humanist principles of Africa'.[43] As Nkrumah specifies,

With true independence regained, however, a new harmony needs to be forged, a harmony that will allow the combined presence of traditional Africa, Islamic Africa and Euro-Christian Africa, so that this presence is in tune with the original humanist principles underlying African society. Our society is not the old society, but a new society enlarged by Islamic and Euro-Christian influences. A new emergent ideology is therefore required, an ideology which can solidify in a philosophical statement, but at the same time an ideology which will not abandon the original humanist principles of Africa.[44]

Hence, Nkrumah's socialism becomes inseparable from African humanism and the spirit of care and solidarity that traditionally existed in Africa. The task of consciencism would thus be to bring together these principles in light of Africa's realities and challenges in the post-independence era. His emphasis on African humanism was meant to stress the egalitarian aspects of traditional Africa and distinguish it from Western humanism, which, according to him, ensued from a non-egalitarian tradition.[45] In addition, he insisted that the 'attitude to the Western and the Islamic experience must be purposeful' and 'accommodated only as experiences of the traditional African society'.[46] This means his consciencism is a clear reinterpretation of Marxism in the context of post-colonial Africa, and he presents it as a philosophy and ideology which will provide a practical framework to the reality of the new Africa.[47] According to Nkrumah:

Our philosophy must find its weapons in the environment and living conditions of the African people. It is from those conditions that the intellectual content of our philosophy must be created. The emancipation of the African continent is the emancipation of man. This requires two aims: first, the restitution of the egalitarianism of human society, and, second, the logistic mobilization of all our resources towards the attainment of that restitution.[48]

In his address at the first seminar at Winneba Ideological Institute, in February 1962, Nkrumah stated, 'Let us not forget that Marxism is not a dogma but a guide to action',[49] and this statement not only guided his political action throughout the struggle for independence but also after independence and during his exile in Guinea. For Nkrumah, from the very beginning it was obvious that there were only two possibilities for African states after independence: either they 'remain under imperialist domination via capitalism and neo-colonialism' or they 'pursue a socialist path by adopting the principles of scientific socialism'. He knew that it was possible to pursue only a socialist path and not a socialist state right away because industrialisation had just begun, and the country had only a small, if strong, proletarian population.[50] However, he was optimistic about the future of the revolutionary process. He asserted:

> The ultimate victory of the revolutionary forces depends on the ability of the socialist revolutionary Party to assess the class position in society, and to see which classes and groups are for, and which against, the revolution. The Party must be able to mobilise and direct the vast forces for socialist revolution already existing, and to awaken and stimulate the immense revolutionary potential which is at present lying dormant.[51]

The Party would back what Nkrumah called 'positive action', which was an amalgamation of a number of strategies – from boycotts to strikes, leafleting and educational campaigns – and that included different social groups such as youth, women, trade unions and farmers. This strategy was first outlined in his small book *Towards Colonial Freedom*, which was written in 1947. The objective was to unite against capitalism, the common enemy, rather than being divided into various parties and pursuing multiple interests. That is why he proposed a one-party system. The Party, dedicated to socialism and representative of the masses, would pave the way towards economic independence and oppose neo-colonial forces. It would also promote a national consciousness, scientific socialism and the philosophy of consciencism.[52] Moreover, Nkrumah emphasised the local roots of the Party: 'the structure of the Convention People's Party has been built up from our own experiences, conditions, environments and concepts, entirely Ghanaian and African in outlook, and based on the Marxist socialist philosophy and worldview'.[53]

However, for Nkrumah, the local and the national were a prerequisite of a broader agenda. As the academic Paul Emiljanowicz has correctly pointed out, 'for Nkrumah the designation of "national" acts as a prerequisite for the achievement of continental-diasporic independence and unity'.[54] In fact, Ghana would become 'a microcosm of his vision for the entire African continent'.[55] Nkrumah constantly asserted that the African struggle for independence should go beyond anti-colonialism and include a quest for autonomous nation-states to transform their economies and socio-political structures to assure a dignified and sufficient living standard for all people and in the context of a united Africa.[56] Shortly after independence, in 1958, the first All-African Peoples' Conference took place in Accra, and Ghana became 'a "base" from which to coordinate "real development" for the African Revolution'.[57] Apart from Nkrumah, who was leading the Conference, a number of other African statesmen such as Ahmed Sékou Touré of Guinea and Léopold Senghor of Senegal also spoke of socialism as a revolutionary tool for Africa's independence and socio-economic reconstruction.[58]

Nkrumah's socialist pan-Africanism offered a practical solution for African states to achieve political and economic unity. Independent zones and countries had three duties: support the ongoing revolutionary struggles in other parts of

Africa, support the organisation and revolutionary practice of people in countries facing neo-colonialism, and cooperate economically and politically with other liberated African nations.[59] In his book *Africa Must Unite*, which was distributed widely among the African heads of state shortly before the establishment of the Organisation of African Unity in May 1963,[60] Nkrumah outlined the reasons why African unity was necessary:

> We need the strength of our combined numbers and resources to protect ourselves from the very positive dangers of returning colonialism in disguised forms. We need it to combat the entrenched forces driving our continent and still holding back millions of our brothers. We need it to secure total African liberation. We need it to carry forward our construction of a socio-economic system that will support the great mass of our steadily rising population at levels of life which will compare with those in the most advanced countries.[61]

The prerequisites for these achievements, according to Nkrumah, were the development of large-scale industry and transport networks, thus easing inter-African trade; creating a central bank; and forming a unified policy on export control and quota arrangements that would ensure Africa would remain 'a viable, single, economic, and political unit'.[62] Moreover, Nkrumah saw Ghana's role as central in imagining a unified Africa which could confront the legacy of colonialism and realities of neo-colonialism. Therefore, Ghanaian development was meant to become a resource in the larger struggle for the liberation of Africa. Ghana needed to assemble its resources and an effective socialist management in order to rid itself of (neo)colonial conditions of underdevelopment.[63] Therefore, economic development became a cornerstone of Nkrumah's national policy. For example, the Volta Dam project – a hydroelectric dam on the Volta River in the south-east of Ghana – became one of the symbols of Nkrumah's Ghana. This project was not only meant to lay the foundations for a stronger nation by providing jobs for the locals and becoming the country's main source of energy supply but also aimed at sending a message that newly independent countries were capable of nurturing economic development and taking care of their own affairs.[64]

As the historian Thomas Hodgkin has correctly stated, 'Nkrumah's Jacobinism and his devotion to the idea of African Union were clearly complementary'.[65] A stable base in Ghana achieved by a unified revolutionary party would allow Nkrumah to contribute to the ideal of a united Africa. Moreover, a large and diverse yet united Africa would enable him resist any counter-revolutionary force or expansion of neo-colonialism in Ghana and would facilitate the move towards creating a socialist society. He believed that 'at the core of the concept of African unity lies socialism and the socialist definition of the new African society'.[66] An independent Africa would be able to confront global capitalism in a more competent way. Moreover, an economically free and politically united Africa would result in monopolists coming 'face to face with their own working class in their own countries, and a new struggle will arise within which the liquidation and collapse of imperialism will be complete'.[67]

Therefore, Nkrumah's pan-Africanism went hand in hand with anti-imperialism and solidarity with the oppressed of the world beyond Africa. Towards the end of his life, while living in exile after the military coup in Ghana and having gone through the experience of failed or successful military coups in other parts of Africa, Nkrumah emphasised the 'need for the founding of an all-African vanguard working-class party, and for the creation of an all-African people's army and militia'.[68] Nkrumah's conclusions at the end of his life were not very different from his earlier work. In fact, throughout his life he insisted on the significance of class struggle by workers and peasants for the success of the socialist revolutionary struggle worldwide.

Kwame Nkrumah's legacy

Nkrumah has been referred to as 'a political prophet ahead of his time'[69] and as both Marx and Lenin for African countries.[70] Ghana under Nkrumah was among the first socialist regimes to emerge in post-colonial Africa and to shape an African perspective for socialism. Nkrumah's socialist policies and Nkrumahism were praised by intellectuals, revolutionaries and politicians around the world. For example, his long-term companion C. L. R. James claimed that if Nkrumahism is 'adopted by the labour and socialist elements of the most advanced countries of the world it will not roll over Africa alone but it will lead to the emancipation of all oppressed peoples and classes in every section of the globe'.[71]

After his death, a number of political parties and social movements emerged in Ghana which identified themselves as 'Nkruhmahist'. Examples include the Pan-African Youth Movement, the African Youth Command and the Socialist Revolutionary Youth League of Ghana. These developments occurred in spite of the fact that, immediately after Nkrumah's death, the CPP was officially banned.[72] In 2007, during Ghana's celebration of its Golden Jubilee, Nkrumah re-emerged in the political life and imagination of the Ghanian people. Also, 2009 marked the centennial of Nkrumah's birth and saw celebrations and commemorations in Ghana and beyond.[73]

While in exile in Guinea, Nkrumah received letters from various activist groups and intellectuals, from student unions and academic faculty members, from Ghanaians and other

Africans outside Ghana but also from around the world.[74] Nkrumah was definitely one of the main figures who contributed to the key debates around decolonisation in the 1950s and 1960s,[75] debates that are very present and relevant today. For example, his discussion of neo-colonialism and the nature of multinational companies, foreign aid, debt and poverty, which would arise due to lack of continental integration, still resonates with many Africans.[76] This is because Africa is still caught in neo-colonial relations, and these exploitative relations that have emerged after independence were the focus of much of Nkrumah's work and vision. The political and cultural philosophy that he developed was intended to address the problems that emerged in the neo-colonial stage and were meant to serve the second phase of the African Revolution.[77]

Writing in the early 1970s, Hodgkin identified six areas of Nkrumah's contribution which would have an enduring legacy: his theoretical concerns, his understanding of history, his egalitarianism, his views on imperialism and neo-colonialism, his Jacobinism and his notion of African unity and union.[78] Although all these areas have remained relevant today, perhaps his ideas regarding African unity have endured the most in contemporary African politics.

The Organisation of African Unity, which was co-founded by Nkrumah, was transformed into the African Union in 2002. Although the African Union falls short of Nkrumah's socialist vision, its main objective remains African unity. In addition, after Nkrumah's death, a number of conferences about continental unity and Africa's decolonisation were organised in places such as Tanzania, Uganda and South Africa, which hosted the Sixth, Seventh and Eighth Pan-African Congresses in 1974, 1994 and 2014, helping the continuation of Nkrumah's ideas after his death. At the end of the Seventh Congress, in a final resolution it was unanimously agreed that resisting recolonisation of Africa by global capitalism should be the main objective of the African nations. This was a reaction to the structural adjustment programmes demanded by the International Monetary Fund (IMF) and World Bank that were adopted by a number of African states during the 1980s and 1990s. As the historian Ama Biney wrote, this unanimity 'echoed the emphases, thinking, and positions expressed by Nkrumah in his famous book *Neo-Colonialism: The Last Stage of Imperialism*'.[79]

Nkrumah's vision of an economically independent and unified Africa that would play a sovereign role in global politics continues in the current consciousness of activists, intellectuals and those concerned with an alternative world vision to the existing status quo. In September 2018, leading pan-Africanist activists, socialists, trade unionists and members of other progressive groups gathered in Accra to celebrate Nkrumah's birthday and to discuss his thought and legacy for the twenty-first century. They were building on two previous meetings held in 2016 and 2017 in Zambia and Tunisia. What brought the three conferences together was, more than anything, discussions around 'the potentials and prospects for Socialist Pan-Africanism'.[80] In the 2018 Accra forum, Nkrumahism was suggested as a model for the liberation of African countries, which reveals Nkrumah's enduring legacy and the need for alternative visions which are rooted in actual anti-colonial struggles and particularities of context and lived experiences of people.[81] As Amílcar Cabral stated in his tribute to Nkrumah:

> For us, as Africans, the best homage we can pay to Kwame Nkrumah and his immortal memory, is reinforced vigilance in all fields of the struggle, more strongly developed and intensified struggle, the total liberation of Africa, success in development and economic, social and cultural progress for

our peoples, and in the building of African unity. That was the fundamental aim of Kwame Nkrumah's action and thought. This is the oath we should all take before history in respect of the African continent.... We are certain, absolutely certain that framed by the eternal green of the African forests, flowers of crimson like the blood of martyrs and of gold like the harvests of plenty will bloom over the grave of Kwame Nkrumah; for Africa will triumph.[82]

Chapter 5

Amílcar Cabral: a charismatic visionary leader

Amílcar Cabral (1924–1973) was the leader of the national liberation movement that freed Guinea-Bissau (formerly Portuguese Guinea, henceforth Guinea) and Cape Verde from Portuguese colonialism. He went to school in Cape Verde and studied agronomy in Lisbon. During his time in Lisbon he became involved in student politics and started to engage with the revolutionary theories of Marx, Engels and Lenin while also learning about revolutionary experiences in China, Cuba, Algeria and Vietnam, among others. Upon his return to Africa after completing his university education, he worked as an agronomist and conducted a nationwide agricultural survey, which helped him gain a deep understanding of colonial rule in Guinea. In 1956, he founded the African Party for the Independence of Guinea and Cape Verde (Partido Africano para a Independência da Guiné e Cabo Verde, or PAIGC), which later waged a decade of successful armed struggle against Portuguese colonialism.

Cabral underlined the significance of the mode of production as the motive force of history and thereby made an important theoretical contribution to Marxist class analysis. He demonstrated that national liberation was more than just self-rule, as it required a change in the mode of production. Therefore, he strongly emphasised changing neo-colonial structures, and in doing so he gave a prominent role to the national petite bourgeoisie. Finally, he highlighted the role of culture and its relation to national liberation struggles.

Cabral became one of the best-known leaders of national liberation movements, and his influence went beyond Guinea, Cape Verde and Africa. In spite of his innovative revolutionary ideas, however, his thoughts were not systematically recorded to the extent that some of the other revolutionary theorists' ideas were. This is because Cabral's writings were peripheral to the struggle, and he never wrote anything for purely intellectual or theoretical purposes. Nevertheless, we can find his ideas in the numerous short articles, essays, notes and speeches he wrote.[1] Apart from the significant role he played in PAIGC, Cabral was also instrumental in the establishment of the People's Movement for the Liberation of Angola (Movimento Popular de Libertação de Angola, or MPLA).

Revolutionary pathways[2]

Amílcar Cabral was born in Bafata, Portuguese Guinea, in September 1924. His father came from a landowning family and was a teacher. His mother was an independent small businesswoman. They were migrants from Cape Verde, escaping drought and other problems, but after a few years they returned to the islands, where Cabral received a high-quality education. From an early age, Cabral's mother was instrumental in giving him a sense of self-determination, discipline and personal ethics. In addition, because of her determination for her children to receive a good education she made sure that Cabral received excellent schooling in Cape Verde. The hardships that his mother endured as an independent woman caring for her kids influenced his views on gender justice and the revolutionary role of women in national liberation struggles. Later in life, he would express his gratitude to his mother by dedicating a poem to her, in which he calls her 'the star of my infancy' and declares, 'Without you, I am nobody'.[3]

Cape Verde at the time had a unique position in the colonial system. Cape Verdeans were considered quasi-citizens by Portugal and played an indirect role in the colonisation of Guinea through their collaboration with the colonial administration. Moreover, Cape Verdeans had gone through periods of famine and drought, which caused thousands of deaths. These issues were seen as political by Cape Verdeans and a consequence of a lack of political will to solve these problems. Guinea was a country divided between the 'civilised' (the Portuguese colonialists) and the 'uncivilised' (the 'natives'). The 'uncivilised' had to pass a 'civilisation' test in order to be officially designated as 'civilised', that is, assimilated into Portuguese structures and assumptions, and the overall percentage of people who attained this status was really low.

Cabral was only twenty years old when, in 1945, he received a scholarship from the Portuguese government to move to Lisbon to train as an agronomist. His decision to study agronomy was related to his lived experience and historical knowledge of the scourge of recurrent droughts and famines in Cape Verde and his consciousness of Portuguese exploitation and neglect. He arrived in Europe at the end of the Second World War and, even though the Allies had prevailed over fascism, the Portuguese people continued to live under the dictatorship of António de Oliveira Salazar, who had developed the Estado Novo (New State), a fascist dictatorship established in 1932 by the 1926 military coup that ended the sixteen-year-old parliamentary democracy which had followed the overthrow of the Portuguese monarchy in 1910. From the very beginning of his time in Portugal, Cabral got involved in the ongoing student movement against Salazar and became a reference point among the small group of African intellectuals living in Lisbon. Also, during these years he began to engage with the revolutionary theories of Marx, Engels and Lenin and familiarised himself with revolutionary experiences from Russia, China, Cuba, Algeria, Vietnam and the Indian independence movement as well as the Négritude movement.[4] Student opposition to the dictatorship was mostly organised by the Movement of Democratic Unity, which was a coalition of various groups, including communists, socialists, labour unionists, liberals and monarchists who were against the regime. However, the Portuguese Communist Party, founded in 1921, was very deeply involved and actively disseminated Marxist-Leninist ideology in this movement, which strongly influenced Cabral and some of the other African students such as Agostinho Neto, the future leader of Angola's liberation movement.

Cabral wrote his dissertation on soil erosion and its relationship to capitalism in the Alentejo – a Portuguese region that had a similar geological and metrological make-up to Cape Verde. The dissertation was dedicated to his mother, in recognition of her sacrifices, and to the labourers of Alentejo. His analysis, inspired by his reading of Marxist texts, was very innovative at the time. He argued that the main reasons for soil damage were property regimes that emphasised profit, harmful use of the soil and an economic agrarian model that left no option for poor peasants but to exploit the soil. Moreover, Cabral criticised the economic-agrarian model in Alentejo, which he asserted was directly linked to unequal distribution of land. Even though agriculture at the time was the main occupation in Portugal, in Alentejo very few people held property.

After finishing his degree, Cabral married Maria Helena Rodrigues, a Portuguese tree specialist from his university cohort. Rodrigues was an intelligent and politically conscious woman. She was among the twenty women admitted in Cabral's initial cohort of 220 students and became acquainted with Cabral during their studies, at a time when there was little interaction between white and black students. Also, their marriage in a racist country became a challenge. Meanwhile, Cabral applied for a position in Portugal but was denied employment. His attempts to find employment in Cape Verde similarly failed and finally he took a position in Guinea, where he devoted his life to anti-colonial political activism.

In summary, Cabral's years in Lisbon were very important. Living in the capital of the metropole gave him a different perspective on the colonial situation; he met comrades with whom he would begin the struggle for the independence of Portuguese Africa, and he learned various techniques of dissident work which he later implemented in the struggle against colonial rule.

Cabral returned to Guinea in September 1952 to work as an agronomist at the agriculture and forestry department, although engaging in politics was his most important goal upon arrival. In spite of being an educated African and 'civilised', Cabral felt he was treated as a second-class engineer and agronomist. Moreover, he was confronted by the brutality and violence of the colonial rulers against the people, as well as the repressive laws implemented by the International Police for the Defence of the State, which was basically a Portuguese secret police aimed at silencing all forms of dissent. His job as an agronomist allowed him to conduct an exhaustive agricultural census and helped him learn at first-hand the realities of Portuguese rule as the majority of the rural population experienced it. Moreover, it was an instrumental way for him to understand the country's social and economic structure. Finally, this job allowed him to realise and assess the rural population's degree of dissatisfaction with their rulers and estimate the potential response to a mobilisation for independence. Cabral was, however, aware that mobilising the urban population, who felt the presence of the colonialists most strongly, was just as important. His covert attempts to assess such discontent and raise political consciousness among the urban population led to him being ousted from Guinea in 1955. He relocated to Lisbon and found consulting work in the private sector, which allowed him to travel across Europe and to different parts of the Portuguese colonies, allowing him to become involved in numerous movements.

In 1956, during a brief visit to Guinea, he co-founded the African Party for the Independence of Guinea and Cape Verde (Partido Africano para a Independência da Guiné e Cabo Verde, or PAIGC), which was initially kept secret and intended to campaign peacefully for independence. However, due to numerous factors, including the bloody response of the colonial state to a strike at the Port of Bissau's Pidjiguiti docks in 1959, it turned to armed conflict in the 1960s. Cabral was confident that socialism was the most meaningful path for an independent nation and, therefore, the ideological orientation of the PAIGC was socialist and overtly influenced by Marxism.

Cabral led a double life for a few years after the establishment of the PAIGC, working in the heart of colonial Portugal and at the same time trying to abolish it by working with the PAIGC and other nationalist groups in Africa. In the same year that he founded that party, Cabral became one of the founding members of the MPLA. The independence of Guinea-Conakry in 1958 and the defeat of the French there impacted Cabral enormously and made it easier for him to envision the end of Portuguese colonial rule in Africa. The socialist Ahmed Sékou Touré, independence leader and first

President of Guinea-Conakry, massively helped Cabral during Guinea's struggle for independence. While guiding the PAIGC through a prolonged armed struggle with the colonialists, Cabral simultaneously constructed infrastructures of social, economic and political institutions within liberated areas. He led an armed struggle against the Portuguese for a decade (1963–1973). Indeed, at the time of his assassination in January 1973 by Portuguese agents who had infiltrated the PAIGC he was in the middle of negotiating with a number of countries to secure their support for Guinean and Cape Verdean independence. In September 1973, a few months after Cabral's assassination, Guinea unilaterally declared independence from Portugal and it was recognised by Portugal a year after recognition by over eighty countries around the world. Cape Verde gained its independence in July 1975.

Amílcar Cabral's Marxism

Cabral was a humanist and had deep concern for human beings. He believed that Marxism 'complemented and validated his humanist ideals'.[5] Moreover, Marxism for Cabral was an attractive theoretical framework to explain the development of societies towards a better future.[6] Like Marx, Cabral believed that the economy is the basis of political power. Hence, for example, in his analysis of the state, he made it clear that it is the class that is in charge of the state that matters, as do the ways the state relates to the specific mode of production in society. He argued that class struggle determines the manner in which the state relates to the development of productive forces, in the sense that certain class configurations hinder the development of those forces.[7]

Although at the time, many believed that political independence was the main objective of national liberation movements,

Cabral saw major problems with a political independence that did not include economic independence. He emphasised the 'destruction of domination' and argued that the national question in the liberation process could be resolved only if profound changes in the productive forces that were created by colonialism were to occur at the same time.[8] He also thought that colonialism hindered the development of productive forces. In other words, for Cabral, national liberation could be completed only if the entire socio-economic system respons-ible for colonialism was rejected. Otherwise, neo-colonialism would simply replace colonialism, and ex-colonies would be further assimilated into the structures of capitalist system and already existing processes of underdevelopment.

Such analysis was the result of Cabral's Marxian under-standing of the history of capitalist development and it enabled him to link the struggle for national liberation in Guinea and Cape Verde with the struggle for socialism. According to Cabral, a socialist revolution would prevent the emergence of neo-colonial conditions and the development of new class contradictions after independence. Moreover, based on a Marxist perspective of history, Cabral developed the idea that it was necessary for the masses to gain not only theoretical and political consciousness but also organisational consciousness.[9] He further believed that revolutionary practice was meaning-less without a revolutionary theory and that national liberation was determined by the conditions and realities of the people involved in the struggle.[10]

Consequently, Cabral believed that Marxist categories could not be externally imposed but needed to be embedded in the particular reality of the people in order to be able to influence praxis. In other words, Marxism for Cabral was a worldview and a guide to action.[11] He believed that one of the most re-markable aspects of Marx's work was the critical analysis of the society he lived in,[12] and this is what Cabral attempted to do himself. As the renowned educator and philosopher Paulo Freire has said, Cabral 'undertook an African reading of Marx, not a German reading of Marx, nor a nineteenth-century reading of Marx. He engaged in a twentieth-century reading of Marxist Africa'.[13]

Therefore, Cabral felt free to develop his own analysis of Guinean society without concern for prevailing political theories. This was largely because he conceived of theory as an analysis of reality rather than as a merely speculative exercise. His writings rarely took up subjects which were not of direct relevance to the situation in Guinea and Cape Verde. This critical view enabled him to develop his own analysis of Guinea and African societies in general and brought him to a very innovative class analysis:

> Those who assert – and in our view rightly – that the motive force of history is the class struggle, would certainly agree to re-examining this assertion to make it more precise and give it even wider application, if they had a deeper knowledge of the essential characteristics of some of the colonised peoples (dominated by imperialism). In fact, in the general evolution of mankind and of each of the peoples in the human groups of which it is composed, classes appear neither as a generalised and simultaneous phenomenon throughout all these groups, nor as a finished, perfect, uniform and spontaneous whole. The formation of classes within one or more human groups is basically the result of progressive development of the productive forces and the way in which the wealth produced by this group – or usurped by other groups – is distributed.[14]

This means that, for Cabral, the category of class as a social and economic phenomenon emerges and develops in relation to the level of productive forces and is based on the system behind the ownership of the means of production. Cabral further explains that 'this development takes place slowly, unevenly and gradually' and only by 'quantitative increases in the essential variables',[15] and that after reaching a certain point in the processes of accumulation, a qualitative change occurs which manifests itself in the emergence of classes and class conflict.[16] External factors can also have an important impact on the development of classes, and they might facilitate or impede the process but in general the process remains 'continuous and progressive'.[17] Unexpected advances happen only as the result of change 'in the level of productive forces or in the system of ownership' and are called revolutions.[18]

Cabral clearly rejects assumptions about the negation of the existence of history before classes and class struggle and warns that such an affirmation would

> place outside history the whole period of life of human groups from the discovery of hunting, and later of nomadic and sedentary agriculture, to cattle raising and to the private appropriation of land. It would also be to consider – and this we refuse to accept – that various human groups in Africa, Asia and Latin America were living without history or outside history at the moment when they were subjected to the yoke of imperialism.[19]

This leads Cabral to argue that class struggle is 'the motive force of history' only 'in a specific historical period' and that the mode of production, that is, 'the level of productive forces and the system of ownership', was and will be the motive force of history before and after the class struggle.[20] Human beings existed before the emergence of classes and class struggle and will outlive classes. Cabral finds this a very logical conclusion since

> the definition of class and class struggle are themselves the result of the development of productive forces in conjunction with the system of ownership of the means of production. It therefore seems permissible to conclude that the level of

productive forces, the essential determinant of the content and form of class struggle, is the true and permanent motive force of history.[21]

Cabral's analysis provides a 'materialist' and 'sociological' analysis of the position of African societies in history, which was at the time for African socialists and proponents of the Négritude movement a discussion point.[22] Moreover, the two dominant paradigms of the time, the Western modernisation theory and the Soviet approach to the Asiatic mode of production, were having difficulties in explaining the reality of post-colonial Africa, particularly in terms of situating this reality in relation to broader historical processes.[23] Cabral, in contrast, identified three stages in the history of human beings:

> In the first, corresponding to a low level of productive forces – of man's mastery over nature – the mode of production is of rudimentary character; private appropriation of the means of production does not yet exist, there are no classes, nor, consequently, is there class struggle. In the second, when the raising of the level of productive forces leads to private appropriation of the means of production, the mode of production is progressively more complicated; conflicts of interest are provoked within the dynamic socio-economic whole, the eruption of the phenomenon of class and hence of class struggle is possible, as the social expression of the contradiction in the economic field between the mode of production and the private appropriation of the means of production. In the third stage, once a given level of productive forces is reached, the elimination of private appropriation as the means of production is made possible and is carried out: the phenomenon of class, and hence of class struggle, is removed and new and unknown forces in the historical process of the socio-economic whole are unleashed.[24]

The first stage matches up with the communal agricultural and livestock-raising society, the second stage with agrarian societies – feudal or agro-industrial – and the third stage corresponds to the socialist and communist societies, in which the economy is mostly industrial – since agriculture has also turned to an industry – and in which the state declines or disappears.[25] This analysis shows that, according to Cabral, it is not necessary to see history in relation to one single mode of production or consider development only with reference to a specific order of stages. In fact, a jump from a primitive form to a socialist society is possible, though it depends on the 'development of the society's productive forces' and 'the nature of the political power ruling that society'.[26] Also, by recognising the fact that 'these three stages (or two of them) can be concomitant, as is shown as much by the current reality as by the past',[27] Cabral was able to explain the existence of various forms of economic and social relations at the same time within Guinea: groups that practised communal agriculture for subsistence could be associated with one mode of production, while larger farmers who were focused on the production of one crop were identified with another mode of production.[28]

Cabral was very much inspired by Lenin[29] and built on his analysis of the mode of production to explain imperialism and neo-colonialism in Africa. He demonstrated that national liberation was more than just self-rule, as it required a change in the mode of production: 'national liberation exists when, and only when, the national productive forces have been completely freed from all and any kind of foreign domination'.[30] According to Cabral, colonialism changed the modes of production of the African colonies by (partly) transforming them through the mechanisation of agriculture and the concentration of land in the hands of a few landowners, which made the colonies dependent on colonial/capitalist technology, machinery and assistance in the production and sale of their produce. In other words, they were caught in exploitative structures of colonial/imperial relations in which the imperialist power controlled the development of the mode of production.

Cabral identified two main forms of imperialist domination: colonialism – a traditional way of imposing direct domination on the colonies; and neo-colonialism – a form of domination in the post-independence period characterised by monopoly capital. While (according to him) colonialism directly blocks development, neo-colonial imperialism expands capitalism through new relations of production.[31] Although Cabral's understanding of imperialism as an extension of capitalist relations of production resulting from the growth of monopoly capitalism in capitalist nations corresponds with a classic Marxist view, Cabral insists on distinguishing between the situation of Portugal and other imperial powers to demonstrate the particularities of the Portuguese colonies in Africa. From the early eighteenth century, Portugal's colonial endeavours in Africa and the imperial relationship between Portugal and its colonies were constantly mediated by the dominance of British capital and political power. This made Portugal an intermediary in the imperialist exploitation of Africa and created a completely different set of realities in Portuguese colonies, which lacked any investment in roads, schools or industry.[32] As Cabral writes:

> imperialism, which everything goes to show is really the last stage in the evolution of capitalism was a historical necessity, a consequence of the development of productive forces and the transformations of the mode of production, in the general context of mankind, considered as a dynamic whole. This is a necessity like those today of the national liberation of peoples, the destruction of capitalism and the advent of socialism. The important thing for our peoples is to know whether imperialism, in its role as capital in action, has or has not fulfilled in our countries its historical mission: the speeding up of the process of development of the productive forces and transformation in

the direction of increasing complexity of the characteristics of the mode of production; sharpening class differentiation with the development of the bourgeoisie and intensification of class struggle; and appreciably raising average standard levels in the economic, social and cultural life of the populations.[33]

After 1945 and the rise of the United States as the main global power, imperialism changed course and focused on preferential investment in the so-called First World and the export of capital through special programmes to the so-called Third World. According to Cabral, this was meant to expand imperialist relations in the colonies. The emergence of the reactionary classes in the post-independence era were, according to Cabral, a consequence of imperialist policies of foreign aid and investment in the colonies which encouraged the growth of a domestic petite bourgeoisie that was trapped in the illusion of progress and with whom an alliance could be formed in the interest of imperial power relations. These local elites were, however, caught in the same old exploitative relations and were prevented from controlling the advancement of the forces of production.[34] According to Cabral,

neocolonialist domination, by allowing the social dynamic to be awakened – conflicts of interest between the native social strata or class struggle – creates the illusion that the historical process is returning to its normal evolution. This illusion is reinforced by the existence of a political power (national state), composed of native elements. It is only an illusion, since in reality the subjection of the native 'ruling' class to the ruling class of the dominating country limits or holds back the full development of the national productive forces.[35]

Based on this analysis, Cabral concludes that

the national liberation of a people is the regaining of the historical personality of that people, it is their return to history through the destruction of the imperialist domination to which they were subjected. Now we have seen that the principal and permanent characteristic of imperialist domination, whatever its form, is the usurpation by violence of the freedom of the process of development of the dominated socio-economic whole. We have also seen that this freedom, and it alone, can guarantee the normal course of the historical process of a people. We can therefore conclude that national liberation exists when, and only when, the national productive forces have been completely freed from all and any kind of foreign domination…. Furthermore, if we accept that national liberation demands a profound mutation in the process of development of the productive forces, we see that the phenomenon of national liberation necessarily corresponds to a revolution.[36]

The exit point from neo-colonial domination occurs in the 'suicide' of the petite bourgeoisie, which volunteers to renounce its advantages within the system and join the revolution. As was mentioned earlier, Cabral believed the only way to depart from neo-colonial relations in the post-independence era was through structural changes. He saw the petite bourgeoisie as an important agent in achieving this structural change because of its particular characteristics:

> By virtue of its objective and subjective position (higher standard of living than that of the masses, more frequent humiliation, higher grade of education and political culture, etc.), it is the stratum that soonest becomes aware of the need to rid itself of foreign domination.[37]

Cabral explains that, of course, the petite bourgeoisie has the option of becoming a 'bourgeoisie' or a 'national pseudo-bourgeoisie' by 'denying the revolution' and 'subjecting itself to imperialist capital'.[38] However,

> In order not to betray these objectives, the petty bourgeoisie has only one road: to strengthen its revolutionary consciousness, to repudiate the temptations to become 'bourgeois' and the natural pretensions of its class mentality; to identify with

the classes of workers, not to oppose the normal development of the process of revolution. This means that in order to play completely the part that falls to it in the national liberation struggle, the revolutionary petty bourgeoisie must be capable of *committing suicide* as a class, to be restored to life in the condition of a revolutionary worker completely identified with the deepest aspirations of the people to which he belongs.[39]

According to Cabral, the petite bourgeoisie, by committing suicide and scarifying itself, would not lose but would revive itself in the circumstances of workers and peasants,[40] and, moreover, this was a significant factor in the success of the socialist revolution.[41] Cabral had identified two factions within the petite bourgeoisie in Guinea: the higher- and middle-ranking officials employed by the state; and petty officials and those working in commerce with permanent contracts. In addition, a number of farmers producing groundnuts on a larger scale than the peasantry was part of this faction. However, Cabral did not make a political distinction between the two and assumed the same role for both.[42]

Another original aspect of Cabral's theoretical work can be found in his analysis of culture and its relation to national liberation struggles. Cabral situated culture in its historical context, as 'an essential element of the history of a people'.[43] Moreover, he argued that culture has its material base at the level of the productive forces and the mode of production and, therefore, situating the development of culture in relationship to the material bases of society makes it possible to clarify its importance in the struggle against imperialist domination and for national liberation.[44] He wrote:

The value of culture as an element of resistance to foreign domination lies in the fact that culture is the vigorous manifestation, on the ideological or idealist level, of the material and historical reality of the society that is dominated or to be dominated.[45]

Since culture is a product as well as a determinant of people's history and holds the capacity for the development of society due to its relationship to the material bases,[46] cultural resistance to imperialist domination becomes an important aspect of the national liberation struggle. In Cabral's words, 'the foundation of national liberation lies in the inalienable right of every people to have their own history, whatever the formulations adopted in international law. The aim of national liberation is therefore to regain this right, usurped by imperialist domination.'[47]

Cabral recognised the cultural diversity of Guinea; for him, the cultural features of each group were important and shaped their attitude towards the liberation struggle besides their economic interests.[48] However, he insisted that 'this complexity cannot and must not diminish the crucial importance of the class nature of culture for the development of this [liberation] movement'.[49] Moreover, Cabral argued that a permanent confrontation between different elements of culture and the demands of the liberation movement needs to exist. Nevertheless, culture and the liberation movement constantly influence each other as the movement develops.[50]

What was supposed to come after independence was a new cultural hegemony. However, this was already being created through the participation of people in the liberated zones during the armed struggle. As the historian Basil Davidson has rightly argued, the 'launching of this new culture, at least in its essentials and foundations, was the central aim of the liberated zones, and of democratic self-organization'.[51] In general, the PAIGC's programme was not limited to political independence but also had the long-term objective of economic and social transformation. The party started its work by helping peasants understand the causes of the conditions within which they were living, for example with low prices for most of their produce and vulnerability to abuses by the government. Peasants were informed that their problems were the consequence of 'the introduction of the colonial means of production'.[52]

Cabral believed that the peasantry in Guinea were not a revolutionary force due to lack of any history of revolt. He argued that they were instead a great physical force because they comprised the majority of the population and produced the nation's wealth. It was in fact through a slow and challenging process of political education which involved hundreds of discussion groups with the peasantry and the distribution of various documents and pamphlets among them that 'the defeat of Portuguese colonialism was begun'.[53]

The PAIGC under Cabral employed three variables to determine the revolutionary capacity of various groups in Guinea, and these were the main components of Cabral's analysis of social structure. First, the position of each group was defined in relation to its dependence on the colonial regime; second, the attitude of each group towards the national liberation struggle was analysed; and finally, the behaviour of each group after independence and towards revolutionary change was assessed.[54]

As the main intellectual force within the PAIGC, Cabral's analysis of the social structure of Guinea, which heavily relied on an analysis of Guinean agriculture, helped the party succeed in its struggle against the Portuguese. His understanding of Guinean agriculture and its relation to Portuguese colonialism became instrumental in his analysis of social classes, culture and the political economy.[55]

Amílcar Cabral's legacy

In the words of Peter Mendy, Cabral's biographer, he was 'a charismatic visionary leader', 'a reconciliation leader' who was 'committed to participatory democratic principles'.[56] The historian Jock McCulloch writes that Cabral's greatest legacy is 'the practical idealism' that forms the foundation of his thinking.[57] According to McCulloch, the most important effect of Cabral's political life was to dismantle the last colonial empire in Africa.[58]

The legacy of Cabral's thought and practice lives in numerus countries and continues in different ways. His most direct legacy can be found in his role in the national liberation struggle in Guinea-Bissau and Cape Verde. Cabral was the man behind the unity between the Guinean and Cape Verdean people in their struggle against colonial rule, in spite of the efforts of Portuguese and nationalists on both sides who were against such unity.[59] 'Cabral ka muri' ('Cabral is not dead') is a common saying in Guinea-Bissau that evokes the spirit of the national liberation struggle and is a tribute to Cabral and his comrades for the sacrifices they made for liberating the people from the last colonial empire in Africa.[60] That is why, in the collective memory of many, Cabral is referred to as the 'father of Guinea and Cape Verde'.[61] In spite of his assassination in January 1973, the liberation movement, which had already been victorious in many parts of Guinea, did not collapse, as was the objective of the assassins. Instead, Cabral's murder intensified the fight and only a few months later resulted in the new nation-state of Guinea-Bissau.[62]

However, in spite of the success of the liberation struggle, Cabral's assassination meant that he was unable to lead the independent nation he dreamt of, and his early loss shaped an important aspect of his legacy.[63] His brother, Luis Cabral, the first President of Guinea-Bissau, tried to put into practice some of Amílcar's ideas after independence. For example, he asked Paulo Freire to build an educational programme for the country based on his discussions with Amílcar.[64]

Apart from his impact in Guinea, Cape Verde and the continent of Africa more generally – including North Africa[65] – Cabral's revolutionary accomplishments and his theoretical insights have been influential in many parts of the global South, and his speeches and writings have been translated and disseminated in numerous languages. Interestingly, Cabral has had a huge influence in Latin America, particularly in Central America. For example, his ideas on culture and liberation were incorporated into the Guatemalan revolution.[66]

The struggle that Cabral waged was particularly fascinating because it came at a time when the French and British colonial empires were being dismantled in Africa. The success of the PAIGC contributed considerably to the collapse of the Estado Novo dictatorship in Portugal, which was followed by the breakdown of the Portuguese empire in Africa.[67] Out of all the problems the Portuguese faced in their colonies, the pressure from the guerrilla fighters in Guinea was a huge challenge. It was also in Guinea that the Portuguese faced difficulties equipping the troops and felt 'a general atmosphere of insubordination'.[68]

However, perhaps Cabral's most important legacy outside of Africa was in the United States. During the 1970s, he was among the first national liberation leaders to speak with African-Americans about the philosophy of liberation and the strategy and tactics of the struggle in Guinea and Cape Verde. On numerous occasions he met informally with activist groups and spoke with them about the interconnections of struggles as well as the importance of understanding each struggle in its particular context. These speeches have been recorded, translated and published in the United States, and his interactions with African-American communities have led to a long-lasting 'tradition of discourse and international solidarity between Africans and African-Americans' rooted in the common history of oppression between African-Americans and the colonies.[69] It was perhaps more than anything Cabral's experience in the PAIGC and his acute understanding of revolutionary theory and practice that helped him link his struggle with those outside of Africa.[70]

In the introduction to their edited volume *Claim No Easy Victories: The Legacy of Amílcar Cabral*, published in 2013 for the fortieth anniversary of Cabral's assassination, Manji and Fletcher write about Cabral's heavily guarded mausoleum and those of some of his PAIGC comrades at the military headquarters of Guinea-Bissau. They believe that such heavy military presence is due to the fact that 'this guarded site of remembrance is a fearful symbol of the profound importance of Cabral's work and achievements'.[71] They are right in this interpretation, as well as in making a point about the tragic disappearance of the memory of Cabral's contributions to the liberation struggle for a long time after his assassination.[72]

However, in recent years, attention to Cabral and his legacy has increased, and he is now often referred to as one of the most important figures of the African liberation struggles, alongside Frantz Fanon and Kwame Nkrumah. For example, Manji and Fletcher's volume brings together thirty-eight essays by a broad range of writers, from activists to social scientists and historians, debating his importance for contemporary issues. It features in-depth discussions on, for example, Cabral's legacy in the formation of anti-colonial culture in former colonies, his contributions to gender equality and emancipation, and his role both in the Black liberation struggle in contemporary America and in the broader worldwide anti-capitalist struggle.

When Amílcar Cabral's foundation based in Praia, the capital of Cape Verde, announced its decision to celebrate Cabral's eightieth birthday, a large number of scholars and specialists responded, and from 9 to 12 September 2004 they gathered to discuss Cabral's impact on today's Africa and his relevance to contemporary African challenges.[73] These are all evidence that Cabral's legacy lives on and, as the academic Reiland Rabaka has put it, his '"organic intellectual" life and political legacy continues to contribute to radical politics, critical social theory, and revolutionary praxis in general, and the Africana tradition of critical theory in particular'.[74]

Chapter 6

Frantz Fanon: the Marx of the Third World

Frantz Fanon (1925–1961) was a psychiatrist and revolutionary from the French colony of Martinique. While serving the Free French Army to fight the Nazis in Europe, he was sent to Algeria, which was at the time a colony of France. This encounter directed him towards questions around the dynamics of colonialism and its effects on colonised people. He joined the Algerian National Liberation Front (Front de Libération Nationale) and became fully involved with Algeria's war of independence, although he did not live to see Algeria's independence in 1962 due to the leukaemia that ended his life only months before the French were ousted.

In the course of his short life he wrote several books and numerous articles on topics such as colonialism, racism, class, national culture and decolonisation. Fanon developed a dialectic analysis of the colonial subject's psychological condition that had been created due to the history and culture of the empire. His emphasis was on the interconnection of racism, colonialism and capitalism and the ways these intersections were manifested. Fanon saw the wide category of 'the wretched of the earth' as being behind the bringing down of the capitalist system. Due to the resilient character of capitalism and colonialism, violence was an absolute necessity for him. Although he was mostly involved in the war of independence in Algeria and in anti-colonisation struggles in Africa, his revolutionary ideas became foundations for many revolutionary struggles around the world, in the global South and North. As the political scientist Anuja Bose has correctly put it, he 'observed and articulated the scope and reach of collective political action that was pitched beyond the nation-state and the continent'.[1] He articulated and was concerned with two dynamic tensions: 'the transcendent sovereignty of the imperial nation-states' and the 'immanent sovereignty of colonized peoples'. Because of his ideas about violence he has sometimes been referred to as someone who preaches a gospel of hate, but others have admired his combined unconditional support for the oppressed with continuous anger towards the oppressor. Apart from various revolutionary struggles, his work has also impacted many academic fields, from postcolonial theory to literary criticism and critical theory, to name just a few.

Revolutionary pathways[2]

Frantz Fanon was born on 20 July 1925 on the Caribbean island of Martinique. His father worked as a customs agent and his mother was a shopkeeper. Martinique was at the time a French colony. Slavery had been abolished there in 1848, but during Fanon's youth, racism was apparent in the economic inequalities that existed between the white colonisers and those of African descent. Fanon grew up in a middle-class family that encouraged him to speak French rather than Creole, which was considered a lower-class language. His mother was an intellectual woman and a central figure in their household. She had ambitious plans for her children and certainly did not want any of them to suffer from poverty.

Fanon attended a prestigious high school during a time when the impacts of the Second World War had reached the

French West Indies, and in 1943 he joined a large number of Martiniquais who left for Dominica to join the Free French Army and fight the Nazis in Europe. Fanon was very passionate about his decision, and at the time of his departure he identified very strongly with France in its struggle against the Nazis and wanted to be 'in the heart of the problem'.[3] In 1944, Fanon was sent to serve in Algeria, then another a French colony, where he also got to know a number of Senegalese soldiers. According to Rabaka, this experience was 'eye-opening and life-altering'.[4] It was during this period that Fanon began to develop a critical understanding of the effects of colonialism on colonised people. Fighting as a black soldier in a white army and for a colonial country was not only disorienting but also made him question many of his assumptions about the very idea of liberation. In a letter to his parents in April 1945, he wrote he was not confident about anything anymore.

In October 1945, Fanon returned to Martinique to complete his secondary education. Aimé Césaire – who was to become one of the most prominent politicians in Martinique and an influential figure in the Négritude movement – was running for parliament as a member of the Communist Party. Fanon joined Césaire's successful campaign and began to be influenced by him politically and intellectually. His intellectual engagement with Césaire lasted throughout his life. Although Fanon could see how remaining in Martinique could be politically rewarding, he was also interested in continuing his education. Because there was no university in Martinique he left for Paris in 1946, and from there soon moved to Lyon to study medicine.

Lyon had a vibrant working class and a rich history of labour organisation, which was attractive to Fanon. He started exploring various intellectual currents, from existentialism (particularly the philosopher Jean-Paul Sartre) to phenomenology, Marxism and psychoanalysis. He attended classes

given by the philosopher Maurice Merleau-Ponty and anthropologist André Leroi-Gourhan; he read Kant, Kierkegaard,
Jaspers, Levi-Strauss, Hegel and Trotsky. It was during this
time that he was introduced to Marx's early works. The publication of the *Economic and Philosophical Manuscripts of 1844*,
which had been translated into French in 1935, and its discussion of alienation and humanism received a lot of attention at
the time from Marxists, Catholics and the psychoanalytic left.
Lyon had turned into a centre of various Marxist tendencies,
and Fanon had developed an interest in the ongoing Marxist
debates of the circles around him. This increasing interest in
Marxist discussions also led him to read the proceedings of
the first three congresses of the Third International. He also
read *Esprit*, one the most important magazines of the wartime
French resistance; *Les Temps modernes*, founded by the philosopher Simone de Beauvoir, Sartre and Merleau-Ponty; and
Présence Africaine, a pan-African French-language magazine
associated with the Négritude movement. Fanon also became
active in student politics and anti-colonial demonstrations in
Lyon. He is reported to have worked with the student branch of
the French Communist Party but never as an official member.

In 1949, Fanon met Marie-Josephe Dublé (known as Josie),
who was a liberal arts student at the time. She was of mixed
Corsican-Roma descent, and her parents were trade unionists
who fully supported their marriage in 1952. Josie played
an important role for the rest of Fanon's life. According to
Peter Hudis, one of Fanon's biographers, she was a 'theorist
and political colleague in her own right'.[5] At some point she
became a staff member of the Algerian magazine *Révolution
africaine*. These qualifications made Josie a great intellectual
companion for Fanon. Apart from her influence on Fanon's
intellectual development, she was a great help to him in
various important endeavours. For example, Fanon never

learned to use a typewriter, and he dictated much of the text of his first book, *Black Skin, White Masks*, to Josie, who produced the typescript.

Over the course of his education, Fanon gradually became interested in psychiatry. He felt the synthesis of psychology, medicine and philosophy that psychiatry offered would make it possible for him to pursue his increasing interest in the effects of colonialism on colonial people. In 1952, he took up an internship at a hospital in Saint Alban in France, under the guidance of François Tosquelles, who was known as the 'red psychiatrist'. Tosquelles was a Freudian and a Marxist and had fought with the Workers Party of Marxist Unification (a Spanish communist political party) on the Republican side in the Spanish Civil War. In Saint Alban, Tosquelles merged psychiatry with politics and turned the hospital into a space where patients could achieve self-liberation. In this space, the study of mental illness was only possible in relation to the patient's social setting. Fanon's exposure to Tosquelles's socio-therapy, which was designed as a political project that aimed to listen to patients and empower them to confront their problems in a group setting, proved to be a significant experience. Above all, it helped him develop the methodology for his book *Black Skin, White Masks* (published in 1952), in which he offers a socio-therapeutic analysis of the colonial subject focused on people's lived experience.

In 1953, Fanon took up a position as a psychiatrist at Blida-Joinville Hospital in Algeria. In a letter to his brother he explained that the French had enough psychiatrists and he would rather be in a country where he was needed. When Fanon arrived in Algeria, the independence movement in the country was barely nascent, but the idea of independence was being discussed in numerous circles. Fanon did not initially plan to move to Algeria because of any particular project, but once there he gradually became involved in the independence movement as his encounters with the Algerian people and their sufferings intensified. During his time at the psychiatric hospital of Blida-Joinville, he gained significant clinical experience and developed his ideas regarding the socio-political causes of mental illnesses. Moreover, he introduced some reforms in the institution and established a model similar to Tosquelles's socio-therapeutic model.

In 1956, Fanon resigned from his role at the hospital to join the National Liberation Front (Front de Libération Nationale, FLN), the revolutionary movement that had initiated an armed struggle to free Algeria from French colonialism. He was aware that this would impact any prospect of a career as a psychiatrist in France or in Martinique and that he would not be able to return to Algeria if he ever left the country. Fanon had been in contact with the FLN for some time; however, after his resignation from Blida-Joinville, it did not take long for him to integrate more fully into the ongoing movement. Fanon was expelled from Algeria at the end of 1956 and shortly afterwards he relocated to Tunisia, which was the FLN's capital in exile. There he would work for the FLN and also practise psychiatry.

In September 1958, the Provisional Government of the Algerian Republic (GPRA) – the FLN's government in exile – was established, and in December of that same year Fanon addressed the All-African People's Congress held in Accra, Ghana, as a member of the Algerian delegation. It was at this Congress that Fanon put forward his rather controversial views on violence and decolonisation and argued that the struggle of the Algerian people was part of a broader pan-African movement.

In 1959, Fanon was appointed as the FLN representative for international occasions and conferences. With the publication of *L'An V de la révolution algérienne* ('Year Five of the Algerian

Revolution', though the English translation was later given the title *A Dying Colonialism*), Fanon began to be widely accepted as a spokesperson for the Algerian Revolution. Fanon's time in Tunisia turned him into a complete political militant. He did not only become a spokesperson for the FLN but also regularly contributed to its newspaper, *El Moudjahid*. Moreover, he developed an interest beyond Algeria and became involved in sub-Saharan African politics in general. In 1960, he was appointed as the GPRA's ambassador to Ghana.

Fanon died of leukaemia in December 1961. He finished his seminal work *The Wretched of the Earth* (which has been referred to as the 'Bible of Third Worldism') after he had been diagnosed. Sartre wrote a preface to the book and called it an 'Extreme Third World manifesto'. Algeria formally became an independent country in July 1962, only a few months after Fanon's passing.

Frantz Fanon's Marxism

The sociologist Dennis Forsythe has referred to Fanon as 'the Marx of the Third World';[6] Rabaka has stated that Fanon is 'a too often unrecognized rightful member of the Marxian pantheon';[7] and the academic Tony Martin has argued that there are clear signs of Fanon's 'affinity to Marx which are evident even without a close look at his philosophy'.[8] In fact, two of Fanon's books have 'titles directly suggestive of a conscious identification with Marx'.[9] His *The Wretched of the Earth* is inspired by the first line of the French translation of *The Internationale* – the anthem of the socialist movement – and *Year Five of the Algerian Revolution* is similar to Marx's *The Eighteenth Brumaire of Louis Bonaparte*. Martin argues that Fanon can be considered a Marxist, but he emphasises the fact that Fanon was Marxist in the sense that Lenin or Castro or Mao are Marxist. That is, he accepted Marx's basic analysis of society as given and proceeded from there to elaborate on that analysis and modify it where necessary to suit his own historical and geographical context.[10]

Fanon was engaged in Marxist debates from early on in his intellectual career, and Marxist ideas were 'integral to his political and theoretical project'.[11] Central to Fanon's work is the Marxist view that the oppressed and the oppressor constitute two conflicting classes. Fanon accepted Marx's economic analyses of conflict and envisioned the anti-colonial struggle in class terms,[12] and in relation to the exploitation of 'one group of men by another which has reached a higher stage of technical development'.[13] In his various writings, but particularly in *The Wretched of the Earth*, he used class-based terminology to refer to the master–slave and colonised–coloniser relations. He concluded that a new humanity will emerge from these class conflicts. He engaged with a Marxian understanding of the material base and ideological superstructure and argued that racism is not separate from modes of production and primitive accumulation. Modes of production and ways of life are destroyed in the colonies and new systems are imposed. Changes in the material base induce changes in the ideological superstructure, which leads to a more sophisticated method of exploitation and racism. The base and superstructure then enter into a dynamic relationship in which they constantly change places.[14]

Fanon dedicated a central point to consciousness in action.[15] In *The Wretched of the Earth*, the consciousness of people who have systematically been dehumanised becomes central to envisioning a new humanity.[16] In addition, like Marx, he highlights that consciousness on its own does not lead to social change and that a radical and uncompromising revolutionary commitment is essential in transforming consciousness into action that could then lead to the emergence of a new society.[17] That is why we can claim that, similar to Marx, Fanon 'advocated an instrumental theory of action' which does not focus on knowing the world but on changing it.[18]

Following Marx, Fanon believed in the revolutionary transformation of society and that the form and the content of revolution is not inherited from the past but is made in the midst of the revolutionary process.[19] For both Marx and Fanon, the revolution is the outcome of the dialectical processes taking place within the capitalist system that create a revolutionary dynamism among oppressed people.[20] In the case of colonised subjects, it is the structures created by capitalist economic expansion as well as the psychological effects of those structures that bring the colonised face to face with their exploitation and humiliation. This ultimately places them at the forefront of struggles for national liberation.[21]

Fanon's emphasis on 'disalienation' – the process of overcoming or transcending alienation – in Black Skin, White Masks (but also in his later writings) is based on Marx's theory of alienation.[22] Marx had argued that, apart from the exploitation of labourers and the appropriation of their surplus value, the alienation of workers from their work and the production process adds a deeper layer to the capitalist relations of production because it robs those workers of their very existence.[23] Fanon argues that blacks and the colonised have developed a self-hatred and an inferiority complex that puts them in constant conflict with their own sense of self and being. In fact, as Fanon writes, 'the true disalienation of the black man implies a brutal awareness of social and economic realities'.[24]

In Black Skin, White Masks, Fanon developed a dialectical analysis of colonial subjectivity in relation to the historical, material and psychological conditions created by colonialism and European hegemony. He argued that colonial subjects' psychological problems had been created by the history and culture of the empire. This crisis was also the crisis of empire, which facilitated the rise of the colonised subject.[25] In other words, social change can happen only 'through the antithesis of the colonial inferiority complex: a liberated native consciousness that eventually crystallizes as a collective quest for native freedom'.[26]

Fanon did not dismiss the universal as the product of the European Enlightenment. As Hudis writes: 'from his first moment of encounter with Hegel's philosophy, Fanon was especially attuned to its central category – the dialectical movement from the individual to the universal through the particular'.[27] This Hegelian understanding of the world – Hegel believed universality develops first into particularity and then into individuality – was apparent not only in *Black Skin, White Masks* but throughout Fanon's entire body of work, up to his last work, *The Wretched of the Earth*. As the sociologist Immanuel Wallerstein has observed, for Fanon, 'universalism and particularism, properly conceived' remained 'obverse sides of one coin'.[28]

In the early pages of *The Wretched of the Earth* Fanon wrote:

Marxist analysis should always be *slightly stretched* when it comes to addressing the colonial issue. It is not just the concept of the pre-capitalist society, so *effectively* studied by Marx, which needs to be re-examined here. The serf is essentially different from the knight, but a reference to divine right is needed to justify this difference in status. In the colonies the foreigner imposed himself using his cannons and machines. Despite the success of his pacification, in spite of his appropriation, the colonist always remains a foreigner. It is not the factories, the estates, or the bank account which primarily characterize the ruling class. The ruling species is first and foremost the outsider from elsewhere, different from the indigenous population, 'the others'.[29]

The task of 'slightly stretch[ing]' Marxist analysis remained one of the most important focal points of Fanon's work throughout his life. This is not only because he found Marx's analysis so 'effective' but also because he believed human beings had the capacity to make history. Marxism provided him with a philosophy of praxis,[30] and became one of the 'theoretical tools' he utilised in his project of history making and his struggle against capitalism, colonialism and racism.[31] Marx had argued that a new crisis can lead to a new revolution. Fanon interpreted racial colonialism as this new crisis, and he argued that a new conception of revolution was needed that could take into account the combined effects of capitalism, colonialism and racism.[32]

Fanon most often underlined the significance of political economy for understanding racial colonialism within the framework of the capitalist economy,[33] and that is perhaps why Martin emphasises that Fanon 'accepted Marx's basic analysis of society as given and proceeded from there to elaborate on that analysis and modify it where necessary to suit his own historical and geographical context'.[34] Consequently, Fanon, similar to many other African thinkers, was in search of a socialism that would be appropriate for Africa and its various cultures and its needs. He encouraged the wretched of the earth and revolutionary intellectuals to advance a radical political theory specific to their own struggles in order to guide their revolutionary praxis.[35] Although Fanon frequently emphasised the destructive nature of capitalism, his true concern was with the interconnections of racism, colonialism and capitalism in Africa and the colonies in general and how these intersections impacted colonised subjects.[36]

One of Fanon's emphases in advancing Marxist theory was the relationship between class conflict and racial conflict. Fanon started with a relatively firm Marxist analysis of racial and class conflict that considered both to be bound up primarily with economic conditions. In *Black Skin, White Masks* he wrote: 'The Negro problem does not resolve itself into the problem of Negroes living among white men, but rather of Negroes exploited, enslaved, despised by a colonialist, capitalist society that is only accidentally white'.[37] But later in his work he acknowledged that, in spite of the existence of various oppressed groups, racial conflict can have a distinctive and resilient character and can exert a significant influence on colonised peoples.[38]

Fanon became interested in understanding 'the interior life of racism, its lived experience in terms of the actual individual'.[39] He showed the significance of slavery and colonialism as fundamental elements of world historical developments, and his focus on the colonial situation drew attention to the status of the coloniser as the oppressor.[40] Moreover, by highlighting numerous ongoing struggles in the global South, from the Algerian war of independence to anti-colonial struggles in the Congo and Guinea, he showed the role the people of the global South actually played in bringing down imperialist forces and relations. By doing this, Fanon did not see the proletariat as the main group behind bringing down the capitalist system but as part of the wider category of 'the wretched of the earth', who included the lumpen-proletariat as well as the peasantry.[41]

Marx had seen the lumpenproletariat as a rather reactionary group. However, Fanon saw revolutionary potential in this group in the colonies. This was because he believed the colonised lumpenproletariat were deprived of the most basic human needs. The lumpenproletariat had been excluded from the colonial world shared by both the European and colonised bourgeoisies and benefited the least from the neo-colonial arrangement.[42] Also, in contrast to the working class, the lumpenproletariat in the colonies included a large population of impoverished rural migrants to urban areas in search of the fulfilment of their basic needs.[43]

In fact, for Fanon, the lumpenproletariat provided the link between the rural and urban movements. The struggle started by the peasantry would spread to the urban areas through the lumpenproletariat, who had been 'blocked on the outer fringe of the urban centres'.[44] Hence, although Fanon said the peasantry played the leading role, he claimed that the lumpenproletariat also played an important one – but he also said they were unreliable and even treacherous if other groupings did not assume a leading role. He wrote:

> In fact, any national liberation movement should give this lumpenproletariat maximum attention. It will always respond to the call to revolt, but if the insurrection thinks it can afford to ignore it, then this famished underclass will pitch itself into the armed struggle and take part in the conflict, this time on the side of the oppressor. The oppressor, who never misses an opportunity to let the blacks tear at each other's throats, is only too willing to exploit those characteristic flaws of the lumpenproletariat, namely its lack of political consciousness and ignorance. If this readily available human reserve is not immediately organized by the insurrection, it will join the colonialist troops as mercenaries.[45]

Fanon's conception of the national bourgeoisie was central to his analysis of the outcome of the anti-colonial movement. He believed that the national bourgeoisie can play a progressive role in at least some contexts in helping to lead the independence movement but he argued it has no progressive role beyond that; once independence is achieved and the task shifts from national to social liberation, it plays a reactionary role. In fact, he saw them as corrupt and chauvinistic instruments of capital.[46] He warned that the national bourgeoisie can recolonise the nation by surrendering to the existing capitalist order of the time as imperial powers readjust themselves to continue the process of colonisation – that is, resource extraction and labour exploitation – after independence.[47] This is different from a Marxian analysis of the national bourgeoisie, which considers it a class, at least in some contexts, sharing the interests of both the peasantry and the working class.[48]

For Fanon, the solution to the problem of the national bourgeoisie was to be found in the masses, that is, in the peasantry. Although Fanon saw the peasantry as the primary agent of decolonisation in Africa, he argued the peasantry needs to enter into 'coalitions and alliances, with radical/revolutionary urban and middle-class militants who would serve as political educators'.[49] In emphasising the role of the peasantry, Fanon was influenced by a broad range of African political thought, particularly that of leaders and thinkers who advocated socialism, such as Julius Nyerere of Tanzania and Léopold Sédar Senghor of Senegal. However, while the approach of these thinkers and revolutionaries to the peasantry was rather pragmatic and usually situated as part of the path to economic development, Fanon gave the peasantry a more 'enhanced status' and considered them 'not just as the inevitable components of the developmental machine but as the repository of the life-force of the emergent nation'.[50] However, according to Hudis, his approach was rather distant from that of Mao, for whom the peasantry was 'the universal class in place of the working class'.[51] This is because Fanon did not see the peasantry as the main driver of revolutions across the world but only as 'the primary subject in Africa at the time he [was] writing'.[52]

While Marx's solution for the oppressed was a communist revolution, Fanon's proposal centred around decolonisation. For Fanon, decolonisation was both a revolutionary transformation and a lengthy process, meaning that political independence was only the beginning and getting rid of colonial values and culture had to be proceeded by political independence.[53]

Also, in his theory of revolution, Fanon emphasises the absolute necessity of violence due to the nature of colonialism and capitalism.[54] Therefore, similar to Mao and Guevara, Fanon justifies violence through the resilient character of the capitalist and non-native system of domination, which can be defeated, according to Fanon, only through armed struggle.[55] In *Toward the African Revolution* he wrote:

> The end of the colonial regime effected by peaceful means and made possible by the colonialist's understanding might under certain circumstances lead to a renewed collaboration of the two nations. History, however, shows that no colonialist nation is willing to withdraw without having exhausted all its possibilities of maintaining itself.[56]

Moreover, for Fanon, violence is a factor which unites the people.[57] He refers to the sociological function of violence as a means to mobilise people and help them develop a certain level of consciousness about themselves and their nation.[58] This national consciousness, according to Fanon, 'is the highest form of culture' and, moreover, 'national consciousness, which is not nationalism, is alone capable of giving us an international dimension'.[59] He urged African intellectuals to focus on building their nations because 'it is national liberation that puts the nation on the stage of history. It is at the heart of national consciousness that international consciousness establishes itself and thrives.'[60] According to Bose, Fanonian international consciousness has two features. It should be understood as 'an intercontinental political community forged between the Third World regions of Asia, Africa, and the Americas' and as an 'intercontinentalism' which is embedded 'in a form of populism that expands beyond nation-states to articulate a collective democratic subjectivity of the Third World'.[61]

According to Fanon, violence functions as a moral force and gives the colonised back their dignity, because in the act of violence the colonised redirect their misery and this helps them reach a certain level of realisation.[62] Therefore, for Fanon, violence is a 'subjective individual act' that cleanses the individual of colonial subjugation.[63] The colonised bear a continuous tendency towards violence because their inherent anger cannot easily find any outlet, and therefore this anger is released in the form of explosions, tribal warfare or fights between individuals. Violence is needed for the decolonisation of the mind and to free colonised subjects from their inferiority complex. Hence, Fanon assumed a therapeutic function for violence. He saw guerrilla strategies and not trade unionism or party politics as the means of initiating the necessary violence against the enduring nature of the colonial powers in Africa. After the conflict started, he posited that a political party would be able to develop out of the revolutionary conflict.[64]

Many Marxists had categorised the colonies as feudal or pre-capitalist and, for them, the capitalist phase could not be avoided on the path towards socialism and communism.[65] Fanon's response to these debates can be seen in the following excerpt from *The Wretched of the Earth*:

> The theoretical question, which has been posed for the last fifty years when addressing the history of the underdeveloped countries, i.e., whether the bourgeois phase can be effectively skipped, must be resolved through revolutionary action and not through reasoning. The bourgeois phase in the under-developed countries is only justified if the national bourgeoisie is sufficiently powerful, economically and technically, to build a bourgeois society, to create the conditions for developing a sizeable proletariat, to mechanize agriculture, and finally pave the way for a genuine national culture.[66]

Furthermore, Fanon differed from Marx in his account of the post-revolutionary situation, in that he did not have a coherent definition of socialism, but his vision implies that, depending on the characteristics of the local condition, different forms of socialism can emerge after the victory of national liberation movements. Facilitating the emergence of these various forms of socialism would be a vital task.[67] In comparison with Marx, Fanon's vision was much more focused on the individual and argued that the liberation of the individual does not automatically follow national liberation and requires its own work. Also, he highlighted the ongoing process of liberation struggles after colonialism had ended by claiming that, after the victory of anti-colonial struggles, people's struggles to fight poverty, illiteracy and underdevelopment would emerge.

Fanon did not advocate total communal ownership. He argued that the economy needs to be nationalised but thought it should not take the form of an inflexible state control. Additionally, the party which has led the victorious revolution needs then to become decentralised.[68] According to Fanon:

> The party must be the direct expression of the masses.... One of the greatest services the Algerian revolution has rendered to Algerian intellectuals was to put them in touch with the masses, to allow them to see the extreme, unspeakable poverty of the people and at the same time witness the awakening of their intelligence and the development of their consciousness.[69]

Fanon proposed a new humanism for the 'post-colony', where abolishing the very condition of exploitation of the wretched of the earth would be the ultimate goal.[70] Similar to Guevara, whose objective was the creation of a new human and a society that would support the existence of this new being, Fanon insisted that creation of a new humanity and returning dignity to human beings should be at the forefront of the revolutionary agenda. In other words, socio-economic changes would not be enough and would need to be accompanied by the formation of a revolutionary consciousness and a new understanding of the human being. According to Fanon, this could be achieved through political education.[71] Decolonisation would be complete only when the ideology of the coloniser was replaced by a new ideology and by pursuit of human potentials, beyond capitalist alienation. Otherwise, people's struggles would lead to a dead-end.[72]

Frantz Fanon's legacy

Fanon wrote four books – *Black Skin, White Masks* (1952), *The Wretched of the Earth* (1961), *A Dying Colonialism* (1959) and *Toward the African Revolution* (1964) – as well as numerous articles and short pieces and even a play[73] in the course of his short life. Although his work and life trajectory reveal him to be an extraordinary critical thinker and revolutionary, it was only after his death that he gradually came to be considered one of the greatest revolutionary thinkers of the twentieth century, alongside Mao Zedong and Che Guevara.

In 1961, Fanon died while receiving treatment for his illness in the United States. After lying in state in Tunisia, he was finally buried in Algeria. His body lies in the martyrs' graveyard at Ain Kerma in eastern Algeria. While bidding farewell to Fanon, the Vice-President of the Provisional Government of the Algerian Republic (GPRA) Belkacem Krim stated: 'Frantz Fanon! You devoted your life to the cause of freedom, dignity, justice and good.... You will always be a living example. Rest in peace. Algeria will not forget you.'[74] Indeed, Algeria has not forgotten Fanon. After independence, his ideas were celebrated widely and an avenue, a school and a hospital were all named after him. With subsequent authoritarian developments in

Algeria, Fanon's ideas started to vanish among the ruling elite, although he has always remained a popular figure among intellectuals as well as many ordinary people of different generations for whom independence is inseparable from the work of a Martiniquais who passionately devoted his life to their liberation from the French, even though their country might not have developed in the direction that Fanon and other revolutionaries wanted.

On the day that the news of Fanon's death reached Paris, the French police started seizing copies of *The Wretched of the Earth* from bookshops, while the GPRA's representatives at the United Nations gave copies of it to diplomats as a Christmas present.[75] It was only for a short period after his passing that Fanon was seen as an original thinker of the Third World, and about twenty years after his death *The Wretched of the Earth* was dismissed in France as out of date.[76]

In spite of this dismissal in the country where he was educated and had spent a significant amount of time, Fanon's work has remained influential in a number of academic and literary disciplines, including postcolonial theory, political science, literary and cultural studies, philosophy, queer theory and black studies, to name but a few. Numerous scholars have extended Fanonian frameworks to discuss issues such as migration, diaspora and apartheid. Hamid Dabashi and Glen Coulthard have dedicated their time to providing a new version of Fanon's first book with their respective works *Brown Skin, White Masks* and *Red Skin, White Masks*.[77] This broad 'appropriation' of Fanon,[78] similar to that of Marx, is an indicator of the depth and breadth of his work and ideas, which have deepened our understanding of the nature of imperialism, capitalism and colonialism. Many of these ideas are key in anti-imperialist struggles around the world and in building national and international solidarities.

Writing over forty years after his death, David Macey, one of Fanon's biographers, stated that 'Fanon remains a surprisingly enigmatic and elusive figure. Whether he should be regarded as "Martiniquan", "Algerian", "French" or simply "Black" is not a question that can be decided easily.'[79] In the global South, Fanon impacted numerous struggles and thinkers. It has been argued that his thought directly influenced the liberation struggle in the Portuguese colony of Mozambique, the Palestinian liberation movement, a Black Power Movement which flourished in Cuba in the 1960s and the anti-apartheid struggle in South Africa.[80]

Although he wrote from within the framework of the so-called Third World, and particularly Africa, his revolutionary ideas and search for a new humanity did not remain confined to the global South. His work also influenced the Black Power Movement in the United States. As Macey has written, 'Every brother on a rooftop who was taking care of business with a gun could, so it was said, quote Fanon. A lot of white students thought they wanted to be on the rooftops too. And so, we read Fanon. It was his anger that was so attractive.'[81] Moreover, the philosophy and strategy of Malcolm X during the American Civil Rights Movement was influenced by Fanonian thought and strategy. In recent years, we have witnessed a revival of Fanon among Black Lives Matter protesters, who have transformed violence against black people into acts of resistance.[82] Moreover, they have used some of his quotes as slogans at demonstrations. As Hudis states, this is because 'his ideas are seen by many to speak to the urgency of the moment'.[83]

With recent increased calls for the decolonisation of academia and the curriculum, Fanon's thought has regained popularity in different academic and intellectual circles, particularly his ideas regarding the construction of a new humanity. Fanon's futuristic mind-set teaches us that while we cannot forget past traumas, we can move beyond them, learn from the emancipatory visions that were behind anti-colonial struggles and self-consciously become future-oriented.[84] As Fanon's daughter, Mireille Fanon Mendès-France, noted:

> Fanon's thought continues today to inspire those who fight for the progress of humanity everywhere on the planet. In a world where the system of oppression and of annihilation of all that is human continues to adapt and renew itself, his thought is an antidote against giving up. That thought is the weapon of a clear passion for the unending fight for freedom, justice and dignity for all men and women. The liberation of peoples and individuals from enslavement and alienation is still a goal, and full emancipation still remains a future attainment.[85]

Chapter 7

Ernesto Che Guevara: the model of a revolutionary man

Ernesto Guevara (1928–1967) (who later in life was known as 'Che' Guevara) was an Argentine revolutionary, intellectual, physician, writer, guerrilla strategist and diplomat, among other things. It was in his early youth that he gradually began to explore socialist thought. He joined the Cuban revolutionaries led by Fidel Castro and played a significant role not only in the victory of the Cuban Revolution but in the process of constructing socialism in its aftermath. After the Revolution, Guevara performed a number of roles in the Cuban government. Based on Marxist ideas, he developed and implemented numerous concrete policies for the country's post-revolutionary transition to socialism. The structural changes he implemented transformed Cuba from a semi-colonial dependent country to an independent country which was fully integrated into the socialist bloc. As a diplomat, he advocated an internationalism that focused on the 'Third World' and encouraged progressives to direct their attention to the (previously) colonised or neo-colonised countries and those populations suffering from American imperialism.

Apart from being a physician and a revolutionary, Guevara was also an original and creative thinker whose ideas were expressed in numerous lectures, speeches, essays and books. Guevara's original contributions to Marxism were his focus on the political economy of transition to socialism and on the significance of the transformation of the human being into a 'new man' (*hombre nuevo*) via the construction of socialism and his theory of the *foco* as a revolutionary strategy for the global South. His practical policies, in particular his Budgetary Finance System of economic management, enhances Marxist theory. Although rooted in the history, culture and politics of Latin America, his ideas bear a universal message and are 'capable of delicate variation as regards forms of application to a complex and changing reality'.[1] At the age of thirty-nine, Guevara was captured and executed, in the course of a guerrilla war he led in Bolivia. Before this, he had led an unsuccessful guerrilla operation in the Congo. The circumstances of his death led to numerous protests and demonstrations worldwide and contributed to the spread of his image and the idealisation of him as a martyr.

Revolutionary pathways[2]

Ernesto Guevara was born in Rosario, Argentina, on 14 June 1928. He was the eldest of five children. His parents were from an upper-middle-class background. His father was an entrepreneur and a builder-architect who also got involved in yacht building and the cultivation of *maté* – the national beverage of Argentina. His mother was from a landowning family and had received a substantial inheritance at a young age. Because of young Ernesto's asthma, in 1932 the Guevara family moved to Alta Gracia for its drier climate. Guevara grew up there and then later in the city of Cordoba.

He had a special bond with his mother which lasted until the end of her life. Celia Guevara was an intelligent woman who gave Ernesto a lot of attention and love. She tutored him during the first years of his primary education when he could not go to school because of his asthma. Moreover, she had an adventurous character and often invited different kinds of people from different backgrounds to their home, which created an interesting atmosphere for the kids. According to Guevara's biographer Jon Lee Anderson, as early as 'the age of five, Ernesto had begun to reveal a personality that reflected his mother's in many ways. Both enjoyed courting danger, were naturally rebellious, decisive, and opinionated; and developed strong intuitive bonds with other people'.[3]

Ernesto's parents were both leftists who identified with the Republican cause during the Spanish Civil War. They were also ardent anti-Nazis and opposed Juan Perón and the populist political movement affiliated with him. Ernesto's parents' interest in politics created a politicised environment in their home which shaped his early views of the world. Moreover, the Guevaras had quite an extensive home library, which provided Ernesto with numerous resources to explore from his early youth. It was in his early youth that he gradually began to explore socialist thought. At a young age, Guevara had already read a biography of Lenin, *The Communist Manifesto*, some speeches by Lenin and part of *Capital*.

In 1947, Guevara's family moved to the capital and he began studying medicine at the University of Buenos Aires. Years later, he stated that he chose to study medicine because he 'dreamed of becoming a famous researcher ... of working indefatigably to find something that could be definitively placed at the disposition of humanity'.[4] At university, Guevara came into contact with some of the militants of the Communist Youth Federation (Federación Juvenil Comunista). He also regularly discussed with his friends the works of Argentine Marxist writer Aníbal Ponce (1898–1938).

In 1950, Guevara journeyed to a number of provinces in Argentina on a motorcycle, and in December 1951, one year before completing his medical degree, he travelled around the South American continent (including visits to Chile, Peru and Colombia) with his friend Alberto Granado. His *Motorcycle Diaries*,[5] which were published years after his death, is an interesting account of this journey. It is in this book that Guevara relates an encounter with mine workers and members of the Chilean Communist Party that touched him deeply. These diaries are also full of references to the social injustices, oppression and discrimination he observed first-hand during his trip, demonstrating his growing political consciousness and interest in socialism.

In 1953, Guevara received his medical degree and shortly after set out on his second journey around Latin America. This time he was accompanied by his friend Carlos (Calica) Ferrer, and their trip included visits to Bolivia, Ecuador and Guatemala. It was during this trip that he met exiled Cuban revolutionaries like Ñico Lopez, who, in addition to introducing him to Raúl Castro (who then introduced him to his brother Fidel), gave him the nickname 'Che' (which is an Argentine expression that roughly translates to 'Hey You!'). It was in Guatemala that Guevara met his future wife, Hilda Gadea. Hilda was a militant member of Peru's leftist political party, the American Popular Revolutionary Alliance. She had been forced to leave Peru because that party had been outlawed. In Guatemala, Guevara started to admire the communists he met. He supported the democratically elected government of President Jacobo Árbenz and the Guatemalan Labour Party (Partido Guatemalteco del Trabajo, which was originally the Communist Party of Guatemala).

While Guevara was in Guatemala, events were taking place in Cuba that would soon dramatically influence his life. On 26 July 1953, a group of young rebels who hoped to spark a national uprising against the military dictator Fulgencio

Batista attacked the army barracks in the city of Santiago de Cuba. A number of soldiers and police officers were killed but the rebels were ultimately defeated, many were executed and a few, including Fidel Castro and his brother Raúl, were taken into custody, tried and imprisoned (however, they were released after two years). Then, in June 1954, Guatemala's President Árbenz was overthrown in a coup planned and supported by the CIA. Guevara joined the resistance to the CIA's attempt to overthrow the government. In the repressive aftermath of the coup, both Guevara and Hilda had to leave Guatemala, and they chose to go to Mexico City. Like Guatemala before the coup, Mexico provided a refuge for Latin American exiles from various countries. Ernesto and Hilda married in August 1955 and their first child, Hildita, was born in February 1956.

It was around this time that Guevara met Fidel Castro through his friend Ñico Lopez, who had also found refuge in Mexico City. Guevara wrote in his diary that from this first meeting he felt a mutual sympathy with Fidel. After meeting the Castros, Guevara undertook a rather systematic reading of Marx, although he had already begun deepening his Marxist education after the coup in Guatemala and moving to Mexico. In November 1956, Guevara was one of the eighty-two revolutionaries aboard the yacht *Granma* which was used to transport the revolutionaries of the 26th of July Movement – a Cuban revolutionary organisation and later a political party led by Fidel Castro – from Mexico to Cuba. Upon landing in Cuba, many of them were killed in battle with the Cuban army. The survivors were joined by some peasants in January 1957, and together they began operating as a guerrilla force in the Sierra Maestra mountains. They were gradually joined by more local peasants, members of different political groups and the urban supporters of the 26th of July Movement. In

July 1957 Guevara was promoted to comandante, the rebel army's highest rank. He led numerous battles, including in the critical city of Santa Clara. Shortly after the Santa Clara battle, on 1 January 1959, the dictator Batista fled Cuba, and Castro's revolutionaries victoriously took power.

Guevara was granted Cuban citizenship. After divorcing Hilda, in June 1959 he married Aleida March, a Cuban member of the 26th of July Movement and one of his close collaborators during the revolutionary war. Initially a school teacher, she had also served as a secret arms courier and messenger for the Movement. Shortly after marrying Aleida, Guevara set out on a trip to establish relations between the revolutionary government of Cuba and governments in the Middle East, Africa, Asia and Europe, when he met with renowned world leaders such as Abdel Nasser of Egypt, Ahmed Ben Bella of Algeria, Jawaharlal Nehru of India, Mao Zedong of the People's Republic of China and Josip Tito of Yugoslavia. After his return, Guevara was appointed head of the Department of Industrialisation at the National Institute for Agrarian Reform (Instituto Nacional de Reforma Agraria, INRA) and was also appointed President of the National Bank of Cuba.

In 1961, Guevara was appointed Minister of Industry. As head of INRA's Department of Industrialisation, he was responsible for overseeing the performance of numerous industries, as well as for developing a plan for industrialising post-revolutionary Cuba. In addition, in his role as the President of the National Bank of Cuba, he was responsible for the country's financial affairs. Finally, Guevara played an important role in making Cuba one of the leaders of the coalition of African, Asian, Middle Eastern and Latin American countries known as the Non-Aligned Movement. This coalition had anti-imperialist sentiments, and the countries involved tried to increase their independence by not aligning themselves with any of the major power blocs during the Cold War.

In 1965, after years of revolutionary leadership, Guevara resigned from his government and party posts and left Cuba to continue what he had long considered his mission – to liberate the Third World from imperialist domination and capitalist exploitation. He first went to the Congo to join the movement that had been founded by Patrice Lumumba, the late leader of the Congolese independence struggle. The rebels against the military coup in the Congo had requested Cuban assistance. Guevara believed that the Congo could serve as a good training base for assisting liberation movements across the African continent. Africa seemed to present a promising battleground as rebel movements were fighting the last remnants of colonial rule throughout the continent. However, shortly after arriving in the Congo, Guevara realised that, because of various issues, such as weakness in the movement's leadership and lack of support from the local population, they would not be successful.

After the failure of their mission in the Congo, Guevara led a guerrilla fight in Bolivia from November 1966 to October 1967. His ultimate aim was to connect with the revolutionary struggles in other countries of Latin America. Unfortunately, Guevara and his group had miscalculated the backing they would receive from the local population and other sympathetic groups. They in fact received minimal support throughout their mission and they suffered many losses. Guevara became increasingly ill because of the shortage of medicine, which he needed for the treatment of his asthma. His guerrilla force was eventually captured by the Bolivian army in an operation assisted by the CIA on 8 October 1967, and he was executed the following day.

Ernesto Che Guevara's Marxism

In 'Notes for the study of the ideology of the Cuban Revolution', originally published in October 1960, Guevara wrote:

> The merit of Marx is that he suddenly produces a qualitative change in the history of social thought. He interprets history, understands its dynamic, foresees the future. But in addition to foreseeing it (by which he would meet his scientific obligation), he expresses a revolutionary concept: it is not enough to interpret the world, it must be transformed.[6]

Based on a Marxist analysis, Guevara envisioned a programme of social change for Cuba. For him, as for Marx, what mattered was the 'politico-ethical warrant' of changing the world.[7] Hence, for Guevara, Marxism was, more than anything, a 'philosophy of praxis' and a 'theory of revolutionary action'.[8]

It is widely agreed that Guevara's political thought was influenced by Marxist humanism and was based on Marx's early writings where he 'identifies communism with humanism' and defines humanism as a community of human beings who are able to grow, flourish and live in harmony with each other. In such a society, no exploitative mechanisms would be at work and no one would feel alienated.[9] Like Marx, Guevara's humanism is a revolutionary humanism and clearly based on a proletarian class outlook. Guevara was most likely influenced by the work of Aníbal Ponce, and his concept of 'proletarian humanism', which puts the humanism of the working people and of the bourgeoisie in sharp contrast.[10]

One Marxist concept that Guevara used was 'the dictatorship of the proletariat', which, according to Marx and Engels, should be understood as the rule of the proletariat. This is exactly what Guevara meant when he used this term in his writings and speeches, and he emphasised that the dictatorship of the proletariat is a method of people's rule.[11] Also, one of the main functions of the dictatorship of the proletariat is to ensure the success of the revolution and eradicate the resistance of the counter-revolutionary forces who aspire to overthrow the revolutionary regime.[12]

Guevara's internationalism was very much a direct manifestation of the Marxist value of proletarian internationalism. Like Marx, Guevara envisioned communist society as an abundant classless society that aims to satisfy the needs of everyone. Furthermore, following a basic premise of Marxism, Guevara insisted that because people's needs will continue to grow, the production and distribution of consumer goods need to grow as well and, therefore, the supply of such goods needs to increase.[13]

Guevara's original contribution to Marxist thought can be summarised in three topics: the political economy of the transition to socialism; the significance of human transformation in the move towards socialism; and a revolutionary strategy for the global South. With regard to the first point, it is important to note that Guevara's focus is on the political economy of the *transition* to socialism, which, according to him, is fundamentally different from the political economy of socialism.[14] After the victory of the Cuban Revolution in 1959, Guevara started to concentrate on Marxist texts with the objective of understanding the problems related to the transition to socialism. According to Marx and Engels, communism would emerge in most advanced capitalist countries where the working class could appropriate the already existing accumulated wealth and the advanced technology to their own benefit and liberate themselves from exploitation. From this theory, it was not very clear what would happen to societies without much wealth and technology in the process of transition to communism.[15] In *Socialism and Man in Cuba*, originally published in 1965, Guevara wrote:

We are not dealing with a period of pure transition as Marx envisaged in his *Critique of the Gotha Program*, but rather a new phase unforeseen by him: an initial period of the transition to communism, or of the construction of socialism. It is taking place in the midst of violent class struggles, and with elements of capitalism within it that obscure a complete understanding of its essence.[16]

'Alienation' and 'antagonism' were characterised by Marx as manifestations of capitalist social relations. Guevara believed these needed to be replaced with 'integration' and 'solidarity', by developing a collective attitude to production which meant perceiving work as a social duty.[17] In *Man and Socialism in Cuba*, Guevara stated:

We are doing everything possible to give work this new status of social duty and to link it on the one side with the development of technology, which will create the conditions for greater freedom, and on the other side with voluntary work based on the Marxist appreciation that man truly reaches his full human condition when he produces without being compelled by the physical necessity of selling himself as a commodity.[18]

Guevara was aware that Cubans' consciousness had been shaped by capitalism and, therefore, he was not against offering material incentives for work. However, he was against using such incentives as the primary tool for motivating people because he believed this would impose an individualistic and competitive logic on relations of production.[19] Moreover, Guevara was aware that the 'new spirit of work' or 'new attitude toward work' would not materialise in the short term and strong policies would thus be required to ensure this transition.[20] He also knew that the 'humanisation of work', as he called it, would require the reorganisation of the entire labour process in order to make all work favourable to human flourishing. For Guevara, it was necessary to make work mild, interesting and humane.[21] This would go hand in hand with the development of workers' consciousness, as communism would be reached much faster if their consciousness would be raised together with the development of productive forces.[22] It is worth mentioning that Guevara's understanding of consciousness, similar to that of Marx, was as a 'commitment to the social and economic justice aims of the Revolution, the conscious integration and participation of individuals in the project of socialist transition'.[23] Moreover, Guevara was aware that the standard of living needed to improve, in order to ensure people remained committed to the Revolution and its goals. These material developments, according to Guevara, should be achieved by 'administrative controls (the plan, the budget, supervision and audits, workers democracy), state investment in skills training, education, science and technology research, exploiting endogenous resources, fostering industry and diversifying agricultural production'.[24]

Guevara placed great emphasis on the role of human transformation in the formation of socialism and he uses the term 'new man' to conceptualise the end result of such a transformation. These new human beings that Guevara theorised, not only in his seminal text *Socialism and Man in Cuba* but also elsewhere, are for him synonymous with communist men and women. In other words, when referring to the characteristics of the new human beings Guevara was envisioning the new men and women within a communist society.[25] This is important because we need to realise that the transformations that Guevara had in mind, and would be the result of the socio-economic policies that he advocated, could not be realised in the short term.[26]

In fact, in *Socialism and Man in Cuba*, Guevara stated 'the road is long and in part unknown. We know our limitations. We will create the man of the 21st century – we, ourselves.'[27]

These new human beings have two main characteristics. First, they are committed to radical egalitarianism, that is, they support equality of condition for everyone. Guevara seldom explicitly advocated this commitment; it is, rather, assumed.[28] Second, what is expected from the new human being is 'a significant expansion of moral concern, in the sense of adherence to a far more comprehensive notion of one's social duty'.[29] This characteristic is elaborated on explicitly throughout Guevara's work. Guevara attributed highest importance to moral concerns and this plays a significant role in his project of creating 'a genuinely communist ethos'.[30]

Guevara often mentioned 'consciousness' in his writings and speeches and referred to certain moral commitments, which include some that define human beings. This consciousness or moral transformation is vital for the project of transitioning to socialism and beyond that to communism. Moral transformation should be at the centre of everyday practices; it transforms human beings as well as wider society.[31]

In addition to the abovementioned characteristics, the new human being would be directed by 'strong feelings of love' for humanity, they would not fall into 'dogmatic extremes' and would be ready to make a great deal of personal sacrifice. Guevara believed that development of this new human being would be possible in spite of the challenges.[32] As the academic Peter McLaren has nicely put it, the 'revolutionary agent of socialism exists dialectically, as both individual and as collective membership, always in process, always beginning anew, as the future immanent in the concrete moment of revolutionary world-making'.[33]

Guevara's ideal of creating a genuine communist society was based on concrete analysis of the economic, social and political conditions of Latin America and other countries exploited by colonialism and imperialism. He repeatedly emphasised the significance of anti-imperialist and anti-colonial struggles in these countries:

> Marx outlined the transition period as resulting from the explosive transformation of the capitalist system destroyed by its own contradictions. In historical reality, however, we have seen that some countries that were weak limbs on the tree of imperialism were torn off first – a phenomenon foreseen by Lenin. In these countries capitalism has developed sufficiently to make its effects felt by the people in one way or another. But it was not capitalism's internal contradictions that, having exhausted all possibilities, caused the system to explode. The struggle for liberation from a foreign oppressor; the misery caused by external events such as war, whose consequences privileged classes placed on the backs of the exploited; liberation movements aimed at overthrowing neocolonial regimes – these are the usual factors in unleashing this kind of explosion.[34]

In his message to the Tricontinental – a celebrated conference held in Havana in January 1966 which gathered representatives of countries mostly from Asia, Africa and Latin America and focused on anti-colonial and anti-imperial issues – Guevara referred to Lenin's classic work *Imperialism, the Highest Stage of Capitalism* and formulated imperialism as the final stage of capitalism in the world system. However, living decades after the publication of Lenin's work and in the era of neo-colonial power relations enabled Guevara to experience the subtleties of neo-colonialism at first hand.[35]

One of Guevara's main contributions to revolutionary theory is his theory of *foco*, a revolutionary situation that can be created in rural areas with highly trained guerrilla fighters. In developing his theory of guerrilla warfare, Guevara was inspired by the military strategy of the Spanish Civil War, the work of Mao Zedong, the experience of the Yugoslav partisans, the freedom fighters in Algeria – mostly inspired by Fanon – and the experience of Vietnamese resistance.[36] Similar to many Marxists, Guevara agreed that certain preconditions are necessary for a revolution. The three preconditions that can be developed before a revolutionary situation and formation of a *foco* are: loss of legitimacy of the governing elites in a country, existence of tensions and lack of any feasible legal way to improve the situation. These are only preconditions but they do create a social and political frame within which the *foco* can function as a catalyst for a revolutionary situation. However, the existence of these preconditions does not guarantee the success of the *foco*. It is the task of the revolutionaries to assess the situation more closely and precisely determine the factors that could make a *foco* successful in a given situation.[37] For Guevara, it is not the task of the *foco* to seize power by itself but, rather, to serve as a catalyst that inspires people, particularly in rural areas, to join the struggle to overthrow the oppressive regime.[38] According to Guevara, guerrilla fighters' knowledge of the environment and ability to collaborate with the local population play a significant role in their success. Based on his knowledge of Latin America, he concluded that the peasants of the region had the potential to make the best guerrillas.[39]

Apart from Guevara's theoretical contributions to Marxist thought, his practical policies, which were based on the concrete praxis of the Cuban Revolution and his work as a member of the Cuban government from 1959 to 1965, are original elaborations of Marxist thought.[40] His practical policies were the result of his reading of Marx's analysis of the capitalist system, his engagement with contemporary socialist debates about political economy and an investigation into the technological and administrative developments in capitalist corporations.[41] As a member of the Cuban government, Guevara was the main figure behind the structural changes which transformed Cuba from a semi-colonial dependent country to an independent nation that was fully integrated into the socialist bloc.

In October 1959, Guevara was appointed head of the Department of Industrialisation within the newly created INRA, and in November he became the President of the National Bank. In 1960, under his leadership, all financial institutions, 83.6% of industry (including all sugar mills) and 42.5% of land were nationalised.[42] In February 1961, the Ministry of Industries (MININD) was created and Guevara was appointed as minister. In this role he created the Budgetary Finance System (BFS) of economic management, which was in place from 1961 to 1965.[43]

Guevara was not happy with the Soviet model of transitioning to communism, which he argued was based on using capitalist tools such as competition, profit, material incentives, credit and interest to accelerate the industrialisation process. Additionally, he believed the Soviet model had failed to raise the collective consciousness of workers that was so essential for socialist and communist societies in which the ultimate objective is the utmost flourishing of human beings.[44] While engaging with Marx's *Capital* and other Marxist texts, Guevara set up the BFS within the Ministry of Industries. The BFS was first developed as a practical measure to solve some specific problems faced by Cuba, but as Guevara intensified his Marxist reading he initiated the Great Debate in 1963 and raised questions about the most appropriate economic management system for Cuba in particular and in socialist countries more generally.[45] Moreover the BFS was designed to test the assumption that consciousness raising and productivity should go hand in hand in the construction of a socialist society.[46]

The BFS was the concrete manifestation of Guevara's Marxism in the format of policies and organisational structures within the social, political and economic conditions that prevailed in Cuba at the time.[47] Therefore, it should not be regarded as something universal and any blank copying of these principles should be avoided. However, it gives us an interesting insight into Guevara's very concrete implementation of Marxism. A summary of the principles of the BFS is as follows:

1. Finances should be centrally controlled.
2. Money serves as a means of account, not as a means of payment.
3. The socialist economy is one big factory.
4. Work should be understood as a social duty.
5. The national economy should be consciously and democratically planned.
6. The key to increasing productivity is lowering production costs.
7. The most advanced technologies and management techniques should be used.
8. Flexibility in relation to (de)centralisation and creativity and participation in resolving production problems is a defining factor.
9. Workers are the collective owners of the means of production.
10. Science and technology must be used to increase production.
11. The full chain of production must be taken into account to secure an independent socialist economy.
12. There is a dialectical relationship between consciousness and production.
13. There is a need to create forums for criticism and open debate.[48]

Guevara's Great Debate was centred around the most suitable economic management system for the transition to socialism (with the focus on the conditions in Cuba). The debate was between Guevara's followers and those who believed in the efficacy of the Soviet model. From the 1950s onward, the Soviet Union and the Eastern European countries of the socialist bloc had gradually begun to liberalise their economies by incorporating more capitalist mechanisms so as to address economic stagnation and bureaucracy. Guevara warned that this was market socialism, which he predicted would eventually lead to the restoration of capitalism. It is worth noting that Guevara had a great respect for the Soviet Union, particularly in light of the assistance it had provided to Cuba, and his criticisms were meant to be constructive. He aspired to highlight the dangers of socialism with capitalist elements and hoped to convince socialist countries to think about their mistakes and develop a different path. In fact, Guevara really hoped for an international debate on the political economy of transition to socialism at the time when the Sino-Soviet split created rancorous debates and challenges within and between communist parties around the world.[49]

The Great Debate, which came to an end in 1965, made a clear contribution to the ongoing discussions around the construction of socialist political economy. During these years, Cubans looking for new perspectives 'were involved in a daily search for administrative and technological mechanisms to organise and stimulate the economy whilst maintaining the enthusiasm and support of the masses'.[50] Guevara argued that undermining the law of value was the main challenge in the period of transition to socialism. The law of value is a central concept in Marx's critique of political economy and refers to the relative exchange values of products made by humans, which is usually measured by money and is determined by the average amount of human labour time which is necessary to produce them. Undermining the law of value was significant for Guevara since it had clear repercussions for the economy and the individual's psyche and their perception of themselves and their role in the society.[51] The task of a socialist country, Guevara believed, was to create circumstances which would lead to the undermining and eventual abolition of the law of value.[52] Unlike the pro-Soviets in the Great Debate, who believed that the law of value and the way it impacts people could be undermined only when there is an abundance of material wealth, Guevara believed that a socialist economy without communist moral values was uninteresting. The fight against poverty was important but fighting alienation of human beings was as important. In fact, elimination of material interest, individual self-interest and profit was at the centre of Guevara's thought.[53]

Ernesto Che Guevara's legacy

Guevara's legacy cannot be separated from the Cuban Revolution. His contribution to developing a socialist political economy in Cuba is incontrovertible. He set up the Budgetary Finance System to show that in the transition to socialism the simultaneous development of productivity and consciousness was not only possible but essential. This approach remains a pillar of Cuban socialism in spite of numerous challenges faced by the revolutionary regime.[54] However, the political character of the venture developed by Guevara and the Cuban Revolution should be considered their most important legacy: an endeavour to create a new society with new social relations, institutions and values.[55]

Today in Cuba, Guevara's political and intellectual virtues are celebrated in various ways, and he remains one of the most important symbols of the Cuban Revolution, alongside Fidel and Raúl Castro. His picture is in every school, and the youth of the country continue to learn about him and his revolution-ary ideas.[56] Above all, he remains 'the model of a revolutionary man', as Fidel Castro referred to him on the twentieth anni-versary of his death, or as a model for the new socialist human being of the twenty-first century, the human being Guevara wrote about in his famous essay *Socialism and Man in Cuba*. After Guevara's execution, Jean-Paul Sartre wrote that he was 'not only an intellectual but also the most complete human being of our age'.[57]

Guevara joined the Cuban Revolution because he believed that liberating Cuba could provide the first step in the liberation of Latin America from imperialism and capital-ist exploitation. Moreover, early on, after the victory of the Cuban Revolution, he argued that the Revolution was not only concerned with the liberation of Latin Americans but that it was also in solidarity with all oppressed people of the world and that it would assist independent struggles in other countries. During the 1960s and 1970s, Cuba's support for revolutionary struggles and socialist and leftist movements extended from Latin American countries to liberation struggles and left-leaning governments in Africa, the Middle East and Asia. During his lifetime, Guevara was instrumental in the provision of this support. Even his unsuccessful mission in the Congo and the lessons he learned from it proved to be extremely helpful for liberation movements and leftist gov-ernments in Africa in the following decades.[58] Apart from the Congo, his interest in Africa led him to establish close relations and exchanges with many progressive leaders on the continent, such as Kwame Nkrumah of Ghana, Julius Nyerere of Tanzania, Abdel Nasser of Egypt and Amílcar Cabral of Guinea-Bissau.[59]

Since his tragic death in 1967, Guevara has become a universal symbol of revolution and resistance against injustice and exploitation and a reference figure among the oppressed or, as Fanon would say, the wretched of the earth – the rebels, intellectuals, activists and revolutionaries. He has inspired generations of activists around the world in both the global South and the global North and in various struggles and on many occasions. His picture can be seen on walls, posters, banners and billboards and in books and magazines in all parts of the world. A large body of literature, films, songs and artworks has celebrated his life and politics. Also, many of his writings have been translated into numerous languages around the world and his revolutionary example has continued to remain important in many countries. As McLaren has correctly put it, Guevara's legacy should be viewed in relation to his ability to put his theoretical Marxist-Leninist approach into practice.[60] He showed the oppressed and exploited of the world that subjective historical conditions play an important role in determining the appropriate method and strategy of struggle. Moreover, he 'reproduced in his life and death a central element of martyrdom: a readiness to lay down his life for the cause of love, freedom and social justice…. Through the example of Che, the crucified peoples of the world are offered hope.'[61]

In addition to numerous speeches, books and articles on various topics, Guevara's *Guerrilla Warfare* (1961) remains a classic work on revolutionary guerrilla strategy, and the renowned *Episodes of the Cuban Revolutionary War* (1963) is a noteworthy history. In spite of his global popularity in both the South and the North, it is not surprising that his ideals have been adopted in a more systematic manner in Latin America by leftist governments, Indigenous and landless people, labour activists as well as by the world-renowned Zapatista movement in Mexico (see Chapter 9 in this volume), among others. In fact, Guevara's death and the failure of the guerrilla operation he led in Bolivia did not discourage revolutionaries in Latin America from taking up armed struggles – on the contrary, it clarified what is actually needed for organising a successful guerrilla campaign. Consequently, the revolutionary movements that started in Central America in the 1970s and 1980s incorporated approaches affiliated with Guevara, including mobilising mass political support in urban and rural areas. The success of the Zapatista movement in southern Mexico and Hugo Chávez's Bolivarian Revolution in Venezuela could both be attributed to this approach.[62] Although the Zapatistas' military tactics have not been as radical as Guevara's, they have been a successful example of his *foco* theory. Also, their charismatic leader, Subcomandante Marcos, who had spent years among Indigenous communities of Chiapas in southern Mexico to organise and train a revolutionary army, has revitalised the image of Guevara in the popular imagination.[63]

Guevara inspired numerous generations of revolutionaries and fighters, not only because of his novel ideas but also 'because of the revolutionary principles he represented – fearlessness, self-sacrifice, honesty and devotion to the cause'.[64] Moreover, in spite of the changes the world has gone through over the past decades, we unfortunately still face many of the issues and problems Guevara confronted during his time, and therefore many of the positions and commitments that he stood for remain relevant today: egalitarianism, internationalism, anti-imperialism, anti-capitalism, solidarity and dedication to radical and transformative education. Given the current condition of the world, decades after Guevara's tragic death, I could not agree more with Fidel Castro, who, in his tribute to Guevara and his comrades after their bodies were found many years after their execution, in October 1997, stated:

Only the world he dreamed of, which he lived and fought for, is big enough for him. The more that injustice, exploitation, inequality, unemployment, poverty, hunger, and misery prevail in human society, the more Che's stature will grow. The more that the power of imperialism, hegemonism, domination, and interventionism grow, to the detriment of the most sacred rights of the peoples – especially the weak, backward, and poor peoples who for centuries were colonies of the West and sources of slave labor – the more the values Che defended will be upheld. The more that abuses, selfishness, and alienation exist; the more that Indians, ethnic minorities, women, and immigrants suffer discrimination; the more that children are bought and sold for sex or forced into the workforce in their hundreds of millions; the more that ignorance, unsanitary conditions, insecurity, and homelessness prevail – the more Che's deeply humanistic message will stand out. The more that corrupt, demagogic, and hypocritical politicians exist anywhere, the more Che's example of a pure, revolutionary, and consistent human being will come through.[65]

Chapter 8

Ali Shariati: an international fighter

Ali Shariati (1933–1977) has been described by many as the main ideologue of the 1979 Iranian Revolution,[1] which was a pro-democracy and anti-imperialist revolution that overturned 2,500 years of monarchy and replaced it with the Islamic Republic. Shariati was an activist in numerous groups and movements in the pre-revolutionary years in Iran and was exposed to Marxist ideas in Paris in the early 1960s. In the years prior to the victory of the 1979 Iranian Revolution, Islamic and Marxist schools of thought were the two major anti-regime political tendencies that animated Iranian politics. In this contentious political atmosphere, Shariati advocated unity by praising both revolutionary tendencies. He combined Marxist and existentialist traditions of thought with a religious and nationalist discourse, which attracted millions of Iranians, particularly the youth. He offered a Marxist view of history, but he was preoccupied with the Islamisation of Marxism or the Marxification of Islam. In order to achieve this goal, he reconstructed the entire history of Islam and highlighted the revolutionary aspects of Shia history and thought, emphasising the fact that social justice and equality were inherent values in Shia Islam. His 'red Shiism', in contrast to the 'black Shiism' of the conservative clergy, was a religion of the masses, a religion which had the capacity to make its adherents aware of the multiple levels of exploitation and injustice forced upon them.

Shariati critiqued Marxism for neglecting culture and believed that non-Western societies' culture was dominated by religion. He agreed with Marx's historical materialist critique of religion, which saw it as a narcotic for the masses, but criticised Marx for failing to understand the dialectical nature of religions. This dialectic is between the religion that legitimises the status quo and the prophetic religion that stands up against it. Many attended (and recorded) his popular lectures and his pamphlets were widely circulated – even when they were banned by the pre-revolution regime. His image was carried in large demonstrations in the years prior to the revolution. Shariati's ideas have remained the cornerstone of the thinking of many Iranians. Outside of Iran, Shariati has been one of the most influential Muslim thinkers of the twentieth century and his ideas have inspired struggles for social justice.

Revolutionary pathways[2]

Shariati was born in 1933 in a village near Mashhad in the north-east of Iran, where he completed his primary and secondary education. His father was a renowned local Islamic scholar and educator whose religious and political thought had a significant influence on Shariati. His father founded a progressive and reform-oriented religious centre – the Centre for the Propagation of Islamic Truths – in 1947, which became involved in the movement to nationalise oil in the 1950s. As a schoolboy, Shariati participated in the activities of the Centre and studied Arabic and the Quran with his father. Also in the late 1940s, Shariati and his father joined a small group called the Movement of God Worshiping Socialists. The establishment of this group was the first attempt in Iran to combine

Shiism – the second largest denomination of Islam after Sunnism – with European socialism. The group believed that Islam and socialism were compatible and that both focused on social justice and equality. Apart from participating in this group, Shariati also wrote newspaper articles for the Mashhad daily newspaper, *Khorasan*, which demonstrate his developing enthusiasm about thinkers such as Jamal al-Din al-Afghani – a political activist and Islamic ideologue – and Muhammad Iqbal – a philosopher and the spiritual father of Pakistan. Both of these thinkers were involved in advancing anti-imperialist and anti-colonial causes.

In 1952, Shariati became a high school teacher. In the following years, he founded the Islamic Students' Association and became a member of the National Front, a political organisation founded by Mohammad Mosaddegh, the leader of the movement to nationalise oil in Iran. Mosaddegh was the first democratically elected Prime Minister of Iran, who was overthrown in 1953 in a coup orchestrated by the United States and the United Kingdom.

Around this time, Shariati translated an Arabic work by the Egyptian thinker Abdul Hamid Jowdat al-Sahar titled *Abu Zar: The God Worshiping Socialist*, which was about the life of the companion of Prophet Muhammad who was critical of the tyrant Caliph and supportive of the poor. For many progressive Muslims, Abu Zar is considered the first Muslim socialist. Shariati received a bachelor's degree in the Arabic and French languages and then was awarded a state scholarship to study for a PhD at the Sorbonne in Paris. In the years prior to his departure for Paris, he was arrested numerous times because of his political activities.

Shariati arrived in Paris in 1959 – at the height of the Cuban and Algerian Revolutions – and soon came into contact with radical political philosophy and revolutionary organisations.

The French left, particularly the work of Jean-Paul Sartre, one of the leading figures in twentieth-century French philosophy, and Marxism attracted him. Moreover, he was influenced by the revision of Marxism by the Russian-born French sociologist and jurist Georges Gurvitch. He corresponded with Frantz Fanon and developed an interest in liberation theology and radical Catholicism. He was particularly impressed by the work of Roger Garaudy, a prominent Christian Marxist intellectual, and Louis Massignon, a Catholic scholar of Islam. He translated into Farsi Sartre's *What Is Literature*, Che Guevara's *Guerrilla Warfare* and a book by a Muslim Marxist on the Algerian war entitled *Le Meilleur Combat*, and he worked on the translation of some of Fanon's books. Furthermore, he joined the Algerian National Liberation Front, the Confederation of Iranian Students (an anti-Shah opposition group made up of Iranians studying abroad) and the Liberation Movement of Iran (a religious nationalist political organisation). Also, he edited two journals: *Free Iran*, the organ of Mohammad Mosaddegh's National Front in Europe; and *Pars Letter*, the monthly journal of the Confederation of Iranian Students in France.

Shariati returned to Iran in 1964, where he was promptly arrested for his political activities in Paris. He was released a few months later, and after initially being denied employment as a lecturer, he eventually started teaching sociology and Islamic and world history at Mashhad University. In 1971 he was sacked from his job because of his growing popularity. From 1967 to 1972 Shariati was one of the main lecturers at Hosseinieh Ershad – an Islamic reform centre in Tehran which was not directly controlled by the government and aimed at engaging young urbanites in debates about society, culture and history. In these lectures, Shariati propagated his revolutionary thought and called for action against injustice and oppression. His lectures were enthusiastically received and became very popular among the educated young urban middle classes. They were tape-recorded and transcribed into numerous pamphlets and booklets. Despite censorship, these were widely circulated. These years marked the most prolific period of Shariati's political life. However, this period did not last long. Being aware of the two most influential political trends of the time, Marxism and Islamism, Mohammad Reza Shah, the monarch of Iran, worked hard to prevent and sabotage any cooperation or alliance between Muslims and Marxists. Moreover, conservative clergy (clergy have historically had a significant influence in Iran) constantly denounced Marxism and dismissed any possibility of such collaboration. By the early 1970s, several Shia clerics accused Shariati of opposing Islam and promoting Marxism.

Hosseinieh Ershad had become a major centre for political activity, and it was closed by the government in 1972. The regime's argument was that the People's Mujahedin of Iran, a radical Muslim group involved in armed struggle against the regime, was affiliated with that institution. Soon after its closure, Shariati was arrested and accused of advocating Islamic Marxism and having connections with the People's Mujahedin. He was released in 1975 but remained under house arrest. In the mid-1970s his books were banned, and one could have been arrested for possessing any of his work.

He left for England in May 1977, where he suspiciously died after a month; the official cause of his death was declared to be a heart attack. His supporters never doubted that SAVAK, the Shah's security and intelligence service, was involved in his untimely passing. Shariati's family decided not to bring his body back to Iran, and he was instead buried in Damascus. In the months after his death, up until the Iranian Revolution, Shariati's speeches became even more widely distributed and popular. In the course of his short life, Shariati wrote numerous books and articles, many of which remain unavailable in English translation.

Ali Shariati's Marxism

There is widespread disagreement about Shariati's relationship with Marxism. According to the sociologist Asef Bayat, more than anything the disagreement is about the nature of Shariati's 'Islamic Marxism' and his attempts to link central concepts and terms of Marxism, such as class exploitation, class struggle and imperialism, with the teachings and lives of Shia icons like Imam Ali and Imam Hussein, the first and third Shia Imams and successors to the Prophet Muhammad, who fought against the tyrannical tendencies of their time.[3] However, the historian Ervand Abrahamian has argued that these ambivalences can be overcome if we understand that, for Shariati, there were three different 'versions' of Marx and hence three different types of Marxism.[4] The young Marx was an atheist philosopher, supporter of dialectical materialism and denier of the existence of God. The second version was the mature Marx, a social scientist who demonstrated the relationship between the exploiter and the exploited and was fascinated with the laws of 'historical determinism' and the interconnection between the superstructure and the base. The third version was the elder Marx, a politician and a revolutionary who did not necessarily remain loyal to his earlier social science methodology. Shariati rejected the first and the third Marx but accepted most of the second. Therefore, he emphasised that some knowledge of Marxism was necessary for understanding history and society, that societies were divided into a base and a superstructure and that human history was essentially one of class struggle.

According to the academic Hamid Dabashi, 'A close reading of Shariati's writings leaves no doubt that his chief frame of reference, his conceptions of history, society, class, state apparatus, economy, culture, his program of political action, his strategies of revolutionary propaganda are all in the classical Marxist tradition'.[5] In a short treatise he wrote, Shariati praised the depth of Marxist analysis and argued that the Marxist conceptualisation of history and a revolutionary proletariat have not only been used by progressives and those in search of social change but also by capitalists and the ruling classes to frustrate the movement towards equality and social justice. In Shariati's view, the socialist revolution did not happen in Europe, as was predicted by Marx and Engels, precisely because of capitalists' awareness of Marxist analysis and its revolutionary premises.[6]

Shariati's adoption of classical Marxist ideas can be summarised in his persistent calls to action and his denunciation of class-bound societies. These views were perfectly aligned with his Shia-inspired call to social justice and the rejection of fatalism.[7] This engagement can be seen throughout Shariati's work but particularly in his *Religion vs Religion*, where he provided a detailed analysis of Shia Islam as an ideology that is opposed to oppression and injustice. Moreover, in his Marxist quest to change the world and not only interpret it, Shariati adopted a Marxian and Hegelian dialectical method in his writings, which eventually led to the development of his Islamic Marxism, a palpable synthesis that emerged from his dialectical engagement with Marxism and Islam.[8]

Nevertheless, Shariati critiqued Marxism for neglecting culture. He argued that 'the spirit dominating the new culture and civilisation is bourgeois: the spirit of moneymaking, business, power seeking, tool making, consumption and hedonism'.[9] His critique of this new culture was close to the ideas circulating within the Western counter-culture of the time.[10] He believed that non-Western societies' cultures were dominated by religion and hence neo-colonialism, which he regarded as the extension of capitalism and colonialism, was attempting to destroy religion in non-Western countries. The destruction of religion, he argued, would ultimately lead to a crisis in cultural identity and the sense of selfhood in non-Western societies. In a collection of essays originally called *Man, Islam and Marxism* (later translated into English with some misinterpretations and the new and absolutely misleading title *Marxism and Other Western Fallacies*), he explicitly demonstrated his concerns about Marxism's notion of super-structure, which asserts economic forces as determinant. Thus, Marx and European Marxists, Shariati argued, have provided a Western and materialistic understanding of humanism and disregard the spiritual dimension of the human being, as well as the unity between humans and God, which in Islam is conceptualised as *tawhid*.[11]

As Dabashi writes, Shariati believed in 'a philosophy of life' which was against capitalism but went beyond the economic preferences. Dabashi quotes Shariati as saying:[12]

> As a universal and scientific principal, Marx makes economics the infrastructure of man; but we [hold] precisely the opposite [view]. That is why we are the enemy of capitalism and hate the bourgeoisie. Our greatest hope in socialism is that in it man, his faith, ideas and ethical values are not superstructural, are not the manufactured and produced goods of economic infrastructure. They are their own cause. Modes of production do not produce them. They are made between the two hands of 'love' and 'consciousness.' Man chooses, creates, and sustains himself.[13]

Moreover, Shariati argued that communism, as a system advocated by Marx and Marxism, is similar to capitalism insofar as they are both practice-based systems that value productivism, mechanism, bureaucracy, competition and materialism.[14] Although Shariati was sympathetic to the Iranian left – who were rather prolific and eminent at the time – and admired their goals and revolutionary enthusiasm, he criticised their strategy, which, according to him, was not culturally sensitive and hence remained incapable of communicating with the religious segments of society. Moreover, Shariati believed they had applied an uncritical perspective on Marxism in Iran, ignoring the fact that Iran had gone through a totally different historical trajectory from Europe: Iran had not experienced the Renaissance, the Reformation, the Industrial Revolution and the rapid transition to capitalism that European countries had. Shariati emphasised that Iran had in fact been characterised by the Asiatic mode of production and hence experienced different labour relations in comparison with its European counterparts. Also, he believed Marxists in Iran had not been sufficiently sensitive to the country's deeply religious society, and he was critical of their publication of atheistic texts. According to Shariati, people of the global South could not defeat imperialism and capitalism without first rediscovering their own national heritage and culture. In a series of lectures, he argued that Shiism represented most aspects of Iranian popular culture.[15]

In spite of his criticism of some aspects of Marxism and Marxist practice, Shariati systematically used Marxist terminology throughout his work, albeit with certain adaptations. For example, he borrowed 'historical determinism' but connected it to the will of God; very often, he spoke of classes, but his understanding of the term was not based on a relation to the means of production but, rather, was political and materialised in culture, that is, norms, beliefs, customs and traditions.[16] In his last two books, *Jahatgiri-ye tabaqati-ye Islam* ('The class bias of Islam') and *Ommat va imamat* ('Community and leadership'), Shariati systematically uses Marxian concepts to discuss the political economy of Islam, but he tries to formulate them in a manner that addresses the particularities of Iranian and Middle Eastern history.[17]

Shariati believed the main problems Iran faced in the second half of the twentieth century were imperialism and inequality. Furthermore, he cautioned against 'Westoxication' (*gharbzadegi*), which had become a popular discourse in the 1960s and focused on the hegemonic power of the West in Iran. He argued that Iran needed two interconnected and simultaneous revolutions: a national revolution which would liberate Iran from imperialism and all forms of imperial domination, including national identity and culture; and a social revolution which would eliminate capitalism and liberate people from all forms of exploitation, poverty, injustice and inequality.[18]

Borrowing from Marxist literature, Shariati emphasised the significance of speaking 'scientifically'. This was addressed to two different groups: the Shia clerics and the secular intellectuals. Shia clerics understood science 'in the context of the Islamic juridical epistemology that divided knowledge into the intellectual sciences and the transmitted sciences'.[19] The secular intellectuals emphasised the 'economic based feature of Marxist socialism that distinguished it from idealist or utopian socialism'.[20] Shariati rejected both understandings of the term and argued that the clerics' understanding was not sociological, while the secular intellectuals' version of scientific socialism could be localised within Persian and Shia culture.

Marxism convinced Shariati of the significance of ideology for advancing any revolution and he considered Islam a powerful force that could be used for revolutionary ends.[21]

Therefore, he translated Marxist ideas into a revolutionary strategy for Iran by creating an 'ideological hybrid' of Marxism and Shiism. Although he agreed with much of Marx's sociological analysis, he felt obliged to promote the idea that one could simultaneously be a Shia and a Marxist.[22] What mattered for him and his attitude towards political forces was not their relation to religion, or their religiosity, but 'how revolutionary they were'.[23]

However, Shariati first needed to reconstruct the entire history of Islam. According to him, the clerics had isolated themselves from the people, and especially the youth, by hiding behind superficial scholasticism. Moreover, they had monopolised the understanding of Shiism and ignored principles of egalitarianism and social justice. He believed the clerical establishment legitimised social oppression in Iran since it had become the official religion of the Safavid dynasty (1501–1736 AD). Safavid Shiism, Shariati argued, was engaged with 'spiritual and metaphysical phenomena' instead of its 'progressive and this-worldly essence'.[24]

Moreover, according to Shariati, the Muslim petite bourgeoisie had historically appropriated Islam, and this had diminished its revolutionary spirit, which is devoted to the liberation of the oppressed. This assertion led him to reject the Shia establishment because of its close connection with and support of the petite bourgeoisie.[25] Historically, clerics and the petite bourgeoisie of the bazaar were allied and tended to act in concert. They were usually from the same families, so the bazaar paid levies for the clerics and the clerics supported the bazaar by holding religious ceremonies for them. Both groups were against Marxist and socialist ideas. In a famous quote, Shariati writes: 'Our mosques, the revolutionary left, and our preachers work for the benefit of the deprived people and are against the lavish and lush. But our *fuqaha* [legal scholars] who teach jurisprudence and give verdicts, are right wingers, capitalists and conservative. In short, our *fiqh* [Islamic law] works for capitalism.'[26]

All the negative characteristics of the bourgeoisie can be summarised in what Iranians refer to as worldliness. Shariati planned to replace 'the struggle against bourgeoisie' with the 'defiance of worldliness', which had its roots in Islam. According to Shariati, the defiance of worldliness could be applied to any revolutionary group that rises against oppression.[27] He believed Islam was an inherently egalitarian religion but that the measures which were designed to combat the enormous accumulation of wealth had been betrayed and misused by the state, clergy and the (petite) bourgeoisie. Muslims needed to recognise this and raise 'the flag of permanent historical revolution' against capitalism and the bourgeoisie.[28]

In his collected work, brought out under the title *On the Sociology of Islam*, and during a series of lectures delivered at the Hosseinieh Ershad from February until November 1972, he systematically sought to reclaim Shiism's progressive core while incorporating some aspects of Marxist ideology. He argued that a revolutionary spirit is inherent in Islam but that modern Muslims had been alienated from their revolutionary past and this was manifest in their Westoxication. The difference between Shariati's Shiism and Safavid Shiism was that the former was a dynamic religion which was constantly being reproduced and the latter was a static institution for the dead and their mourners.

Shariati's Shiism was a religion through which the masses could become aware of their social location, class position and national and global conditions.[29] For Shariati, Islam and Shiism were not only the basis of Iranian cultural identity but also had the potential to politicise the masses. Hence, he sought to revive forgotten aspects of revolutionary Shiism and transform them into 'a political ideology of monolithic revolutionary proportions'.[30] He considered this to be a counter-hegemonic denunciation of the culture of stagnation associated with the clerics' view of Islam, which did not have any emancipatory potential.[31] Through this counter-hegemonic denunciation, he created a unique form of Muslim leadership which was not based on old traditions or any political party. His widely popular lectures were regarded as 'an extensive work of intellectual organization' and became 'the meeting ground of a new generation of young, otherwise Marxist, Muslim intelligentsia'.[32]

Unlike what is commonly believed, Marx did not blame the misery of the masses on religion but argued that religion becomes the 'opium of the people' because of the material conditions in which people find themselves. In fact, religion for Marx is an expression of people's suffering. Shariati completely agreed with Marx's historical materialist critique of religion that characterised religion as a narcotic for the masses that soothes their suffering and pain. Such religion fails to motivate people to change their situation and instead pushes them into their faith and creates static subjects who surrender to their situation. However, Shariati argues that Marx failed to understand the dialectical nature of Abrahamic religions that stands up against the religion that legitimises the status quo. The recovery of this prophetic aspect of religion was at the heart of Shariati's theory of emancipation.[33]

Shariati assumed that, after capitalism, socialism was both inevitable and preferable. Socialism was, for him, a 'philosophy of life', 'the course, and the end of salvation, delivering man from the destiny of capitalism' rather than an economic system based on collective ownership of the means of production.[34] Shariati's socialism was a utopia he referred to as a 'monotheistic classless society' (*jame ye bi tabaqe ye tawhidi*) where all forms of oppression would be eradicated.[35] *Tawhid*, or Islamic monotheism, is central to the realisation of Shariati's ideal society. Shariati defends the Quranic position that first there was monotheism and then out of human corruption and oppressive relations polytheism emerged. He considered *tawhid* to be a life philosophy based on the unity of humans, nature and God. Through this definition he politicised *tawhid* and ultimately argued that only in a classless society can true monotheism be achieved or, in other words, based on a genuinely monotheistic theology, a just, classless society can be established. This classless society was to be achieved by a union of humans in a communal brotherhood and sisterhood, accompanied by the truth of Allah and the abolition of all social, political and economic hierarchies.[36]

Shariati constantly attacked polytheism, which, according to him, propagated inequality and class difference. He traced the roots of polytheistic religions to economic factors and the ownership of wealth and resources by a minority. True monotheists would rebel against such injustice and oppression and would seek refuge in God.[37] He insisted on the values and ethics inspired by Imam Ali, Imam Hussein and other martyrs whose deaths had become symbols for the struggle to material-ise *ummah* and *nezam-e tawhidi* – the activist community and unitary society that Islam advocates.[38] For Shariati, this meant that Shia Islam could be revolutionary and as red as Marxism. However, as mentioned before, his praise for his homeland's religion came along with his fierce criticism of the official presentation of Islam, a problem which was also raised by liberation theologists.[39]

Shariati believed that such a society would not be possible without the emergence of a revolutionary mass movement which could unite and mobilise the masses – religious and non-religious alike and not only the proletariat. Within this context, he was in search of a radical political ideology with egalitarian premises that would appeal to the masses and the oppressed and which would go beyond the traditional Islamic political imagination propagated by the conservative clerics. Moreover, he emphasised the role of power in the creation of inegalitarian and oppressive relations. He argued that the transformation of the egalitarian pastoralist society into class- and property-based agricultural society was the result of oppression and power imbalance, and not the uneven development of productive forces. Thus, he emphasised the social, political and economic significance of oppression.

Finally, by glorifying Imam Hussein's figure of classical Shiism, in which Hussein is killed during his fight against a tyrant centuries ago, he turned Hussein into a revolutionary and a martyr (*shahid*). Also, martyrdom (*shahadat*) was presented as a valuable symbol which would assure the continuation of the revolutionary struggle. Iranian intellectuals and youth had previously seen Islam encouraging Muslims to mourn Hussein, because he was murdered in a very sad way. But Shariati presented Hussein as a revolutionary icon who fought and died for social justice,[40] hence connecting Hussein's struggle to a Marxist ideal.

All this was ultimately driven by Shariati's assessment of the overall socio-political and economic conditions in Iran and his search for a revolutionary praxis. The transcripts of his lectures were widely circulated and his writings were regularly republished and sold on the streets of Tehran and other big cities. His pictures were seen in demonstrations and protest events and his nickname, *moallem-e enghelab* (revolutionary mentor), was chanted by millions in demonstrations. His ideas were passionately debated by revolutionaries and, interestingly, his ideas enjoyed a wider audience than even those of Ayatollah Khomeini, who had emerged as the leader of the Iranian Revolution.[41]

Shariati's red Islam offered a framework to unite the Muslim and secular left in their revolutionary efforts. Because this posed a serious threat to the Pahlavi dynasty, Mohammad Reza Shah constantly tried to undermine this unity through various means.[42] Shariati theorised a way towards fundamental social change and provided a language that revolutionary masses and the youth could identify with. In this sense, he not only provided justification for social change but also provided a template for achieving it by reconciling Marxism with Islam. Shariati's enormous appeal should be understood in light of the originality of his position, which was a combination of a modest religious background and belief in a version of Islam with many similarities to Marxism, although he never considered himself a Marxist.

Ali Shariati's legacy

Commenting on the Iranian Revolution of 1979, the philosopher Michel Foucault referred to Shariati as someone who appeared in all spheres of political and religious life in the country.[43] Similarly, Dabashi credits Shariati with capturing 'the revolutionary imagination of an entire generation',[44] while Abrahamian believes that, during the years prior to and during the Iranian Revolution, Shariati was the most popular modern Iranian writer.[45] For Bayat, Shariati possessed 'a unique moral leadership', which was due to 'his ability to interweave his seeming intellectual sophistication with unrelenting revolutionary politics which captured the spirit of his audience'.[46] However, because of his constant and systematic criticism of the clerics, Shariati and his work gradually became a threat to their authority and legitimacy. They felt their prestige was being eroded by someone who had not studied theology and yet accused theologians of misrepresenting religion for their own benefit.[47]

Understanding Shariati's thought helps us discover the roots of the 1979 Iranian Revolution and its success in overthrowing the monarchy. Through his 'revolutionary Islam' and 'red Shiism', he attracted many young and educated Iranians who were fascinated by various premises of leftist politics but were in search of an Islamic alternative.[48] This alternative that Shariati created was 'an Islamic liberation theology'.[49] His ideas influenced and radicalised a new generation of Iranian Muslim Marxists who not only impacted the upheavals of the pre-revolutionary years but who also remained important actors in the years after the revolution.

Soon after his death Shariati became a 'mythical figure of militant Islam'.[50] In the years after the Iranian Revolution, due to his exceptional popularity, different political groups started to fight over his name, each trying to associate him and his legacy with their own group and ideology. The clerics who had managed to hijack the revolution and appeared as the main successor of the monarchy started to praise him. They particularly referred to his emphasis on Shia roots, the shortcomings of Marxist orthodoxy in the global South and the importance of anti-imperialist struggle but denied his anti-clerical views, his Marxism and his connections to the West. The People's Mujahedin of Iran were among the most dedicated admirers of Shariati, and many of his followers joined this group.[51] However, they ignored Shariati's emphasis on national unity against imperialism by destabilising the country through bombings shortly after the revolution and later by joining Saddam Hussein's forces against Iran during the American-backed Iran–Iraq war.

Many of Shariati's supporters remained loyal to the Islamic Revolution and his anti-capitalist project was infiltrated by his followers, who took charge of the new post-revolutionary institutions.[52] However, as Hamid Algar, the English translator of some of Shariati's works, has stated, 'one of the tragic results of his death was to deprive Iranian public opinion of the assessments he would undoubtedly have offered of post-revolutionary developments, in all their complexity'.[53] Although ruling elites praised Shariati and named streets and schools after him in the immediate aftermath of the revolution, it did not take long before Shariati lost his credibility among post-revolutionary officials and elites. Many of his followers were censored, imprisoned or otherwise restricted. Also, a number of political organisations associated with him have been declared illegal and counter-revolutionary over the years. Within such a political environment, Shariati's family and associates have often stated that, had he been alive, he would have ended up in prison after the revolution.[54]

Despite all these challenges, Shariati's ideas have remained the cornerstone of the thinking of many Iranian radical Muslims and, along with the ideas of the Marxist left, shaped the ideological foundation of the post-revolutionary movements that emerged in the years immediately after the Iranian Revolution.[55] The late Gholam Abbas Tavassoli, sociologist and a senior member of the Liberation Movement of Iran – one of the political groups Shariati had joined during his time in Paris – wrote that Shariati's works and ideas 'have been sought out by the younger generation with such interest and eagerness that their profound impact can never be effaced from our memories or hearts'.[56]

By the early 1990s, due to social, political and cultural changes in Iran, Shariati's ideas had lost their relevance and were no longer embraced by the Iranian public.[57] However, in the 1990s a new generation of Muslim intellectuals had emerged, sometimes referred to as post-Islamists, who rejected the orthodoxy of the post-revolutionary years.[58] By offering a new reading of Shariati's thoughts, they argued that he viewed concepts such as freedom, equality and democracy as universal parts of the historical process of human development. These concepts were introduced into public discourse in Iran and fed the evolving reform movement that culminated in the presidency of the reformist candidate Mohammad Khatami in 1997 and his re-election four years later. During the reform era, new progressive discourses were introduced in the Iranian political sphere, and the development of a strong civil society led to the emergence of numerous social movements.[59] Since then, Shariati's work has experienced a revival in popularity, and books, newspaper and magazine articles are regularly published which debate Shariati's relevance in post-revolutionary Iran. He has also been celebrated in several conferences and symposiums.

Outside of Iran, Shariati has been one of the most influential Muslim thinkers of the twentieth century. At a major event organised by his family and friends on the fortieth day after his death – which is a Shia tradition – numerous liberation organisations from across the world were present. Some of the attendees included the Palestine Liberation Organisation, the Lebanese Amal Movement, the People's Front for the Liberation of Eritrea, the National Liberation Movement of Zanzibar, the National Movement for the Freedom of Zimbabwe and the National Movement for the Freedom of Southern Philippines.[60]

Shariati's reputation beyond Iran can be judged by the translation of his work into English, German, Arabic, Turkish and Malay, among other languages. Recently, his influence has been recognised by renowned scholars such as Farid

Alatas and Raewyn Connell as an important figure of southern theory. Moreover, by underlining the emancipatory as well as repressive aspects of Shiism, Shariati offered a unifying reading of Islam which goes beyond the Shia–Sunni divide. Moreover, for many Muslim and leftist intellectuals, Shariati's position towards Western domination and hegemony, his emphasis on local knowledges, his egalitarian and revolutionary interpretation of Islam which went hand in hand with combining Islam and Marxism provided an emancipatory yet localised discourse for social change.[61]

His sudden death and the suspicions surrounding it made him a martyr in the minds of many Iranians, and he was mourned through various ceremonies inside and outside Iran. Thanking him for his lifetime support of the Palestinian liberation movement, the political leader Yasser Arafat referred to him as 'an international fighter'.[62] In London, a large crowd comprising the members of a large number of associations and groups attended the ceremony. The mourners, many wearing masks to hide their identity from the regime's security and intelligence services, praised him in their chants as someone who symbolised 'the moment of their anti-colonial awakening'. Perhaps Shariati's most important legacy lies in the fact that he 'radicalised Islam by a future-oriented return to its most radical roots' and brought together the Muslim community with an interpretation of Islam that 'represented the universal longing for human emancipation, human flourishing and human solidarity'.[63] In doing so, he not only convinced the Muslim community of the radical potential of their faith, but he also convinced secular intellectuals outside of Iran who were suspicious of religion of the emancipatory nature of their struggle against imperialism and global capitalism.[64]

Chapter 9

Subcomandante Marcos: a guerrilla with a difference

In the final years of the twentieth century, when the socialist bloc had collapsed and, to many, capitalism seemed to be the ultimate winner of the Cold War, a group of mostly Indigenous people declared war on the Mexican state and on global capitalism, on the very day that the North American Free Trade Agreement (NAFTA) came into force (1 January 1994). The group called themselves the Zapatista Army of National Liberation (Ejército Zapatista de Liberación Nacional, EZLN). Its spokesperson (appearing masked) and military leader was a man named Marcos (born 1957), who had left his university position in Mexico City to move to the Lacandón jungle in Chiapas, southern Mexico. Initially a member of a Marxist-Leninist organisation in Mexico City, Marcos's encounter with the Indigenous Mayans and the subsequent rise of the EZLN has led to the emergence of one of the most inspiring anti-capitalist social movements of the late twentieth and early twenty-first centuries. Rafael Sebastián Guillén Vicente, who is generally known by his *nom de guerre* Subcomandante Insurgente Marcos (shortened to Subcomandante Marcos), became instrumental in bringing together the struggles of the rural Indigenous communities of Mexico and the urban (global) civil society.[1] He revitalised the Marxist political language in the post-Soviet era in an innovative way that merged with the literary traditions of Latin Americans and the political reality of Indigenous people. He became the representative not only of the Indigenous community but of all Mexico's oppressed and marginalised populations.

He has been known as one of the most fierce anti-capitalist figures and his vision for another world has been manifested in the three main pillars of the Zapatistas' national project, democracy, freedom and justice. Through these pillars the Zapatistas have expanded the horizons of political possibility, and their vision for a freer, more honest and more just society has not remained limited to Chiapas or Mexico. The global vision they have advocated has been received by various struggles throughout the world. Marcos's writings have appeared in numerous languages and have been instrumental in the internationalisation of the Zapatistas' plea.

Revolutionary pathways[2]

Subcomandante Marcos came to fame as the spokesperson and military leader of the EZLN, a militant political group that controls large parts of Chiapas State in southern Mexico. Although Mexico had gone through a revolution in the early years of the twentieth century (1910–1920), which led to various socio-political changes such as progressive land and labour reforms, Marcos was born in an era of repression and dictatorship that witnessed the suppression of railroad workers, the massacre of hundreds of students and the disappearance and assassination of members of militant and left-wing groups.

He was born on 19 June 1957, in Tampico, on the central east coast of Mexico, to a middle-class family. His parents were both former teachers and gave a lot of attention to the education of their eight children (Rafael was their fourth child). He was exposed to literature at a young age and was surrounded by books. As he states in an interview with Gabriel García Márquez and Roberto Pombo:

> We went out into the world in the same way that we went out into literature. I think this marked us. We didn't look out at the world through a news-wire but through a novel, an essay or a poem. That made us very different. That was the prism through which my parents wanted me to view the world, as others might choose the prism of the media, or a dark prism to stop you seeing what's happening.... Strictly speaking we were already, as the orthodox would say, very corrupted by the time we got to existential literature and, before that, to revolutionary literature. So that when we got into Marx and Engels we were thoroughly spoilt by literature; its irony and humour.[3]

The quote shows that Marcos's exposure to Marxism was mediated and influenced by literary forms which deeply influenced his language as well as the points of reference that he employed later in life. It led to creation of an engaging and inspiring political language for communicating with a large and diverse audience. His future writings would be influenced by world literature but also Indigenous literature and reality. He would constantly emphasise that 'our words are our weapons'. It is believed that his innovative language in expressing Marxist terminology and discourse became instrumental in successful communication and bringing public support to the particular historical moment of the collapse of the Soviet Union and after.

Marcos moved to Mexico City to study political philosophy at the National Autonomous University of Mexico. During his education he was profoundly influenced by the thought of Karl Marx, Louis Althusser, Nicos Poulantzas and Michel Foucault. In 1979, he started to teach at Mexico City's Metropolitan Autonomous University and in the same year he also joined the ranks of the Forces of National Liberation (Fuerzas de Liberación Nacional, FLN), a clandestine Marxist-Leninist revolutionary organisation which was heavily influenced by the Cuban Revolution (1959) and Che Guevara, a figure Marcos had admired since his youth. In fact, the example of Guevara played an important role in Marcos's decision to join the FLN. Joining this organisation was in fact a Guevaran act on his side, since it involved leaving the world of books and getting 'out there', in search of real experiences.

Marcos's exposure to Marxist and Leninist thought was mostly through his involvement with the Marxist-Leninist FLN and during his university studies, particularly while he was conducting research for his award-winning graduation thesis, which he submitted in October 1980. According to his biographer, Nick Henck, his thesis was Marxist at its core and provided 'a picture of capitalist society as being a class-based social system in which the bourgeoisie exploit the proletariat based on their privileged relationship to the means of production, and the history of which is the history of class struggle'.[4] Apart from the work of Marx, Engels and to some extent Lenin, traces of Louis Althusser's influence were apparent in the thesis.

The 1979 victory of the Sandinistas in Nicaragua strengthened the revolutionary convictions of the FLN, whose aim was to respond to the corrupt practices of Mexico's ruling Institutional Revolutionary Party (Partido Revolucionario Institucional, PRI) by establishing a popular socialist republic. For five years, Marcos took on more responsibilities within the FLN and during this time visited Nicaragua. Moreover, he regularly visited Mexico's south-eastern state of Chiapas to meet with the FLN's local contact and to undertake rural guerrilla training. In 1984, assuming the pseudonym Marcos, he left Mexico City to permanently join the FLN's recently established wing in Chiapas, which was called the Zapatista Army of National Liberation (EZLN). Chiapas was chosen as the place to launch a guerrilla insurgency because it was geographically isolated, the FLN had established connections in the area and most of Chiapas's Indigenous peasants were exploited and living in harsh poverty, which would facilitate the groundwork for rebellion.

At first, the EZLN was a small and clandestine guerrilla group that moved throughout Chiapas in order to establish contacts with local communities and build a support base. It was in the late 1980s and early 1990s that the organisation's membership started to grow. By 1993, the Indigenous majority of the EZLN believed they were experiencing an existential dilemma as the result of exploitation, repression, racism and impoverishing neoliberal policies which intensified in the run-up to the implementation of NAFTA on 1 January 1994. Consequently, the EZLN decided to make use of the large membership it had gained. Marcos seemed an obvious military leader for the uprising and he ended up spending the next two decades of his life (1994–2014) as the chief military adviser and spokesperson for the EZLN, which became independent of the FLN after the uprising began in Chiapas in early 1994.

From the first days of the uprising, Marcos became the main representative and icon of the Zapatista movement, and his masked face and hidden identity only added to his popularity. The author Naomi Klein, in a piece in the *Guardian* in 2001, describes Marcos as follows:

> an urban Marxist intellectual and activist, Marcos was wanted by the state and was no longer safe in the cities. He fled to the mountains of Chiapas in southeast Mexico filled with revolutionary rhetoric and certainty, there to convert the poor indigenous masses to the cause of armed proletarian revolution against the bourgeoisie. He said the workers of the world must unite, and the Mayans just stared at him. They said they

weren't workers and, besides, land wasn't property but the heart of their community. Having failed as a Marxist missionary, Marcos immersed himself in Mayan culture. The more he learned, the less he knew.[5]

In February 1995, the Mexican government revealed Marcos's identity as part of its attempt to undermine the Zapatistas and the broad-based support the group enjoyed. This came after the government's failures to arrest Zapatista leaders. Arrest warrants were issued for Marcos as well as other key figures of the movement. Marcos and others fled into the Lacandón jungle, and in response to the unmasking and a renewed offensive against the Zapatistas, large demonstrations were organised in Mexico City by civil society organisations, at which tens of thousands chanted 'Todos somos Marcos!' (We are all Marcos!), expressing their deep solidarity with the Zapatistas.

Although Marcos is known as the spokesperson of the movement, it is important to highlight that he initially was a guerrilla leader and in charge of several hundred troops, as well as being responsible for political education and military training in his local zone. He handed over his leadership roles to the younger and Indigenous Subcomandante Moisés in 2014. In his farewell speech he criticised the obsession with his figure and underlined the significance of collective struggle over individual contributions. In 2016 a federal court ruled that criminal charges that were brought against Marcos in 1995 were no longer valid. Marcos has continued to remain active as an author of Zapatista communiqués, which have been voluminous, and has since attended, participated in and hosted Zapatista events, in most cases together with Subcomandante Moisés. Zapatistas have remained in conflict with the Mexican state since 1994, in spite of on-and-off peace talks.

Subcomandante Marcos's Marxism

Marcos's transformation upon his arrival in Chiapas and coming up against Indigenous communities who had been living decentralised and communal lives has been described by himself as a process of re-education which questioned all the presumptions he and his FLN comrades had about a potential successful guerrilla campaign.[6] Marcos has also talked about the exchange that took place with community groups about the initial proposals of the EZLN and how the conversation transformed some orthodox Marxist-Leninist aspects of their proposals, such as seeing the proletariat as the vanguard of the revolution or taking state power and putting in place a dictatorship of the proletariat. This has been explained by Marcos as a confrontation between the university Marxist-Leninist culture and the Indigenous culture.[7] As has been described by the sociologist Denis O'Hearn:

> Marcos was originally a Marxist guerrillero (and professor) from the city. But in the end he was the right kind of Marxist guerrillero (and professor), because when he went into the jungle of Chiapas he kept his eyes and ears open. Instead of trying to teach Marxism-Leninism to the Mayans, he listened first. He learned that the best way to lead is by obeying.[8]

This 'reconstruction of his political identity' happened within the context of a turn towards even greater authoritarianism on the part of the Mexican government, combined with privatisation of communal land, negligence of Indigenous communities and increasing connections to international capital, particularly in relation to NAFTA.[9]

Marcos has described the stages which led to initiation of the Zapatista uprising on 1 January 1994 as follows. In 1983, the EZLN was founded by six FLN insurgents in Chiapas. Beginning in 1984, the EZLN insurgents started to prepare themselves for the armed struggle. Marcos arrived in Chiapas at this time. During the latter half of the 1980s, the first contacts between EZLN insurgents and the local Indigenous community were made and the EZLN started to grow. In the next stage, the preparation for the 'war' started. In the last days of 1993, the final preparations for an uprising took place.[10] However, what is most interesting is that the encounter between Marcos and his comrades and the Indigenous community resulted in the incorporation of Indigenous reality and history into the preconceptions and ideological discourse of Marxism.[11] This manifested itself in the development of an innovative language and discourse which remained loyal to the fundamentals of Marxism but expanded it in an accessible language which merged smoothly within the context of the Zapatista uprising.

The First Declaration of the Lacandón Jungle, which is believed to have been written by Marcos, begins with the following words:

> We are a product of five hundred years of struggle: first, led by insurgents against slavery during the War of Independence with Spain; then to avoid being absorbed by North American imperialism; then to proclaim our constitution and expel the French empire from our soil; later when the people rebelled against Porfirio Diaz's dictatorship, which denied us the just application of the reform laws, and leaders like Villa and Zapata emerged, poor men just like us who have been denied the most elemental preparation so they can use us as cannon fodder and pillage the wealth of our country. They don't care that we have nothing, absolutely nothing, not even a roof over our heads, no land, no work, no health care, no food or education, not the right to freely and democratically elect our political representatives, nor independence from foreigners. There is no peace or justice for ourselves and our children. But today we say: enough is enough![12]

In March 1995, reflecting on 'A year of the Zapatista government', Marcos wrote:

We, our blood already in the voices of our oldest grand-
parents, walked this land when it was not yet known by this
name. But later in this eternal struggle, between being and
not being, between staying and leaving, between yesterday
and tomorrow, it came into the thinking of our ancestors,
with the blood of two branches, that this piece of land and
water and sky and dreams, a land which we had because it
had been a gift from our earlier ancestors, would be called
Mexico. Then we became that other and had more, and
then the history of the way that we all got the name was
good and thus all who were born had a name. And we were
called Mexicans, and they called us Mexicans. Later history
continued delivering blows, giving pain. We were born
between blood and gunpowder; and between blood and
gunpowder we were raised. Every so often the powerful from
other lands came to rob us of tomorrow. For this reason it
was written in a war song that unites us: 'If a foreigner with
his step ever dares profane your land, think, Oh beloved
motherland, that heaven gave you a soldier in each son.' For
this reason we fought.[13]

For Marcos, 'Neoliberalism, as a global system, is a new
war to conquer territories'.[14] In an article initially published
by *Le Monde diplomatique* in 1997 and titled 'The Fourth
World War has begun', Marcos argues that the 'Cold War'
was misidentified and, in fact, the era should be called 'the
Third World War', which eventually led to the collapse of the
socialist bloc.

The misnamed 'Cold War' reached very high temperatures:
from the catacombs of international espionage to the sidereal
space of Ronald Reagan's famous 'Star Wars'; from the sands
of the Bay of Pigs in Cuba to the Mekong Delta in Vietnam;
from the unbridled nuclear arms race to the savage coups in
Latin America; from the reprehensible manoeuvres of NATO
armies to the intrigues of CIA agents in Bolivia, where Che
Guevara was assassinated. All these events culminated in the
collapse of the socialist camp as a world system and in its dissolution as a social alternative.[15]

Since the dissolution of the socialist alternative, neoliberalism, which Marcos describes as 'the American way of life', has been imposed on people around the globe, from the Indigenous populations of Americas to Europe, Asia and Africa. Marcos calls this 'a planetary war, of the worst and cruellest kind, waged against humanity'.[16] But he also acknowledges and underlines the fact that people – from women to the young and the old; from Indigenous people to ecologists and workers – organise themselves and rebel. And it is within this context that one should understand the Zapatistas, who believe that 'in Mexico, the re-conquest and defence of national sovereignty are part of the anti-neoliberal revolution'.[17] For Marcos, resistance to the status quo and building a new world, 'a world that can contain many worlds, that can contain all worlds', is the only solution.[18]

In an interview with Marta Durán De Huerta and Nicholas Higgins (two academics) in 1999, Marcos defines the three main pillars of the Zapatistas' national project: democracy, freedom and justice.[19] He explains that democracy in the Zapatistas' understanding cannot be limited to elections but is also about creating 'a new relationship between those who govern and those who are governed'.[20] This entails 'balancing' representative democracy with direct democracy and 'the continual participation of the citizens not only as electors or as consumers of electoral proposals, but also as political actors' who regularly participate in societal matters and evaluate the government's work, and not only during elections.[21] There should be a mechanism at work to allow citizens to change their elected representatives at any time if they stop fulfilling their roles. Moreover, citizens should be able to play a significant role in presenting political proposals – beyond economic and media power – and to engage in political activity at all levels, including running for any governmental posts they wish. Finally, a fundamental aspect of a democracy that the Zapatistas work towards is the recognition of the rights and differences of different groups in society.[22]

The Zapatistas define freedom, the second component of their national project as follows:

> The citizen and the nation should be free to choose their own path, and to subscribe to a political proposal and make from it what they will. That means they should be free from external forces, like the forces of money and the forces of financial power, which can often dictate the destiny of a country.[23]

As for justice, the third pillar, two senses are at work: justice in life, which includes having access to the means that are necessary for a dignified life, such as housing, food, health care, education and a fair salary; and administrative justice, which is about the just administration of laws and the just punishment of those who have committed criminal offences, regardless of their political or economic power.[24]

On different occasions and in various writings, Marcos has explicitly explained these main pillars of the Zapatista uprising and their objectives, but he has also made it clear that

> Zapatismo is not an ideology, it is not a bought and paid for doctrine. It is … an intuition. Something so open and flexible that it really occurs in all places. Zapatismo poses the question: 'What is it that has excluded me?' 'What is it that has isolated me?' … In each place the response is different. Zapatismo simply states the question and stipulates that the response is plural, that the response is inclusive….[25]

Marcos has brought together various groups of oppressed populations. More than being the champion of Indigenous people, who have faced systematic discrimination and neglect, Marcos has been the champion of Mexico's downtrodden, defending the rights of different marginalised and oppressed groups, such as women and LGBTQ people. He has been an outspoken critic of the political elite in Mexico, and played an important role in ousting the Institutional Revolutionary Party, which was in power for over seven decades.[26]

Since the beginning of the Zapatista rebellion, Marcos has issued a large number of communiqués and given various interviews and speeches along with press conferences, and other media events. The language he uses is political and poetic, bringing a fresh understanding of how certain Marxist concepts can be communicated. His discourse and the language he employs are very different from traditional political language, and this allows him to communicate complicated political matters without binding them to a certain terminology. This has led to the creation of an innovative, and often anecdotal, political language for the left.[27] For example, in a 2009 tale called 'Marxism according to Insurgent Erika', a female insurgent ascribes Marxism to a woman, Karla Marxism.[28] The incorporation of literary forms and influences derived from literature (mostly Indigenous literature) and linguistic practices has had a very positive impact on the appeal of the Zapatistas' message, its popularisation and 'the new political language' that was born from it.[29]

In Mexico, Marcos quickly became the face of an emerging social force advocating 'another Mexico' and 'another politics'.[30] That social force – the Zapatistas – emerged with a powerful vision and robust organisational practices and strategies. They introduced a 'new politics of the imagination' and 'a different version of the popular' in which forgotten men and women who wore masks and carried guns focused on an 'ancient struggle for the land' and disturbed the image of modernity that had been advocated by the Mexican government, as manifested in its association with NAFTA.

Moreover, as the sociologist John Holloway has argued, when the Zapatistas on the first day of 1994 cried '¡Ya Basta!'

(Enough!) and occupied San Cristóbal de las Casas and six other towns in Chiapas, they cried for dignity and refused 'to accept humiliation and dehumanisation, the refusal to conform', and dignity became the core of their revolution.[31] According to Holloway, the idea of dignity *per se* is nothing new, but the Zapatistas managed 'to put dignity at the centre of oppositional thought',[32] and their revolution's objective became achieving a society based on dignity, that is, democracy, freedom and justice. However, what this exactly means and what concrete steps need to be taken towards it are not defined. In other words, 'the revolution is a moving outwards rather than a moving towards',[33] and therefore it is an undefined revolution.[34] Although this aspect of the Zapatistas' uprising has been at times criticised, Holloway believes that precisely this aspect forces us to understand revolution and revolutionary processes in a new way: 'if the revolution is built on the dignity of those in struggle, if a central principle is the idea of "preguntando caminamos – asking we walk", then it follows that it must be self creative, a revolution created in the process of struggle'.[35] In this sense, dignity is 'a category of struggle' which is constantly defined and redefined but at its core is a struggle against the negation of that dignity in an oppressive society. Therefore, the cry for dignity cannot be separated from the experience of oppression.

Oppression has various forms and cannot be total, but dignity is the other side of it: it is a cry for recognition and disalienation (à la Marx). Moreover, dignity crosses the boundaries of morality and politics, the private and public, the personal and the political. Holloway writes that dignity

is rather an attack on the separation of politics and morality that allows formally democratic regimes all over the world to coexist with growing levels of poverty and social marginalisation. It is the 'here we are!' not just of the marginalised, but of the horror felt by all of us in the face of mass impoverishment and starvation. It is the 'here we are!' not just of the growing numbers shut away in prisons, hospitals and homes, but also of the shame and disgust of all of us who, by living, participate in the bricking-up of people in those prisons, hospitals and homes. Dignity is an assault on the conventional definition of politics, but equally on the acceptance of that definition in the instrumental conception of revolutionary politics which has for so long subordinated the personal to the political, with such disastrous results.[36]

The acronym EZLN stands for Ejército Zapatista de Liberación Nacional. Therefore, 'national liberation' is a clear component of the movement. However, the national liberation Zapatistas have fought for does not fit into the typical understanding of national liberation, which aims at liberating a national territory from a foreign colonial or neo-colonial power and seeks to establish a post-liberation government. What is radically new is that nation/national for the Zapatistas does not have a clear definition of a homeland and is rather loosely defined as 'the place where we happen to live, a space to be defended not just against imperialists but also (and more directly) against the state'.[37] In this sense, national liberation can also mean liberation from a particular state or a defence against the state. Therefore, 'nation' 'refers to the idea of struggling wherever one happens to live, fighting against oppression, fighting for dignity'.[38] Hence, the Zapatista movement of national liberation is not confined to a place or national borders and should, rather, be understood as a movement of 'liberation' and as a 'revolution' with a lower-case 'r' and not a 'Revolution', because it does not have any grand plans to change the world; rather, its claim to be revolutionary lies 'in the present inversion of perspective, in the consistent insistence on seeing the world in terms of that which is incompatible with the world as it is: human dignity'.[39]

As Holloway emphasises, 'Dignity is a class concept, not a humanistic one'.[40] Although Marxism has played an important role in shaping their struggle, the Zapatistas have preferred to develop a new language and not use more conventional Marxist terminology because they believe 'the old words had become so worn out that they had become harmful for those that used them'.[41] Yet, not using a definitional concept of class, that is, categorising the working class as those who sell their labour power to the owners of the means of production in order to survive and thereby are subject to exploitation, does not mean that dignity is not a class concept because

> the starting point is no longer a relation of subordination but a relation of struggle, a relation of insubordination/ subordination. The starting point of dignity is the negation of humiliation, the struggle against subordination. From this perspective there does not exist a settled, fixed world of subordination upon which definitions can be constructed. Just the contrary: the notion of dignity points to the fact that we are not just subordinated or exploited, that our existence within capitalist society cannot be understood simply in terms of subordination. Dignity points to the fact that subordination cannot be conceived without its opposite, that is, the struggle against subordination–insubordination.[42]

Holloway argues that this is consistent with Marx's approach, since his analysis of capitalism was not based on the antagonism between two groups but on the antagonism that existed in the organisation of human social practice. Our existence in a capitalist society is an antagonistic existence, and this antagonism acts in various forms of conflict inherent in capitalism. The conflict in the first place is 'between humanity and its negation', 'between subordination and insubordination' and therefore, we can speak 'of insubordination (or dignity) as a central feature of capitalism'. In other words, 'class struggle does not take place within the constituted forms of capitalist social relations: rather the constitution of those forms is itself class struggle'.[43]

According to Marcos, what the Zapatistas have wanted is to '[open] a crack in history'.[44] This is closely interlinked with the idea of reclaiming dignity and seeking a world with justice, freedom and democracy. Of course, each of these terms could have a particular meaning, depending on the context within which people live. Therefore, one's understanding of these terms should not be limited to their liberal democratic senses. Even within each context, these terms do not have a fixed meaning.[45] As the academic Luis Lorenzano has argued, 'the radical nature of any particular need or demand cannot be defined in the abstract, but only as a critique of a critical situation'.[46] In this sense, the Zapatistas' pursuit of justice, freedom and democracy is radical because it entails a radical disapproval of the socio-political system in Mexico and beyond. However, by refusing to impose a blueprint for revolutionary change, to seize power or insist on one path for social transformation, the Zapatistas have promoted a process for social change 'that is collaborative, democratic, imaginative and unclosed', a process that is based on 'the mutual recognition of dignity – a "world capable of holding many worlds"'.[47] In this sense, the Zapatistas have not only been a symbol of resistance but 'a school of resistance' that tells us how to resist the destructive forces of neoliberal capitalist globalisation.[48]

However, the Zapatistas not only have put forward a broad revolutionary vision for social change but at the same time have issued some concrete demands: access to land for everyone who needs it to work (the central issue for peasants), as well as housing, health care, schools, social services and the right of children to play and learn.[49] This shows the significance of revolutionary planning on both broad/abstract and narrow/concrete levels.

The Zapatistas tend to speak of dignities – in the plural – and not of dignity. The emphasis on plurality demonstrates that, for the Zapatistas, different forms of struggle and opinions matter, although this does not entail a total relativism in which everyone's opinion matters equally; however, the conflict of dignities is inevitable and for the Zapatistas the solution lies in remaining open to articulating and recognising various dignities in a variety of ways. While they organise their discussions on the basis of village assemblies, they acknowledge that the articulation of dignities in another context would need another form.[50]

The Zapatistas introduced a view of resistance and alternative world-building that is open and, while based on certain common principles, looks different in different contexts. However, these 'pockets of rebellion' or 'pockets of resistance' are inherently interconnected because they all target the global neoliberal capitalist system.[51] Slogans such as 'one no, many yeses' help popularise this vision and emphasise that, while there is only one shared goal – of destroying neoliberalism – there are numerous needs, priorities and struggles, and therefore it is a heterogeneous post-capitalist world that can be seen on the horizon.[52] The notions of hope, dignity, imagination and 'a radical sense of possibility' have been prominent elements of Zapatista struggle.[53] It is this radical sense of possibility that has inspired many people around the world to interpret that struggle from their own position, experience and context; the Zapatistas thereby encourage further attempts to rethink contemporary revolutionary politics. In other words, they offer a way forward by reinventing revolution.[54] It has been put beautifully by Holloway and Eloína Peláez: with the occupation of San Cristóbal de las Casas and other towns, the Zapatistas 'sent flares of hope, dignity and revolutionary enthusiasm into the sombre night sky of the world'.[55]

Subcomandante Marcos's legacy

Some Indigenous people in Chiapas believe Marcos is a 'god', while for others Marcos is a shaman with unique power and capabilities. Above all, in the Zapatista social imaginary he is 'a quasi-mythological persona who incarnates the past, present and future of the Maya world'.[56] Régis Debray, the French philosopher and Guevara's comrade during his 1967 mission in Bolivia, has referred to Marcos as 'A guerrilla with a difference' and has compared Marcos's life to that of Robin Hood:

> From all directions, this fugitive receives the mail of a president to which he can obviously not reply, and which, moreover, has to be burned in the most dangerous moments. There are all kinds of things. Letters of detained people from all corners of the world asking him to come and liberate them – he opened the prisons in Chiapas during the first days of the insurrection. Letters from authors of plays which are never performed, of apprentice novelists in search of publishers, of social reformers who in their paranoia seek a brother. But also, and more seriously, from widows and orphans. The role of Robin Hood has its inconveniences, especially in the absence of secretaries.[57]

It has been argued (correctly) that the Zapatistas' significance and relevance cannot be assessed in terms of their 'concrete victories or their control of physical or political space'[58] but by looking at the ways they have 'radically reshaped the Mexican political landscape – and the expanded political horizons of other radical actors in Mexico'.[59] The Zapatistas became the basis for debates on NAFTA, democracy, land reform and social justice, and they have used their social struggle to transform society at large.[60]

However, from the early days of the Zapatista uprising, it was clear that the Zapatistas' vision was not going to remain limited to Chiapas, or Mexico for that matter. During the

first months of 1994, Marcos made it clear that they were envisioning not only a 'new Mexico' but a 'new world' which
is freer, more honest and more just. In the summer of 1996,
the Zapatistas organised an international meeting (*encuentro*)
in Chiapas 'For Humanity and against Neoliberalism', and
Marcos, who wrote the invitation to the gathering, stated that
there were 'no universal recipes, lines, strategies, tactics, laws,
rules or slogans. There is only a desire: to build a better world,
that is, a new world.'[61]

This global vision has been received by various actors
through different channels. Through Marcos's work it has
become possible for different groups of people to resonate
with Zapatistas, to connect with them in a way that makes
sense in their own particular context, history and imagination.[62] As Marcos has put it, 'we are just an experience ... from
which any other struggle may adopt or adapt whatever it finds
useful for its own peculiar geographic conditions'.[63] Marcos's
work has been published in numerous languages, contributing
to an internationalisation of the Zapatistas' appeal.

The most significant manifestation of the Zapatistas' impact
outside of Mexico has been the inspiring role they played
(and particularly the 1996 *encuentro*) in the alter-globalisation
movement and founding of Peoples' Global Action. In
particular, some 3,000 delegates from more than seventy
countries returned home from the 1996 *encuentro* and 'sought
to connect their struggles by building equal, non-hierarchical
relationships so as to resist neoliberal capitalist globalisation
through civil disobedience and non-violent direct action'.[64]
In 1997, the European Zapatista support network organised
another meeting in Spain and again brought together
numerous social movements from around the world and
drafted the primary objectives and organisational principles
of Peoples' Global Action. The movement was officially

launched in 1998 in Geneva. As part of the alter-globalisation movement, the main objective of Peoples' Global Action was to resist capitalism and advocate social and environmental justice. For a number of years, it continuously organised both centralised as well as decentralised demonstrations against the World Trade Organization (WTO), the World Bank, the International Monetary Fund (IMF) and the G8, to name but a few. The Zapatistas marked the beginning of an era that is still ongoing and which has come to be known as an era of resistance against global capitalism. Although such resistance was not new at the time, the rise of the Zapatistas seemed like a qualitatively different form of resistance that had manifested itself in a bundle of networks and was rethinking radical politics and the revolutionary imaginary.[65]

Through Marcos, the Zapatistas offered a global vision to an emerging global civil society that was not linked to any particular group or national politics but, rather, a completely different politics that was inspired by the Zapatista experience 'of real, lived struggle: as Indigenous peoples resisting half a millennium of colonial exploitation; as Chiapan peasants organizing politically to oppose the inroads of neoliberal capitalist globalization; and (under Marcos) as clandestine rural guerrillas confronting state repression and violence at the hands of local landowning elites'.[66] The global vision that Marcos proposes has been very important for the identity and success of the Zapatistas, not as a movement bound to a particular territory, but as part of a struggle against neo-liberalism in Mexico and on the global stage.[67] Marcos's role in offering this global vision has been exemplary. Over the years and through different means of communication Marcos has drawn on Marx's analytical framework and core concepts from *Capital*, while adding his own analysis of capitalism. The result has been a revolutionary global vision that fights against all types of domination, cherishes diversity of opinion, builds consensus, seeks horizontality and a new relationship between power and citizens, and endeavours to transform the world from below.[68]

Marcos and the Zapatistas have 'become symbols of the struggles of all those marginalized, oppressed and exploited by dominant political and economic systems'.[69] To many, Marcos, with gun in hand, his Maoist cap, Guevaran pipe and bandoliers criss-crossing his chest in imitation of Mexican revolutionary Emiliano Zapata, became a clear successor to Guevara, whose execution in 1967 left a vacuum for many in Latin America and globally. The end of the Cold War and the collapse of the socialist bloc contributed to this void, and the appearance of Marcos gave those who were still in shock and despair 'a shot in the arm' and acted 'as a morale booster'.[70] As Naomi Klein writes:

This masked man who calls himself Marcos is the descendant of King, Che Guevara, Malcom X, Emiliano Zapata and all the other heroes who preached from pulpits only to be shot down one by one, leaving bodies of followers wandering around blind and disoriented because they lost their heads. In their place, the world now has a new kind of hero, one who listens more than speaks, who preaches in riddles not in certainties, a leader who doesn't show his face, who says his mask is really a mirror.[71]

Conclusion: whatever happened to global Marxism?

In the preceding pages I have shown how Marxism is a living tradition that has been the cornerstone of revolutionary practice and theory for leaders and revolutionaries of the global South and for the collective struggles they led or inspired. Nine figures have been discussed – Jawaharlal Nehru, Hồ Chí Minh, Mao Zedong, Kwame Nkrumah, Amílcar Cabral, Frantz Fanon, Ernesto Che Guevara, Ali Shariati and Subcomandante Marcos – and various regions of the global South have been covered – Asia (China, India and Vietnam), Africa (Algeria, Guinea-Bissau, Ghana), Latin America (Cuba and Mexico) and the Middle East (Iran). Importantly, the impact of each revolutionary extends beyond a single country to a region, continent and very often to the world.

What do the figures and struggles in this book tell us about how to understand Marxism and its global significance? As discussed in the Introduction, Marx(ism) has been repeatedly accused of being Eurocentric. Critics charge that Marxism is born out of European history, and therefore it is irrelevant to the majority of the world's population who reside in the global South. This perspective, as this book shows, is disingenuous. These critiques fail to account for the scope of Marx's work and tend to reduce him to a certain period, publication or even a few lines of text. More importantly, they barely speak of global Marxism and its enduring influence on decolonisation and revolutionary politics. For an honest and accurate evaluation of Marxist theory and practice, we need to know what Marxism means in different contexts and how it has been adapted in local and national struggles. To this end, studying the revolutionary leaders who adapted Marxism to local contexts is instructive. The book has underlined the place of Marxism in the account of the leaders and revolutionaries of the outstanding anti-colonial, anti-imperialist and anti-capitalist struggles that swept across the global South in the twentieth century. One of my hopes for this book is that it redresses some of the misgivings and misunderstandings that perpetuate the notion that Marxism is inherently Eurocentric.

The book has demonstrated various ways in which revolutionaries' engagement with Marxism helped mobilise support and ultimately prevail in hard-fought struggles. It has also tried to show how and to what extent these figures contributed to Marxism. In fact, their creative engagement not only localised and indigenised Marxism, but also globalised it. For example, Mao Zedong intervened in Marxist revolutionary theory by focusing on the role of the peasantry as the main driver of the revolution. He also proposed the idea of permanent revolution and embraced mass mobilisation. Kwame Nkrumah tried to develop Lenin's analysis of imperialism to a new level by incorporating it into the context of neo-colonial Africa. His concept of conscience, which is about reconstruction of social cohesion, became the cornerstone of his socialist pan-Africanism and was clearly linked to the African traditional spirit of care and solidarity. Meanwhile, Fanon advanced a dialectical analysis of the colonial subjects' psychological condition in relation to colonialism and empire. According to this analysis, the wretched of the earth would ultimately bring down the capitalist system. Marcos's encounter with the Indigenous Mayans and the subsequent rise of the Zapatista Army of National Liberation in Chiapas has led to emergence of one of the most inspiring anti-capitalist social movements in recent history. Importantly, Marcos revitalised Marxist political language in the post-Soviet era and influenced numerous struggles around the world.

Moreover, the book shows that despite local adaptations, Marxism has remained a coherent set of ideas as it developed historically and spread geographically. None of the figures failed to emphasise the importance of economic relations in underpinning structures of dominance, inequality and exploitation. However, in their adaptation, many insisted on calling attention to cultural aspects. Mao Zedong claimed that although the Chinese Revolution was against capitalism, its goal beyond combating capitalism was to forge a new nation and a new culture out of a semi-colonised and feudal society. The Cultural Revolution was in fact an attempt to establish an enduring revolutionary culture. Cabral situated culture in its historical context and emphasised its role as a significant element of people's history. He determined that culture has its material base at the level of the productive forces and the mode of production. Hence, by situating the development of culture in relationship to the material bases of society, Cabral was able to explain its importance in the struggle against imperialist domination and for national liberation. However, according to Cabral, culture and the liberation movement constantly influence each other as the struggle develops. Similarly, Shariati argued that Marxism needed to pay more attention to culture and emphasised that non-Western societies' culture was dominated by religion. He agreed with Marx's historical materialist critique of religion that saw it as a narcotic for the masses but criticised Marx for failing to understand the dialectical nature of Abrahamic religions. This dialectic is between the kind of religion that legitimises the status quo and the prophetic strand that challenges it.

Some of the figures focused on practical aspects of building socialism. Nehru was heavily influenced by Soviet Marxism and the Soviet model, and attempted to use the resources of the state to build a self-sufficient economy. His efforts were focused on building heavy industry and making technological advancements in farming. Che Guevara, in contrast, was not happy with the Soviet model, which he believed was too reliant on capitalist tools such as competition, profit, material incentives, credit and interest to accelerate the industrialisation process. He focused on the challenges that arise from the political economy of transition to socialism and argued that undermining the law of value was the main challenge.

In each period, revolutionary leaders faced very different challenges and Marxism offered a methodology that enabled them to link the local and national to the global in a way that engendered specific forms of political engagement. For example, Nehru faced colonialism, Guevara imperialism and Marcos neoliberalism. The changing global context gave rise to new challenges that were addressed in distinctive ways, dependent on the local and national context. In each case, Marxism proved to be a useful methodology and framework. Marxism helped Nehru combine nationalism and socialism. He reconstructed nationalist thought by situating it within the framework of an ideology. During the struggle for Indian independence, his efforts were focused on moving the ideology of the Indian National Congress towards socialism. Guevara's theory of *foco*, a revolutionary situation that can be created in rural areas with highly trained guerrilla fighters, would provide a catalyst that inspires people, particularly those living in rural areas, to join the revolutionary struggle. In addition, he focused on the political economy of the transition to socialism in Cuba, which, according to him, was fundamentally different from the political economy of socialism. Marcos joined the Zapatista Army of National Liberation to launch a guerrilla insurgency in southern Mexico, where Indigenous peasants were exploited and poor. They chose to declare war on the Mexican state and on global capitalism, on the very same day that the North American Free Trade Agreement was officially implemented.

A clear circulation of ideas and practices is apparent in global Marxism. Due to the specificity of their experience and their social reality – even though with some similarities in some instances – the individuals discussed in this book remain embedded in their own context but some have influenced others. For example, Guevara insisted on publishing *The Wretched of the Earth* in Cuba and Shariati translated Guevara's *Guerrilla Warfare*. Interestingly, a number of them became acquainted with Marxism and Marxists in Europe. Those who did not, such as Mao and Guevara, were influenced by classical Marxist texts such as *The Communist Manifesto*, *Capital* and Kautsky's *Class Struggle*. In addition, it was important to understand colonialism not only from the position of the colony or colonised but also from the standpoint of the metropole or coloniser in order to fully comprehend and also communicate the complexities that arise from colonial domination and advancement of ideas such as justice, freedom and democracy that oversaw anti-colonial and anti-imperialist struggles. For instance, Hồ Chí Minh went to Paris, the capital of French colonialism, because he believed a better understanding of the oppressive system from the centre of the empire would make it easier to resist. Although Nkrumah's purported objective for going to London, the capital of the British empire, was to study and complete his thesis, he ended up getting earnestly involved in political activism, which became instrumental for the independence of his country from British rule.

Internationalism was a cornerstone of revolutionary politics for many of the figures discussed. They all insisted that their particular situation needed to be seen in the larger context of capitalism, colonialism and imperialism. Hồ Chí Minh became a prominent member of the international communist movement and actively participated in the Comintern. Shortly after his arrival in Paris, he joined the French Socialist Party and later became one of the founders of the French Communist Party. Moreover, he cooperated with Chinese revolutionaries in mobilising Chinese peasants and collaborated with the Chinese Communist Party. In his final testament, he requested the unity of the world communist movement. Amílcar Cabral not only freed Guinea-Bissau and Cape Verde from Portuguese colonialism but also became one of the founding members of the People's Movement for the Liberation of Angola. Fanon was a Martiniquais who passionately devoted his life to the struggles of the African continent and particularly the Algerian liberation struggle from the French. Argentine Guevara became one of the revolutionary leaders in Cuba and joined the struggles in Congo and Bolivia. He constantly insisted that the Cuban Revolution should remain in solidarity with all oppressed people of the world and assist their struggles.

Each of the revolutionary figures was an organic intellectual (à la Antonio Gramsci). They joined, engaged and lived with the subjugated and subaltern classes for a significant amount of time and operated within that unique space where the privileges of the rather powerful meet with the disadvantages of the powerless and oppressed. Thus, they left their comfort zones to go beyond armchair philosophising. Many expressed a longing to experience the plight of the disadvantaged, whom they sought to champion. Many of them had middle-class or petite-bourgeois backgrounds but worked within and towards a revolutionary counter-hegemonic narrative. Nehru came into direct contact with rural India. His visits to villages where he observed the misery of the peasantry opened his eyes to the plight of the majority of people subjugated by British colonial rule. His encounter with the hungry masses led to his constant insistence that the Indian National Congress should link its demands for independence to the economic and social demands of the peasantry and the proletariat. Hồ Chí Minh spent two years at sea, working as a cook's assistant on a steamship, where he observed the life of people in different parts of the world. During these years, his understanding of the misery of people throughout the world deepened. In many places he visited, he observed conditions similar to those in Vietnam. This period of travel abroad laid the foundations for his revolutionary worldviews. Guevara's plight perhaps provides one of the most striking examples of an organic intellectual. He left his home at a young age to travel around a continent with deeply entrenched social injustice, oppression and discrimination. Rising to the highest official posts in Cuba did not satisfy him. He resigned from his government and party posts to continue to liberate the oppressed from imperialist domination and capitalist exploitation, a task he had long considered his mission.

Possibilities amidst challenges

The past two decades have seen an enormous number of mass protests around economic issues and, more recently, an escalation in labour disputes. Meanwhile, we have witnessed the rise of the right-wing nationalist movements, which at times, in a terrifying manner, resemble fascism. In addition, the unprecedented climate crisis and its horrifying impact on humans and non-humans has made the limits and contradictions of global capitalism more apparent than ever. The violence in Palestine has convinced millions of people around the world that an urgent response is required. This unsettling conjuncture provides a possibility for the revival of Marxian thought and practice. However, the practicality of putting Marxism on the agenda as a theory of social change and a method of socio-economic analysis remains a challenge.

There are unlimited examples of Marxism's impact on the world and social struggles. Nevertheless, this book shows that a very substantial and continuous engagement with Marxism has come from the global South and by people involved in actual political struggles, who found in Marxism a powerful framework that helped understand and change the world. The task is up to us to engage with the ideas of these revolutionaries to determine their contemporary relevance as theoretical and practical blueprints of emancipation and liberation. Ultimately, challenges of our times are not discontinuous from the pressures and hurdles faced by Nehru, Mao and Guevara.

Critics might point to occasional failure or even the devastating impact of some of the policies implemented by the revolutionaries in this book. It is unfortunate that some policies did not lead to the desired outcomes or turned problematic. However, an honest appraisal of the life, work and legacy of these revolutionaries reminds us that struggles unfold in challenging circumstances and it is not always apparent what the best way forward is. Moreover, a complex amalgamation of various factors influences the outcome of a particular policy. As Marx wrote, people make history not under circumstances they choose but under circumstances that are inherited. For example, the revolutionary situation within which many of the figures rose encouraged vanguardism. Within the historical period of the Cold War, this seemed an appropriate strategy to advance the objectives of the new social order that emerged after the victory of these struggles. The idea was originally coined by Marx and Engels in *The Communist Manifesto* but was later developed as a revolutionary strategy by Lenin within the context of the tsarist regime and the autocracy of the Russian empire. For Lenin, the objective of the vanguard party was to establish the rule of the working class and a dictatorship of the proletariat. Marx and Engels introduced the concept of the dictatorship of the proletariat as a necessity of a transitional period and form of authority that stands between the overthrow of capitalist relations and communist society, which is itself a period of revolutionary transformation. In fact, this concept is inherently democratic because it is meant to ensure the just rule of the majority, that is, the working classes and the oppressed, and to enable them to control the conditions of their emancipation. However, it is important to note that the dictatorship of the proletariat has a transitional character and needs to be replaced by an alternative when the society is fundamentally transformed and humans are liberated from material conditions and structures of domination.[1]

The Marxist critique of bourgeois democracy was based on the idea that in such a democracy workers do not have the means to participate equally in societal affairs and, therefore, that democracy will not be beneficial for them. For example, freedom of the press, without having the means to establish a newspaper or a television channel which is read or seen by millions, automatically disadvantages certain groups. Marx constantly repeated that a bourgeois democracy would not take into account the fundamental inequalities and disparities in power relations that exist in capitalism. Throughout his life, Marx remained committed to democratic ideas in theory and practice and in fact it was this commitment that led him to fierce critiques of bourgeois democracy.

However, in spite of the very democratic nature of the concept of the dictatorship of the proletariat, which is supposed to enable the rule of the majority (the workers), in practice, vanguardism on some occasions led to absolute control and the silencing of any oppositional voice. These unfortunate failures have made it easy for the critics of Marx(ism) to equate vanguardism, or for that matter Marxism, with authoritarianism. These critics advocate liberal and representative democracy as the most suitable form of governance for humanity. They ignore the fact that in 1973, Salvador Allende, the world's first democratically elected Marxist head of state, was violently overthrown by a coup supported by the United States and was replaced by a military dictatorship. Recent declassified documents show that the United States had earlier tried to block Allende from the presidency. Moreover, critics need to be constantly reminded that, as Nehru rightly argued, democracy without socialism is meaningless because democracy cannot be achieved or sustained with exceedingly high rates of poverty and inequality.

Instead of focusing on occasional failures of some figures or movements in creating ideal societies, freed from any shortcomings, the emphasis should be on the theory that has reordered the world and inspired millions of people. Since the many crises we are facing today are rooted in the failures of the capitalist system, Marxism, with its sophisticated and all-encompassing analysis of capitalism and ideas for a post-capitalist future, still provides a fundamental point of departure for universalistic and egalitarian efforts to envision another world beyond capitalist destruction and oppression.

Towards the end of the twentieth century, the Zapatista uprising in Chiapas inspired the left to reinvent itself for the twenty-first century. In some ways it distanced itself from earlier versions of Marxist practice, but in other ways it built on them and forged new ideas and an imaginary for the future. As the case of the Zapatistas shows, this reinvention is not an easy task, but it is possible. The first step in the process of building a new revolutionary imagination and future vision is the rediscovery of twentieth-century struggles and their legacies. Moreover, a twenty-first-century Marxism needs to be localised and adapted to the context of struggle, while retaining a coherent set of ideas and concepts that continue to challenge the destructive forces of the global capitalist economy. The Zapatistas are not struggling for piecemeal reforms – their struggle is age-old and it pits those subordinated by capital against oppressive power structures fundamentally and in total. They have put justice, democracy and freedom at the centre of their struggle. Their efforts to forge an alternative to global capitalism has contributed to a change in global political consciousness and has led to experimentation in new politics grounded in egalitarian, democratic and ecological alternatives to capitalism.

The chronicles of decolonisation and revolutionary politics narrated in this book offer examples for understanding the possibilities inherent in the advancement of critical agency. The unique version of Marxism and revolutionary practice that each figure pursued was related to the ways they associated with the oppressed at the local, regional and global level. Their efforts opened up Marxist categories and revealed the complexity of revolutionary politics, and in the process they contributed to *global Marxism* – a dynamic and diverse Marxism that is rooted in the lessons of various sites of historical and cultural struggles, a Marxism that is underpinned by common principles that are valuable for analysing the changing historical conditions of capitalism and the complex world in which we live.

Notes

Introduction

1 E. Hobsbawm, *The History of Marxism, Vol. 1* (London: Harvester Press, 1982), vii–viii.

2 G. Therborn, 'Dialectics of modernity: on critical theory and the legacy of twentieth-century Marxism', *New Left Review* (1996), 73.

3 E. Traverso, *Revolution: An Intellectual History* (London: Verso, 2021), 18.

4 While movements for social justice might draw on socialism more broadly, Marx advanced socialist thought by defining it in contrast to capitalism. According to Marx, socialism would lead to communism or communist society, which is classless and stateless.

5 C. L. R. James, *Nkrumah and the Ghana Revolution* (Durham: Duke University Press, 2022), 60.

6 V. Prashad, *Red Star Over the Third World* (London: Pluto Press, 2017).

7 M. Burawoy, 'Marxism after communism', *Theory and Society*, 29:2 (2000), 151.

8 *Ibid.*, 152.

9 E. W. Said, *Orientalism* (New York: Pantheon Books, 1978).

10 See for example A. Ahmad, *In Theory: Nations, Classes, Literatures* (London: Verso, 1992); K. B. Anderson, 'Marx's late writings on non-western and precapitalist societies and gender', *Rethinking Marxism*, 14:4 (2002), 84–96; B. Parry, *Postcolonial Studies: A Materialist Critique* (London: Routledge, 2004); A. Loomba, *Colonialism/ Postcolonialism* (London: Routledge, 2005).

11 See K. B. Anderson, *Marx at the Margins: On Nationalism, Ethnicity and Non-Western Societies* (Chicago: University of Chicago Press, 2010); L. Pradella, 'Postcolonial theory and the making of the world working class', *Critical Sociology*, 43:4–5 (2017), 573–586.

12 L. Pradella, 'Imperialism and capitalist development in Marx's *Capital*', *Historical Materialism*, 21:2 (2013), 134.

13 Anderson, *Marx at the Margins*.

14 K. Lindner, *Marx, Marxism and the Question of Eurocentrism* (London: Palgrave Macmillan, 2022), 16.

15 S. Mezzadra and R. Samaddar, 'Colonialism'. In Musto, M. (ed.), *The Marx Revival: Key Concepts and New Interpretations* (Cambridge: Cambridge University Press, 2020), 259.

16 *Ibid.*, 260,

17 J. B. Foster, B. Clark and H. Holleman, 'Marx and the indigenous', *Monthly Review*, 71:9 (2020), 16.

18 Lindner, *Marx, Marxism and the Question of Eurocentrism*.

19 See P. Emiljanowicz, 'From Karl Marx to Kwame Nkrumah: towards a decolonial political economy'. In Ndlovu-Gatsheni, S. and Ndlovu, M. (eds), *Marxism and Decolonisation in the 21st Century: Living Theories and True Ideas* (London: Routledge, 2021), 68–88.

20 K. Marx, *Capital, Vol. 1* (London: Penguin, 1976), 915.

21 Foster et al., 'Marx and the indigenous', 2–3.

22 *Ibid.*

23 See for example Anderson, 'Marx's late writings', 87–88.

24 L. Pradella, 'Marx and the global South: connecting history and value theory', *Sociology*, 51:1 (2017), 146–161. See also Lucia Pradella, *Globalisation and the Critique of Political Economy: New Insights from Marx's Writing* (London: Routledge, 2015).

25 Pradella, 'Marx and the global South', 157.

26 *Ibid.*, 158.

27 Pradella, 'Imperialism and capitalist development in Marx's *Capital*'.

28 Mezzadra and Samaddar, 'Colonialism'.

29 A. Dirlik, 'The postcolonial aura: Third World criticism in the age of global capitalism', *Critical Inquiry*, 20:2 (1994), 334.

30 D. Chakrabarty, *Provincializing Europe: Postcolonial Thought and Historical Difference* (Princeton: Princeton University Press, 2008).

31 Dirlik, 'The postcolonial aura', 356.

32 See B. Parry, 'Directions and dead-ends in postcolonial studies'. In Goldberg, D. T. and Quayson, A. (eds), *Relocating Postcolonialism* (Wiley-Blackwell, 2002); B. Parry, 'Edward Said and Third-World Marxism', *College Literature*, 40:4 (2013), 105–126.

33 See M. N. Smith, 'The limits of postcolonial critique of Marxism: a defence of radical universalism'. In S. Ndlovu-Gatsheni, S. and M. Ndlovu, M. (eds), *Marxism and Decolonisation in the 21st Century: Living Theories and True Ideas* (London: Routledge, 2021), 49–67.

34 V. Chibber, *Postcolonial Theory and the Specter of Capital* (London: Verso, 2013).

35 *Ibid.*, 23.
36 *Ibid.*, 123–124.
37 *Ibid.*, 243.
38 Chakrabarty, *Provincializing Europe.*
39 Chibber, *Postcolonial Theory and the Specter of Capital*, 291.
40 Comintern, also known as the Communist International or the Third International, was an organisation founded by Lenin in 1919 to advocate communism worldwide. It was led by the Communist Party of the Soviet Union and was preceded by the dissolution of the Second International, an organisation of socialist and labour parties that existed from 1889 to 1916.
41 See Prashad, *Red Star Over the Third World.*
42 K. N. Brutens, *National Liberation Revolutions Today* (Moscow: Progress Publishers, 1977), 8.
43 V. L. Lenin, *Imperialism: The Highest Stage of Capitalism* (London: Penguin, 2010); Brutens, *National Liberation Revolutions Today*, 14.
44 N. Knight, 'Applying Marxism to Asian conditions: Mao Zedong, Hồ Chí Minh and the "universality" of Marxism'. In Glaser, D. and Walker, D. M. (eds), *Twentieth Century Marxism: A Global Introduction* (London: Routledge, 2007), 141–153.
45 A. Hughes, 'The appeal of Marxism to Africans', *Journal of Communist Studies and Transition Politics*, 8:2 (1992), 5.
46 See W. E. Willmott, 'Thoughts on Hồ Chí Minh', *Pacific Affairs*, 44:4 (1971), 585–590.
47 J. McCulloch, *In the Twilight of Revolution: The Political Theory of Amílcar Cabral* (London: Routledge, 2020), 12.
48 E. W. Said, 'Traveling theory'. In: Said, E. W. (ed.), *The World, the Text, and the Critic* (Cambridge: Harvard University Press, 1983), 226–247.
49 F. A. Bardawil, *Revolution and Disenchantment* (Durham: Duke University Press, 2020), 8.
50 See M. Musto (ed.), *The Marx Revival: Key Concepts and New Interpretations* (Cambridge: Cambridge University Press, 2020).
51 E. Tuck and K. W. Yang, 'Decolonization is not a metaphor', *Decolonization: Indigeneity, Education and Society* 1:1 (2012), 1–40.
52 *Ibid.*, 7.
53 James, *Nkrumah and the Ghana Revolution*, 24; emphasis in the original.
54 See G. K. Bhambra, *Connected Sociologies* (London: Bloomsbury, 2014); G. K. Bhambra and J. Holmwood, *Colonialism and Modern Social Theory* (Cambridge: Polity Press, 2021).
55 See for example R. Connell, *Southern Theory: The Global Dynamics of Knowledge in Social Science* (London: Routledge, 2007); S. Patel

(ed.), *The ISA Handbook of Diverse Sociological Traditions* (London: Sage, 2009); S. F. Alatas and V. Sinha, *Sociological Theory Beyond the Canon* (London: Palgrave Macmillan, 2017); A. Meghji, *Decolonizing Sociology: An Introduction* (Cambridge: Polity Press, 2020).

56 B. de Sousa Santos, *Epistemologies of the South: Justice Against Epistemicide* (London: Routledge, 2014); B. de Sousa Santos, *The End of the Cognitive Empire: The Coming of Age of Epistemologies of the South* (Durham: Duke University Press, 2018).

57 P. Gopal, *Insurgent Empire: Anticolonial Resistance and British Dissent* (London: Verso, 2019).

58 P. Gopal, 'On decolonisation and the university', *Textual Practice*, 35:6 (2021), 873–899.

59 *Ibid.*, 873.

60 *Ibid.*, 882.

61 M. Ahmad, 'Movement texts as anti-colonial theory', *Sociology*, 57:1 (2023), 58.

62 M. Lugones, 'Heterosexualism and the colonial/modern gender system', *Hypatia*, 22:1 (2007), 186–209; A. Quijano, 'Coloniality and modernity/rationality', *Cultural Studies*, 21:2 (2007), 168–178.

63 See S. Fadaee, 'Bringing in the south: towards a global paradigm for social movement studies', *Interface: A Journal For and About Social Movements*, 9:2 (2017), 45–60.

64 Ahmad, 'Movement texts as anti-colonial theory', 59.

65 M. Burawoy, 'Decolonizing sociology: the significance of W. E. B. Du Bois', *Critical Sociology*, 47:4–5 (2021), 545–554; M. Burawoy, 'Why is classical theory classical? Theorizing the canon and canonizing Du Bois', *Journal of Classical Sociology*, 21:3–4 (2021), 245–259.

66 W. E. B. Du Bois, *The World and Africa* (New York: Oxford University Press, 2007 [1947]).

67 Burawoy, 'Decolonizing sociology', 545–546.

68 T. Piketty, *Capital in the Twenty-First Century* (Cambridge: Harvard University Press, 2014).

69 Burawoy, 'Decolonizing sociology', 550.

70 M. Burawoy, 'Walking on two legs: Black Marxism and the sociological canon', *Critical Sociology*, 48:4–5 (2022), 571–586.

71 *Ibid.*, 583.

72 Burawoy, 'Marxism after communism', 155.

73 Hobsbawm, *The History of Marxism*, 110.

74 A. Mayer, *Naija Marxisms: Revolutionary Thought in Nigeria* (London: Pluto Press, 2016), 2.

Chapter 1. Jawaharlal Nehru

1 S. Gopal, 'The formative ideology of Jawaharlal Nehru', *Economic and Political Weekly*, 11:21 (1976), 787–792.

2 B. G. Gokhale, 'Nehru and history', *History and Theory*, 17:3 (1978), 311–322; K. Singh, 'Jawaharlal Nehru as a humanist', *India International Centre Quarterly*, 6:2 (1979), 115–118.

3 B. R. Nanda, *Jawaharlal Nehru: Rebel and Statesman* (New Delhi: Oxford University Press, 1998).

4 L. S. Rathore, 'Political ideas of Jawaharlal Nehru: some reflections', *Indian Journal of Political Science*, 46:4 (1985), 466.

5 C. A. Bayly, 'The ends of liberalism and the political thought of Nehru's India', *Modern Intellectual History*, 12:3 (2015), 605.

6 S. Seth, 'Nehruvian socialism 1927–1937: nationalism, Marxism, and the pursuit of modernity', *Alternatives*, 18:4 (1993), 468.

7 I am heavily indebted to Jawaharlal Nehru, *An Autobiography* (New Delhi: Penguin Books, 2004), which was originally published in 1936, and Nehru's biography by Nanda, *Jawaharlal Nehru*.

8 Nehru, *An Autobiography*, 17.

9 *Ibid.*, 21.

10 Rathore, 'Political ideas of Jawaharlal Nehru', 452.

11 See M. L. Louro, *Comrades against Imperialism: Nehru, India, and Interwar Internationalism* (Cambridge: Cambridge University Press, 2018).

12 Nehru, *An Autobiography*, 172.

13 S. B. Gupta, 'Growth of socialism in Congress and Nehru's role', *Indian Journal of Political Science*, 29:4 (1968), 360.

14 Seth, 'Nehruvian socialism 1927–1937'.

15 *Ibid.*, 458.

16 Quoted in V. V. Rao, 'Socialist thought of Jawaharlal Nehru', *Indian Journal of Political Science*, 48:2 (1987), 196.

17 Nehru, *An Autobiography*, 378–379.

18 *Ibid.*, 610–611.

19 *Ibid.*, 463–464.

20 Gokhale, 'Nehru and history', 313.

21 P. F. Power, 'Indian foreign policy: the age of Nehru', *Review of Politics*, 26:2 (1964), 257–286.

22 S. Purushotham, 'World history in the atomic age: past, present and future in the political thought of Jawaharlal Nehru', *Modern Intellectual History*, 14:3 (2017), 837–867.

23 Seth, 'Nehruvian socialism 1927–1937'.

24 Power, 'Indian foreign policy', 268–269.

25 S. Sherlock, 'Berlin, Moscow and Bombay: the Marxism that India inherited', *South Asia: Journal of South Asian Studies*, 21:1 (1998), 71.

26 Nehru, *An Autobiography*, 611.

27 J. Nehru, 'The basic approach', *AICC Economic Review: Fortnightly Journal of the Economic and Political Research Department of the All India Congress Committee*, 10:8–9 (1958).

28 India has a long and strong Marxist and socialist tradition. The Communist Party of India, the oldest communist party in India, was established in 1925.

29 This was a communist-led insurrection of peasants in the Telangana region of India (1946–1951).

30 Gopal, 'The formative ideology of Jawaharlal Nehru'.

31 Nehru, *An Autobiography*, 611.

32 T. A. Nizami, 'Marxism and the Communist Party of India', *Indian Journal of Political Science*, 29:2 (1968), 108.

33 J. Mohan, 'Jawaharlal Nehru and his socialism', *India International Centre Quarterly*, 2:3 (1975), 183.

34 *Indian Affairs Record*, 2:9 (October 1956), 13. Consulted at https://books.google.co.uk/books?id=JncPAQAAIAAJ&pg (accessed March 2024).

35 Gokhale, 'Nehru and history', 317.

36 K. V. Viswanathaiah, Jawaharlal Nehru's concept of democratic socialism', *Indian Journal of Political Science*, 26:4 (1965), 95.

37 P. Chatterjee, *Nationalist Thought and the Colonial World: A Derivative Discourse?* (London: Zed Books, 1986).

38 Seth, 'Nehruvian socialism 1927–1937'.

39 *Ibid.*, 455.

40 Rao, 'Socialist thought of Jawaharlal Nehru', 204–205.

41 K. N. Raj, 'Nehru, the Congress and class conflict', *Economic Weekly*, Special number (1964), 1231.

42 *Ibid.*

43 *Ibid.*, 1231–1232.

44 Quoted in A. Appadorai, 'Recent socialist thought in India', *Review of Politics*, 30:3 (1968), 353.

45 Viswanathaiah, 'Jawaharlal Nehru's concept of democratic socialism', 96.

46 *Ibid.*, 94.

47 *Ibid.*, 93.

48 Hazary, 'Democratic socialism and Jawaharlal Nehru', 103.

49 Viswanathaiah, 'Jawaharlal Nehru's concept of democratic socialism', 95.

50 Rao, 'Socialist thought of Jawaharlal Nehru'; Rathore, 'Political ideas of Jawaharlal Nehru'.

51 N. Hazary, 'Democratic socialism and Jawaharlal Nehru', *Indian Journal of Political Science*, 26:4 (1965), 102.
52 Rao, 'Socialist thought of Jawaharlal Nehru', 196.
53 Hazary, 'Democratic socialism and Jawaharlal Nehru', 104.
54 Rao, 'Socialist thought of Jawaharlal Nehru', 196.
55 Quoted in Hazary, 'Democratic socialism and Jawaharlal Nehru', 104.
56 Rao, 'Socialist thought of Jawaharlal Nehru'; Rathore, 'Political ideas of Jawaharlal Nehru'.
57 Hazary, 'Democratic socialism and Jawaharlal Nehru', 104.
58 Rathore, 'Political ideas of Jawaharlal Nehru', 472.
59 Nehru, *An Autobiography*, 571.
60 *Ibid.*, 548.
61 Hazary, 'Democratic socialism and Jawaharlal Nehru', 104.
62 G. von Hatzfeldt, 'Agonistic democracy: the endurance of the Gandhi and Nehru legacy', *Contemporary South Asia*, 24:2 (2016), 157.
63 Seth, 'Nehruvian socialism 1927–1937'.
64 Mohan, 'Jawaharlal Nehru and his socialism', 192.
65 A. Mukherjee, 'Nehru's legacy: inclusive democracy and people's empowerment', *Economic and Political Weekly*, 50:16 (2015), 38.
66 von Hatzfeldt, 'Agonistic democracy', 157.
67 Gopal, 'The formative ideology of Jawaharlal Nehru'.
68 M. L. King and C. West, *The Radical King* (Boston: Beacon Press, 2015), 159.

Chapter 2. Hồ Chí Minh

1 Pierre Brocheux, *Hồ Chí Minh: A Biography* (Cambridge: Cambridge University Press, 2007), ix.
2 William J. Duiker, *Hồ Chí Minh: A Life* (New York: Hyperion, 2000), 3.
3 I am heavily indebted to the biographies by Duiker, *Hồ Chí Minh*; Brocheux, *Hồ Chí Minh*; and David M. Crowe, *Hemingway and Hồ Chí Minh in Paris: The Art of Resistance* (Minneapolis: Fortress Press, 2020).
4 Hồ Chí Minh had many pseudonyms, including the name Hồ Chí Minh itself. Throughout this chapter I will not match his many names to the appropriate historical moment but, for the reader's benefit, I briefly mention the more important names and pseudonyms he had throughout his life. At his birth in 1890, he was given the 'milk name' of Nguyen Sinh Cung by his parents. Following

the Vietnamese tradition, he was given another name, Nguyen Tat Thanh, when he turned ten. He should have kept this name throughout the rest of his life, but he chose many pseudonyms instead. When he left Vietnam at the age of eleven, he took the name Ba, until he moved to Paris in 1919 and called himself Nguyen Ai Quoc, meaning 'Nguyen who is a patriot'. In 1942, shortly before the Việt Minh secured Vietnamese independence, he began to call himself Hồ Chí Minh, meaning 'He who has been enlightened'. He used this name until his death in 1969. He also at different times used other pseudonyms for security reasons, but because they were only used very briefly I have not mentioned them here.

5 R. K. Brigham, 'Hồ Chí Minh, Confucianism, and Marxism'. In Anderson, D. L. and Ernst, J. (eds), *The War That Never Ends: New Perspectives on the Vietnam War* (Lexington: University Press of Kentucky, 2007), 110.

6 H. C. Minh, *Hồ Chí Minh on Revolution: Selected Writings 1920–66* (New York: Praeger, 1967), 24.

7 P. A. DeCaro, *Rhetoric of Revolt: Hồ Chí Minh's Discourse for Revolution* (New York: Praeger, 2003), 12–13.

8 Minh, *Hồ Chí Minh on Revolution*, 40.

9 Duiker, *Hồ Chí Minh*, 62.

10 C. Fenn, *Hồ Chí Minh: A Biographical Introduction* (London: Studio Vista, 1973), 41.

11 Duiker, *Hồ Chí Minh*, 62.

12 *Ibid.*, 63.

13 Brocheux, *Hồ Chí Minh*, 184.

14 Duiker, *Hồ Chí Minh*, 63.

15 Minh, *Hồ Chí Minh on Revolution*, 23.

16 *Ibid.*, 23–24.

17 *Ibid.*, 24.

18 *Ibid.*, 26.

19 *Ibid.*, 49.

20 *Ibid.*, 255.

21 *Ibid.*, 256–257.

22 N. Knight, 'Applying Marxism to Asian conditions: Mao Zedong, Hồ Chí Minh and the "universality" of Marxism'. In Glaser, D. and Walker, D. M. (eds), *Twentieth-Century Marxism: A Global Introduction* (London: Routledge, 2007), 141–153.

23 Duiker, *Hồ Chí Minh*, 74.

24 Brocheux, *Hồ Chí Minh*, 27.

25 *Ibid.*

26 Knight, 'Applying Marxism to Asian conditions', 148.

27 *Ibid.*, 148–149.

28 Duiker, *Hồ Chí Minh*, 124.
29 *Ibid.*, 99.
30 *Ibid.*, 101–102.
31 *Ibid.*, 115–116.
32 W. J. Duiker, 'What is to be done? Hồ Chí Minh's Road Kach Mei'. In Taylor, K. W. and Whitemore, J. K. (eds), *Essays into Vietnamese Pasts* (New York: Cornell University Press, 1995), 211.
33 Duiker, 'What is to be done?', 207–208.
34 Duiker, *Hồ Chí Minh*, 132.
35 Duiker, 'What is to be done?', 211–212.
36 See DeCaro, *Rhetoric of Revolt*; Brigham, 'Hồ Chí Minh, Confucianism, and Marxism'; B. N. Son, 'The Confucian foundations of Hồ Chí Minh's vision of government', *Journal of Oriental Studies*, 46:1 (2013), 35–59.
37 Brocheux, *Hồ Chí Minh*, x–xii.
38 Brigham, 'Hồ Chí Minh, Confucianism, and Marxism', 110.
39 *Ibid.*, 119.
40 *Ibid.*, 109.
41 See Duiker, *Hồ Chí Minh*.
42 *Ibid.*, 137.
43 See Duiker, 'What is to be done?'
44 *Ibid.*
45 Duiker, *Hồ Chí Minh*.
46 *Ibid.*, 571.
47 DeCaro, *Rhetoric of Revolt*, 92.
48 Minh, *Hồ Chí Minh on Revolution*, 275.
49 Duiker, *Hồ Chí Minh*, 522.
50 *Ibid.*, 560–563.
51 Fenn, *Hồ Chí Minh*, 46.
52 M. Marouda, 'The unending death of an immortal: the state commemoration of Hồ Chí Minh in contemporary Viet Nam', *South East Asia Research*, 21:2 (2013), 303; Duiker, *Hồ Chí Minh*, 3.
53 Brocheux, *Hồ Chí Minh*, xiv.
54 Asia News Monitor, 'Vietnam: Vietnamese leaders celebrate legacy of Hồ Chí Minh', 4 September 2009. https://www.proquest.com/docview/1027266451 (accessed March 2024).
55 Duiker, *Hồ Chí Minh*, 577.
56 Fenn, *Hồ Chí Minh*, 44; T. Harper, *Underground Asia: Global Revolutionaries and the Assault on Empire* (London: Penguin, 2020).
57 S. K. Singh, 'Hồ Chí Minh and Vietnam's struggle for freedom', *Proceedings of the Indian History Congress, Indian History Congress*, 70 (2009), 800.
58 Duiker, *Hồ Chí Minh*, 576.

59 Asia New Monitor, 'Vietnam: Paris seminar spotlights Hồ Chí Minh's legacy', 23 September 2011. https://www.proquest.com/docview/893614154 (accessed March 2024).
60 Duiker, *Hồ Chí Minh*, 562.
61 *Time Magazine*, 'The legacy of Hồ Chí Minh', 12 September 1969. https://content.time.com/time/subscriber/article/0,33009,901394,00.html (accessed March 2024).

Chapter 3. Mao Zedong

1 R. Terrill, *Mao: A Biography* (Stanford: Stanford University Press, 1999), 459.
2 A. Dirlik, *Marxism in the Chinese Revolution* (Lanham: Rowman and Littlefield, 2005), 75.
3 *Ibid.*
4 I am heavily indebted to the following biographies: S.R. Schram, *Mao Tse-tung* (Harmondsworth: Penguin Books, 1971 [1967]); and Terrill, *Mao*.
5 Terrill, *Mao*, 77.
6 B. Womack, *The Foundations of Mao Zedong's Political Thought, 1917–1935* (Honolulu: University Press of Hawaii, 1982), 186.
7 J. M. Koller, 'Philosophical aspects of Maoist thought', *Studies in Soviet Thought*, 14:1–2 (1974), 55.
8 Womack, *The Foundations of Mao Zedong's Political Thought*, 191–193.
9 S. R. Schram, 'Mao Zedong a hundred years on: the legacy of a ruler', *China Quarterly*, 137 (1994), 128.
10 *Ibid.*
11 N. Knight, *Rethinking Mao: Explorations in Mao Zedong's Thought* (Lanham: Lexington Books, 2007), 103–104.
12 *Ibid.*, 9.
13 *Ibid.*, 257.
14 *Ibid.*, 128.
15 Z. Mao, *Selected Works of Mao Tse-tung, Vol. 1* (Peking: Foreign Languages Press, 1965), 297.
16 Womack, *The Foundations of Mao Zedong's Political Thought*, 196.
17 H. Xiaorong, *Chinese Discourses on the Peasants, 1900–1949* (Albany: State University of New York Press, 2005), 149.
18 S. R. Schram, 'Chinese and Leninist components in the personality of Mao Tse-tung', *Asian Survey*, 3:6 (1963), 268–269.
19 Knight, *Rethinking Mao*, 128.
20 Dirlik, *Marxism in the Chinese Revolution*.

21 Koller, 'Philosophical aspects of Maoist thought'.
22 Schram, *Mao Tse-tung*, 223.
23 Knight, *Rethinking Mao*.
24 J. Friedman, *Shadow Cold War: The Sion–Soviet Competition for the Third World* (Chapel Hill: University of North Carolina Press, 2015), 11.
25 Koller, 'Philosophical aspects of Maoist thought'.
26 Knight, *Rethinking Mao*, 157.
27 A. Dirlik, 'The predicament of Marxist revolutionary consciousness: Mao Zedong, Antonio Gramsci, and the reformulation of Marxist revolutionary theory', *Modern China*, 9:2 (1983), 183.
28 *Ibid.*, 193.
29 *Ibid.*
30 Womack, *The Foundations of Mao Zedong's Political Thought*, 193.
31 S. R. Schram, 'Mao Tse-tung and the theory of the permanent revolution, 1958–69', *China Quarterly*, 46 (1971), 238.
32 Knight, *Rethinking Mao*, 227.
33 *Ibid.*, 229.
34 Schram, 'Chinese and Leninist components', 260.
35 Z. Mao, *Selected Works of Mao Tse-tung*, Vol. 2 (Peking: Foreign Languages Press, 1965), 381.
36 Schram, *Mao Tse-tung*, 223.
37 S. R. Schram, 'Mao Tse-tung's thought from 1949 to 1976'. In MacFaquhar, R. and Fairbank, J. K. (eds), *The Cambridge History of China* (Cambridge: Cambridge University Press, 1991), 43.
38 *Ibid.*
39 Dirlik, *Marxism in the Chinese Revolution*.
40 B. L. Schwartz, 'The reign of virtue – some broad perspectives on leader and part in the cultural revolution', *China Quarterly*, 35 (1968), 1–17.
41 See for example B. L. Schwartz, *Chinese Communism and the Rise of Mao* (New York: Harper and Row, 1951); Schram, 'Chinese and Leninist components'; V. Holubnychy, 'Mao Tse-tung's materialist dialectics', *China Quarterly*, 19 (1964), 3–37; S. R. Schram, *The Political Thought of Mao Tse-tung* (Harmondsworth: Penguin Books, 1969); Koller, 'Philosophical aspects of Maoist thought'; N. Knight, 'Soviet philosophy and Mao Zedong's "Sinification of Marxism"', *Journal of Contemporary Asia*, 20:1 (1990), 89–109; Dirlik, *Marxism in the Chinese Revolution*; and Knight, *Rethinking Mao*.
42 Koller, 'Philosophical aspects of Maoist thought', 56.
43 Knight, 'Soviet philosophy', 99.
44 Schram, 'Chinese and Leninist components', 273.
45 *Ibid.*, 260.

46 Dirlik, 'The predicament of Marxist revolutionary consciousness', 197.

47 Dirlik, *Marxism in the Chinese Revolution*, 94–95.

48 Knight, *Rethinking Mao*.

49 Dirlik, 'The predicament of Marxist revolutionary consciousness', 189.

50 Dirlik, *Marxism in the Chinese Revolution*, 84.

51 *Ibid.*, 85.

52 Terrill, *Mao*, 17.

53 Knight, *Rethinking Mao*.

54 M. Gao, *The Battle for China's Past: Mao and the Cultural Revolution* (London: Pluto Press, 2008), 3.

55 *Ibid.*, 5.

56 *Ibid.*, 6.

57 Terrill, *Mao*, 469.

58 Womack, *The Foundations of Mao Zedong's Political Thought*.

59 See C. X. G. Wei, 'Mao's legacy revisited: its lasting impact on China and post-Mao era reform', *Asian Politics and Policy*, 3:1 (2011), 23.

60 *Ibid.*, 3–27.

61 G. T. Yu, 'Africa in Chinese foreign policy', *Asian Survey*, 28 (1988), 849–862.

62 Terrill, *Mao*, 475.

63 Womack, *The Foundations of Mao Zedong's Political Thought*, 197.

64 A. Dirlik, P. Healy and N. Knight (eds), *Critical Perspectives on Mao Zedong's Thought* (Atlantic Highlands Humanities Press, 1997).

65 See for example N. Sundar, *The Burning Forest: India's War Against the Maoists* (London: Verso, 2019).

66 M. Rothwell, 'The road is tortuous: the Chinese revolution and the end of the global sixties', *Izquierdas*, 50 (2021). http://dx.doi.org/10.4067/s0718-50492021000100219 (accessed March 2024).

Chapter 4. Kwame Nkrumah

1 D. Z. Poe, *Kwame Nkrumah's Contribution to Pan-Africanism: An Afrocentric Analysis* (New York: Routledge, 2003), 3.

2 I am heavily indebted to Kwame Nkrumah's autobiography, *The Autobiography of Kwame Nkrumah* (Edinburgh: Thomas Nelson and Sons, 1957), and the biography of Nkrumah by Basil Davidson, *Black Star: A View of the Life and Times of Kwame Nkrumah* (Oxford: James Currey, 2019).

3 Nkrumah, *The Autobiography*, 5.

4 *Ibid.*, 14.

5 *Ibid.*, 27.
6 *Ibid.*, 45.
7 *Ibid.*, 52.
8 *Ibid.*, 52–53.
9 K. Nkrumah, *Class Struggle in Africa* (New York: International Publishers, 1972 [1970]), 87–88.
10 *Ibid.*, 88.
11 *Ibid.*, 10.
12 *Ibid.*, 17.
13 *Ibid.*
14 *Ibid.*, 19.
15 *Ibid.*, 64.
16 *Ibid.*
17 *Ibid.*, 75.
18 *Ibid.*, 80.
19 Nkrumah, *The Autobiography.*
20 S. Metz, 'In lieu of orthodoxy: the socialist theories of Nkrumah and Nyerere', *Journal of Modern African Studies*, 20:3 (1982), 386.
21 Nkrumah, *Class Struggle in Africa*, 26.
22 P. K. Tunteng, 'Kwame Nkrumah and the African revolution', *Civilisations*, 23–24:3–4 (1973), 241–242.
23 T. F. Zak, 'Applying the weapon of theory: comparing the philosophy of Julius Kambarage Nyerere and Kwame Nkrumah', *Journal of African Cultural Studies*, 28:2 (2016), 156.
24 A. Biney, 'The legacy of Kwame Nkrumah in retrospect', *Journal of Pan African Studies*, 2:3 (2008), 134.
25 K. Nkrumah, *Consciencism: Philosophy and ideology for Decolonization* (New York: Monthly Review Press, 1970 [1964]).
26 Nkrumah, *Class Struggle in Africa*, 26.
27 T. Hodgkin, 'Nkrumah's radicalism', *Présence Africaine*, 85 (1973), 65.
28 A. Mazrui, 'Nkrumah: the Leninist czar', *Transition*, 75–76 (1966), 106.
29 Hodgkin, 'Nkrumah's radicalism', 70.
30 K. Nkrumah, *Towards Colonial Freedom: Africa in the Struggle Against World Imperialism* (London: Heinemann, 1962), xv.
31 V. Dodoo, 'Kwame Nkrumah's mission and vision for Africa and the world', *Journal of Pan African Studies*, 4:10 (2012), 87.
32 K. Nkrumah, *Neo-Colonialism: The Last Stage of Imperialism* (New York: International Publishers, 1965), xi.
33 Mazrui, 'Nkrumah: the Leninist czar', 113.
34 Dodoo, 'Kwame Nkrumah's mission and vision for Africa and the world', 88.
35 Nkrumah, *Class Struggle in Africa*, 14.

36 P. Emiljanowicz, 'Tensions, ambiguities, and connectivity in Kwame Nkrumah: rethinking the "national" in postcolonial nationalism', *Interventions*, 21:5 (2019), 626.

37 Nkrumah, *Consciencism*, 73.

38 *Ibid.*, 75.

39 *Ibid.*, 76.

40 J. D. Elam, 'Conscience and conscious in the global South: B. R. Ambedkar, Kwame Nkrumah, and anticolonial sociology', *Comparative Literature Studies*, 58:3 (2021), 613–614.

41 Nkrumah, *Consciencism*, 68.

42 A. Biney, *The Political and Social Thought of Kwame Nkrumah* (New York: Palgrave Macmillan, 2011), 126–127.

43 Nkrumah, *Consciencism*, 70; see also Dodoo, 'Kwame Nkrumah's mission and vision for Africa and the world', 87.

44 Nkrumah, *Consciencism*, 70.

45 D. M. C. Ude, 'Kwasi Wiredu's critique of Marxism: its philosophical application to the "African socialism" via Nkrumah, Nyerere and Touré', *Africology: The Journal of Pan African Studies*, 12:5 (2018), 185.

46 Nkrumah, *Consciencism*, 78.

47 K. Botwe-Asamoah, *Kwame Nkrumah's Politico-Cultural Thought and Policies: An African-Centered Paradigm for the Second Phase of the African Revolution* (New York: Routledge, 2005), 43.

48 Nkrumah, *Consciencism*, 78.

49 Cited in K. Nkrumah, *Revolutionary Path* (London: Panaf, 1973), 171.

50 Nkrumah, *Class Struggle in Africa*, 84.

51 *Ibid.*, 85.

52 Nkrumah, *The Autobiography*; also see Emiljanowicz, 'Tensions, ambiguities, and connectivity in Kwame Nkrumah'.

53 Nkrumah, *Revolutionary Path*, 168.

54 Emiljanowicz, 'Tensions, ambiguities, and connectivity in Kwame Nkrumah', 629.

55 Biney, 'The legacy of Kwame Nkrumah in retrospect', 135.

56 D. Rooney, *Kwame Nkrumah: Vision and Tragedy* (Accra: Sub-Saharan Publishers, 2007), 14.

57 Emiljanowicz, 'Tensions, ambiguities, and connectivity in Kwame Nkrumah', 629.

58 C. A. Boateng, *The Political Legacy of Kwame Nkrumah of Ghana* (Lewiston: Edwin Mellen Press, 2003), 40.

59 Emiljanowicz, 'Tensions, ambiguities, and connectivity in Kwame Nkrumah', 630.

60 Biney, 'The legacy of Kwame Nkrumah in retrospect', 136.

61 K. Nkrumah, *Africa Must Unite* (New York: Praeger, 1964 [1963]), 2017–2018.

62 Biney, *The Political and Social Thought of Kwame Nkrumah*, 132.

63 P. Emiljanowicz, 'From Karl Marx to Kwame Nkrumah: towards a decolonial political economy'. In Ndlovu- Gatsheni, S. J. and Ndlovu, M. (eds), *Marxism and Decolonization in the 21st Century: Living Theories and True Ideas* (London: Routledge, 2021), 68–88.

64 J. Amankwah-Amoah and E. L. Osabutey, 'Newly independent nations and large engineering projects: the case of the Volta River Project', *Critical Perspectives on International Business*, 14:2–3 (2017), 154–169.

65 Hodgkin, 'Nkrumah's radicalism', 71.

66 K. Nkrumah, *Handbook of Revolutionary Warfare: A Guide to the Armed Phase of the African Revolution* (New York: International Publishers, 1968), 28.

67 Nkrumah, *Neo-Colonialism*, 256.

68 Nkrumah, *Class Struggle in Africa*, 54.

69 Biney, 'The legacy of Kwame Nkrumah in retrospect', 150.

70 Rooney, *Kwame Nkrumah. Vision and Tragedy*, 11.

71 C. L. R. James, *Nkrumah and the Ghana Revolution* (Durham: Duke University Press, 2022), 136.

72 Biney, *The Political and Social Thought of Kwame Nkrumah*, 182–184.

73 *Ibid.*, 188.

74 Emiljanowicz, 'From Karl Marx to Kwame Nkrumah', 85.

75 Biney, 'The legacy of Kwame Nkrumah in retrospect', 132.

76 *Ibid.*, 150.

77 Botwe-Asamoah, *Kwame Nkrumah's Politico-Cultural Thought and Policies*, 174.

78 Hodgkin, 'Nkrumah's radicalism'.

79 Biney, *The Political and Social Thought of Kwame Nkrumah*, 178.

80 Emiljanowicz, 'From Karl Marx to Kwame Nkrumah', 86.

81 *Ibid.*, 86–87.

82 A. Cabral, *Unity and Struggle: Speeches and Writings* (New York: Monthly Review Press, 1979), 117–118.

Chapter 5. Amílcar Cabral

1 J. McCulloch, *In the Twilight of Revolution: The Political Theory of Amílcar Cabral* (London: Routledge, 2020), 130.

2 I am heavily indebted to the biographies by Peter Karibe Mendy,

Amílcar Cabral: Nationalist and Pan-Africanist Revolutionary (Athens: Ohio University Press, 2019); and António Tomás, *Amílcar Cabral: The Life of a Reluctant Nationalist* (London: Hurst and Company, 2021).

3 Mendy, *Amílcar Cabral*, 36.

4 A movement aimed at raising black consciousness across Africa and its diaspora.

5 *Ibid.*, 202.

6 P. Chabal, 'The social and political thought of Amílcar Cabral: a reassessment', *Journal of Modern African Studies*, 19:1 (1981), 33.

7 A. M. Mukandabantu, 'The political thought of Amílcar Cabral: a review article', *Review of African Political Economy*, 27–28 (1983), 212–213.

8 B. Magubane, 'Toward a sociology of national liberation from colonialism: Cabral's legacy', *Contemporary Marxism*, 7 (1983), 7.

9 Magubane, 'Toward a sociology of national liberation from colonialism', 5–27.

10 R. H. Chilcote, 'The theory and practice of Amílcar Cabral: revolutionary implications for the Third World', *Latin American Perspectives*, 11:2 (1984), 3–14.

11 Magubane, 'Toward a sociology of national liberation from colonialism', 12.

12 Chabal, 'The social and political thought of Amílcar Cabral', 56.

13 P. Freire, 'South African freedom fighter Amílcar Cabral: pedagogue of the revolution'. In Marcine, S. L. (ed.), *Critical Pedagogy in Uncertain Times: Hopes and Possibilities* (New York: Palgrave Macmillan, 2020), 178.

14 A. Cabral, *Unity and Struggle: Selected Speeches and Writings* (Pretoria: Unisa press, 2012), 154–155.

15 *Ibid.*, 155.

16 *Ibid.*

17 *Ibid.*

18 *Ibid.*

19 *Ibid.*, 156.

20 *Ibid.*

21 *Ibid.*

22 B. Magubane, 'Amílcar Cabral: evolution of revolutionary thought', *Ufahamu: A Journal of African Studies*, 2:2 (1971), 76.

23 McCulloch, *In the Twilight of Revolution*, 3.

24 Cabral, *Unity and Struggle*, 156–157.

25 *Ibid.*, 157.

26 *Ibid.*, 157; Chilcote, 'The theory and practice of Amílcar Cabral', 10.

27 Cabral, *Unity and Struggle*, 157.

28 J. McCulloch, 'Amílcar Cabral: a theory of imperialism', *Journal of Modern African Studies*, 19:3 (1981), 511.
29 Chabal, 'The social and political thought of Amílcar Cabral'; G. Nzongola-Ntalaja, 'Amílcar Cabral and the theory of the national liberation struggle', *Latin American Perspectives*, 11:2 (1984), 43–54.
30 Cabral, *Unity and Struggle*, 161.
31 Chilcote, 'The theory and practice of Amílcar Cabral', 6–7.
32 McCulloch, *In the Twilight of Revolution*.
33 Cabral, *Unity and Struggle*, 158–159.
34 McCulloch, *In the Twilight of Revolution*.
35 Cabral, *Unity and Struggle*, 160–161.
36 *Ibid.*, 161.
37 *Ibid.*, 165.
38 *Ibid.*, 166.
39 *Ibid.*, emphasis added.
40 B. Davidson, 'On revolutionary nationalism: the legacy of Cabral', *Latin American Perspectives*, 11:2 (1984), 22.
41 T. Meisenhelder, 'Amílcar Cabral's theory of class suicide and revolutionary socialism', *Monthly Review*, 45:6 (1993), 40–48.
42 McCulloch, *In the Twilight of Revolution*, 77.
43 Cabral, *Unity and Struggle*, 172.
44 *Ibid.*, 173.
45 *Ibid.*, 172.
46 M. Hubbard, 'Culture and history in a revolutionary context: approaches to Amílcar Cabral', *Ufahamu: A Journal of African Studies*, 3:3 (1973), 79.
47 Cabral, *Unity and Struggle*, 173.
48 Hubbard, 'Culture and history in a revolutionary context', 80.
49 A. Cabral, *Resistance and Decolonisation* (London: Rowman and Littlefield, 2016), 174.
50 *Ibid.*, 175.
51 Davidson, 'On revolutionary nationalism', 31.
52 Tomás, *Amílcar Cabral*, 60.
53 McCulloch, *In the Twilight of Revolution*, 19.
54 *Ibid.*, 63–64.
55 *Ibid.*, 3.
56 P. K. Mendy, 'Amílcar Cabral and the liberation of Guinea-Bissau: context, challenges and lessons for effective African leadership', *African Identities*, 4:1 (2006), 19.
57 McCulloch, *In the Twilight of Revolution*, 131.
58 *Ibid.*, 138.
59 Mendy, 'Amílcar Cabral and the liberation of Guinea-Bissau', 17–18.
60 *Ibid.*, 7.

NOTES TO CHAPTER 6

61 A. Wick, 'Manifestations of nationhood in the writings of Amílcar Cabral', *African Identities*, 4:1 (2006), 46.

62 Mendy, 'Amílcar Cabral and the liberation of Guinea-Bissau', 19.

63 F. Manji and B. Fletcher Jr (eds), *Claim No Easy Victories: The Legacy of Amílcar Cabral* (Dakar: Codesria and Daraja Press, 2013).

64 B. Lundy, 'The importance of cultural capital in rebuilding a successful education system in Guinea-Bissau'. In Manji, F. and Fletcher Jr, B. (eds), *Claim No Easy Victories: The Legacy of Amílcar Cabral* (Dakar: Codesria and Daraja Press, 2013), 365–378.

65 See Z. El Nabolsy, 'Amílcar Cabral's modernist philosophy of culture and cultural liberation', *Journal of African Cultural Studies*, 32:2 (2020), 231–250.

66 Chilcote, 'The theory and practice of Amílcar Cabral'.

67 Mendy, *Amílcar Cabral*, 22.

68 Tomás, *Amílcar Cabral*, 207.

69 S. Hill, 'International solidarity: Cabral's legacy to the African-American community', *Latin American Perspectives*, 11:2 (1984), 67–68.

70 *Ibid.*, 72.

71 Manji and Fletcher, *Claim No Easy Victories*, 3.

72 *Ibid.*

73 See C. Lopes (ed.), *Africa's Contemporary Challenges: The Legacy of Amílcar Cabral* (London: Routledge, 2010).

74 R. Rabaka, 'The weapon of critical theory: Amílcar Cabral, Cabralism, and Africana critical theory'. In Cabral, A., *Resistance and Decolonisation* (London: Rowman and Littlefield, 2016), 11.

Chapter 6. Frantz Fanon

1 A. Bose, 'Frantz Fanon and the politicization of the Third World as a collective subject', *Interventions*, 21:5 (2019), 673.

2 I am heavily indebted to the following biographies: David Macey, *Frantz Fanon: A Biography* (London: Verso Books, 2012); and Peter Hudis, *Frantz Fanon: Philosopher of the Barricades* (London: Pluto Press, 2015).

3 Macey, *Frantz Fanon*, 86.

4 R. Rabaka, *Africana Critical Theory: Reconstructing the Black Radical Tradition, from W. E. B. Du Bois and C. L. R. James to Frantz Fanon and Amílcar Cabral* (Lanham: Lexington Books, 2009), 166.

5 Hudis, *Frantz Fanon*, 23.

6 D. Forsythe, 'Frantz Fanon – the Marx of the Third World', *Phylon*, 34:2 (1973), 160–170.

7 R. Rabaka, 'Revolutionary Fanonism: on Frantz Fanon's modification of Marxism and decolonization of democratic socialism', *Socialism and Democracy*, 25:1 (2011), 138.

8 T. Martin, 'Rescuing Fanon from the critics', *African Studies Review*, 13:3 (1970), 384.

9 *Ibid.*

10 *Ibid.*, 385.

11 Hudis, *Frantz Fanon*, 9.

12 Forsythe, 'Frantz Fanon', 161.

13 F. Fanon, *A Dying Colonialism* (New York: Grove Press, 1994 [1964]), 38.

14 N. Gibson, 'Fanon and Marx revisited', *Journal of the British Society for Phenomenology*, 51:4 (2020), 328.

15 *Ibid..*

16 F. Fanon, *The Wretched of the Earth* (New York: Grove Press, 2011 [1961]).

17 W. W. Hansen, 'Another side of Frantz Fanon: reflections on socialism and democracy', *New Political Science*, 19:3 (1997), 92.

18 Forsythe, 'Frantz Fanon', 162.

19 N. Gibson, 'Beyond Manicheanism: dialectics in the thought of Frantz Fanon', *Journal of Political Ideologies*, 4:3 (1999), 342.

20 Forsythe, 'Frantz Fanon', 161.

21 P. Nursey-Bray, 'Race and nation: ideology in the thought of Frantz Fanon', *Journal of Modern African Studies*, 18:1 (1980), 138.

22 See Hudis, *Frantz Fanon*, 10.

23 *Ibid.*

24 F. Fanon, *Black Skin, White Masks* (London: Pluto Press, 2008 [1952]).

25 *Ibid.*

26 L. T. Parris, 'Frantz Fanon: existentialist, dialectician, and revolutionary', *Journal of Pan African Studies*, 4:7 (2011), 16.

27 Hudis, *Frantz Fanon*, 8.

28 I. Wallerstein, 'Frantz Fanon: reason and violence', *Berkeley Journal of Sociology*, 15 (1970), 225.

29 Fanon, *The Wretched of the Earth*, 5, emphasis added.

30 Gibson, 'Fanon and Marx revisited', 322.

31 Rabaka, *Africana Critical Theory*, 179.

32 *Ibid.*, 178.

33 *Ibid.*, 183.

34 Martin, 'Rescuing Fanon from the critics', 385.

35 Fanon, *The Wretched of the Earth*; Rabaka, *Africana Critical Theory*, 184.

36 Rabaka, *Africana Critical Theory*, 186.

37 Fanon, *Black Skin, White Masks*, 157.
38 Forsythe, 'Frantz Fanon', 163.
39 Hudis, *Frantz Fanon*, 23.
40 Forsythe, 'Frantz Fanon', 165.
41 *Ibid.*, 166.
42 Rabaka, *Africana Critical Theory*, 197–198.
43 Gibson, 'Fanon and Marx revisited', 329.
44 Forsythe, 'Frantz Fanon', 167.
45 Fanon, *The Wretched of the Earth*, 87.
46 Gibson, 'Fanon and Marx revisited'.
47 Bose, 'Frantz Fanon and the politicization of the Third World as a collective subject', 682.
48 Macey, *Frantz Fanon*, 481.
49 R. Rabaka, *Forms of Fanonism: Frantz Fanon's Critical Theory and the Dialectics of Decolonization* (Lanham: Lexington Books, 2010), 157.
50 P. Nursey-Bray, 'Marxism and existentialism in the thought of Frantz Fanon', *Political Studies*, 20:2 (1972), 152–168.
51 Hudis, *Frantz Fanon*, 126.
52 *Ibid.*
53 Rabaka, *Africana Critical Theory*, 187.
54 Forsythe, 'Frantz Fanon', 167.
55 *Ibid.*, 169.
56 F. Fanon, *Toward the African Revolution* (New York: Grove Press, 1994 [1964]), 154–155.
57 Macey, *Frantz Fanon*, 479.
58 Forsythe, 'Frantz Fanon', 167–168.
59 Fanon, *The Wretched of the Earth*, 179.
60 *Ibid.*, 180.
61 Bose, 'Frantz Fanon and the politicization of the Third World as a collective subject', 681.
62 Nursey-Bray, 'Marxism and existentialism in the thought of Frantz Fanon', 159.
63 *Ibid.*, 160.
64 Forsythe, 'Frantz Fanon, 169.
65 D. Hanley, 'Frantz Fanon – revolutionary nationalist?', *Political Studies*, 24:2 (1976), 129.
66 Fanon, *The Wretched of the Earth*, 119.
67 Hanley, 'Frantz Fanon', 128.
68 Forsythe, 'Frantz Fanon', 169–170.
69 Fanon, *The Wretched of the Earth*, 130.
70 Hudis, *Frantz Fanon*, 95.
71 Nursey-Bray, 'Race and nation', 140–141.

72 P. Hudis, 'Frantz Fanon's contribution to Hegelian Marxism', *Critical Sociology*, 43:6 (2017), 865–873.

73 See Frantz Fanon, *Alienation and Freedom* (London: Bloomsbury Publishing, 2018).

74 Quoted in Macey, *Frantz Fanon*, 5.

75 *Ibid.*, 487.

76 *Ibid.*, 25.

77 Hamid Dabashi, *Brown Skin, White Masks* (London: Pluto Press, 2011); Glen Coulthard, *Red Skin, White Masks: Rejecting the Colonial Politics of Recognition* (Minneapolis: University of Minnesota Press, 2014).

78 P. N. Nayar, *Frantz Fanon* (London: Rutledge, 2013).

79 Macey, *Frantz Fanon*, 7.

80 *Ibid.*, 24; Nayar, *Frantz Fanon*, 134.

81 Macey, *Frantz Fanon*, xiv.

82 F. Ekotto, 'Frantz Fanon in the era of Black Lives Matter', in Kim, D. D. (ed.), *Reframing Postcolonial Studies* (London: Palgrave Macmillan, 2021), 249–259.

83 Hudis, *Frantz Fanon*, 1.

84 Nayar, *Frantz Fanon*.

85 M. Fanon Mendès-France and D. Fhunsu, 'The contribution of Frantz Fanon to the process of the liberation of the people', *Black Scholar*, 42:3–4 (2012), 11–12.

Chapter 7. Ernesto Che Guevara

1 M. Löwy, *The Marxism of Che Guevara: Philosophy, Economics, Revolutionary Warfare* (Lanham: Rowman and Littlefield, 2007), xxxiii.

2 I am heavily indebted to the following biographies: Jon Lee Anderson, *Che Guevara: A Revolutionary Life* (London: Bantam Books, 2010); and Richard Harris, *Che Guevara: A Biography* (Santa Barbara: Greenwood Press, 2011).

3 Anderson, *Che Guevara*, 16.

4 Quoted *ibid.*, 43.

5 E. C. Guevara, *The Motorcycle Diaries: A Journey Around South America* (London: Verso, 1995).

6 E. C. Guevara, *Che Guevara Speaks* (New York: Pathfinder, 2000), 28.

7 P. McLaren, 'Revolutionary leadership and pedagogical praxis: revisiting the legacy of Che Guevara', *International Journal of Leadership in Education*, 2:3 (1999), 287.

8 Löwy, *The Marxism of Che Guevara*, 11.
9 R. Llorente, *The Political Theory of Che Guevara* (Lanham: Rowman and Littlefield, 2018), 110.
10 Löwy, *The Marxism of Che Guevara*, 9.
11 Llorente, *The Political Theory of Che Guevara*, 71.
12 P. McLaren, 'Foreword'. In Löwy, M., *The Marxism of Che Guevara: Philosophy, Economics, Revolutionary Warfare* (Lanham: Rowman and Littlefield, 2007), xvii.
13 Llorente, *The Political Theory of Che Guevara*.
14 *Ibid.*, 64.
15 H. Yaffe, 'Che Guevara's enduring legacy: not the *foco* but the theory of socialist construction', *Latin American Perspectives*, 36:2 (2009), 51.
16 E. C. Guevara, *Socialism and Man in Cuba* (New York: Pathfinder, 2009 [1968]), 18.
17 H. Yaffe, 'Che Guevara and the Great Debate, past and present', *Science and Society*, 76:1 (2012), 30.
18 Guevara, *Socialism and Man in Cuba*, 18.
19 H. Yaffe, 'Che Guevara: cooperatives and the political economy of socialist transition'. In Piñeiro Harnecker, C. (ed.), *Cooperatives and Socialism: A View from Cuba* (Basingstoke: Palgrave Macmillan, 2013), 4.
20 Llorente, *The Political Theory of Che Guevara*, 32–33.
21 *Ibid.*, 40.
22 H. Yaffe, *Che Guevara: The Economics of Revolution* (Basingstoke: Palgrave Macmillan, 2009), 202.
23 *Ibid.*, 231.
24 Yaffe, 'Che Guevara: cooperatives and the political economy of socialist transition', 18–19.
25 Llorente, *The Political Theory of Che Guevara*, 12.
26 *Ibid.*, 13.
27 Guevara, *Socialism and Man in Cuba*, 27.
28 Llorente, *The Political Theory of Che Guevara*, 14.
29 *Ibid.*, 15.
30 *Ibid.*, 112.
31 *Ibid.*
32 Guevara, *Socialism and Man in Cuba*; Harris, *Che Guevara*, 128.
33 McLaren, 'Revolutionary leadership and pedagogical praxis', 258.
34 Guevara, *Socialism and Man in Cuba*, 12–13.
35 Llorente, *The Political Theory of Che Guevara*, 50–51.
36 Löwy, *The Marxism of Che Guevara*, 82.
37 J. A. Moreno, 'Che Guevara on guerrilla warfare: doctrine, practice and evaluation', *Comparative Studies in Society and History*, 12:2 (1970), 115–116.

38 Harris, *Che Guevara*, 105.
39 *Ibid.*, 108.
40 See Löwy, *The Marxism of Che Guevara*; Yaffe, *Che Guevara*.
41 Yaffe, *Che Guevara*, 2.
42 Yaffe, 'Che Guevara and the Great Debate, past and present', 14.
43 Yaffe, *Che Guevara*, 2.
44 Yaffe, 'Che Guevara's enduring legacy', 51.
45 Yaffe, *Che Guevara*, 2.
46 *Ibid.*, 45–46.
47 Yaffe, 'Che Guevara's enduring legacy', 53.
48 See Yaffe, *Che Guevara*, 261–262.
49 *Ibid.*, 234.
50 *Ibid.*, 67.
51 *Ibid.*
52 Yaffe, 'Che Guevara and the Great Debate, past and present', 25.
53 *Ibid.*, 30–31.
54 Yaffe, 'Che Guevara's enduring legacy'.
55 Yaffe, *Che Guevara*, 260.
56 Harris, *Che Guevara*, 197.
57 Quoted in Anderson, *Che Guevara*, 446.
58 Harris, *Che Guevara*.
59 R. L. Harris, 'Cuban internationalism, Che Guevara, and the survival of Cuba's socialist regime', *Latin American Perspectives*, 36:3 (2009), 33.
60 P. McLaren, *Che Guevara, Paulo Freire, and the Pedagogy of Revolution* (Lanham: Rowman and Littlefield, 2000), 43.
61 McLaren, 'Revolutionary leadership and pedagogical praxis', 291.
62 Harris, *Che Guevara*; also see Löwy, *The Marxism of Che Guevara*, xxviii–xxix.
63 Anderson, *Che Guevara*, 726.
64 *Ibid.*, xi.
65 Quoted in E. C. Guevara, *Che Guevara Talks to Young People* (New York: Pathfinder, 2000), 134.

Chapter 8. Ali Shariati

1 N. Keddie, *Roots of Revolution: An Interpretive History of Modern Iran* (New Haven: Yale University Press, 1981); E. Abrahamian, 'Ali Shariati: ideologue of the Iranian Revolution', *Merip Reports*, 102 (1982), 24–28; S. A. Arjomand, *The Turban for the Crown: The Islamic Revolution in Iran* (New York: Oxford University Press,

1988); A. Bayat, 'Shari'ati and Marx: a critique of an Islamic critique of Marxism', *Alif: Journal of Comparative Poetics* (1990), 19–41; H. Dabashi, *Theology of Discontent: The Ideological Foundation of the Islamic Revolution in Iran* (New York: New York University Press, 1993).

2 I am heavily indebted to the biography by Ali Rahnema, *An Islamic Utopian: A Political Biography of Ali Shari'ati* (London: I. B. Tauris, 1998).

3 Bayat, 'Shari'ati and Marx', 24.

4 Abrahamian, 'Ali Shariati', 26–27.

5 Dabashi, *Theology of Discontent*, 137.

6 *Ibid.*

7 B. M. Al-Saif, 'Musulman-e Marksisti: the Islamic modernism of Ali Shariati in *Religion vs. Religion*'. In Byrd, R. and Miri, S. J. (eds), *Ali Shariati and the Future of Social Theory: Religion, Revolution and the Role of the Intellectual* (Leiden: Brill, 2018), 274.

8 See S. Fadaee, 'Marxism, Islam and the Iranian Revolution'. In Kirkpatrick, G., McMylor, P. and Fadaee, S. (eds), *Marxism, Religion and Emancipatory Politics* (London: Palgrave Macmillan, 2022).

9 A. Shariati, *Man and Islam*. Translated by Hamid Algar (Berkeley: Mizan Press, 1981), 25.

10 R. Connell, *Southern Theory: The Global Dynamics of Knowledge in Social Science* (Cambridge: Polity, 2007), 130.

11 A. Shariati, *Marxism and Other Western Fallacies*. Translated by R. Campbell (Berkeley: Mizan Press, 1980).

12 Dabashi, *Theology of Discontent*, 143.

13 Shariati quoted *ibid.*, 47.

14 Shariati, *Marxism and Other Western Fallacies*.

15 Abrahamian, 'Ali Shariati', 27.

16 Bayat, 'Shari'ati and Marx', 30–31.

17 A. Bayat, *Revolution without Revolutionaries: Making Sense of the Arab Spring* (Stanford: Stanford University Press, 2017), 41.

18 Abrahamian, 'Ali Shariati', 26.

19 Dabashi, *Theology of Discontent*, 139.

20 *Ibid.*

21 *Ibid.*, 110.

22 *Ibid.*, 137.

23 Bayat, *Revolution without Revolutionaries*, 43.

24 B. Ghamari-Tabrizi, 'Contentious public religion: to conceptions of Islam in Revolutionary Iran. Ali Shariati and Abdolkarim Soroush', *International Sociology*, 19:4 (2004), 511.

25 Dabashi, *Theology of Discontent*, 142.

26 Quoted in Bayat, 'Shari'ati and Marx', 32.

27 Dabashi, *Theology of Discontent.*

28 *Ibid.,* 143.

29 Ghamari-Tabrizi, 'Contentious public religion', 512.

30 Dabashi, *Theology of Discontent,* 110.

31 A. Shariati, *On the Sociology of Islam.* Translated by H. Algar (Berkeley: Mizan Press, 2017 [1979]).

32 Ghamari-Tabrizi, 'Contentious public religion', 513.

33 D. Byrd, 'Ali Shariati and critical theory: from black affirmation to red negation'. In Byrd, D. and Miri, S. J. (eds), *Ali Shariati and the Future of Social Theory: Religion, Revolution and the Role of the Intellectual* (Leiden: Brill, 2018), 98–127.

34 Dabashi, *Theology of Discontent,* 143.

35 Shariati, *On the Sociology of Islam.*

36 Dabashi, *Theology of Discontent*; Ghamari-Tabrizi, 'Contentious public religion'.

37 See Al-Saif, 'Musulman-e Marksisti', 274.

38 S.R. Arjana, 'The new Islamism: remembrance and liberation'. In Byrd, D. and Miri, S. J. (eds), *Ali Shariati and the Future of Social Theory: Religion, Revolution and the Role of the Intellectual* (Leiden: Brill, 2018), 192.

39 R. Witzler, 'Ali Shariati: red Shiism and revolution in Iran', *Religious Studies Honors Projects,* paper 8 (2010), 15.

40 K. Matin, 'Decoding political Islam: uneven and combined development and Ali Shariati's political thought'. In Shilliam, R. (ed.), *International Relations and Non-Western Thought: Imperialism, Colonialism and Investigations of Global Modernity* (London: Routledge, 2010), 124–140.

41 Abrahamian, 'Ali Shariati', 28.

42 Bayat, *Revolution without Revolutionaries.*

43 See J. Afary and K. B. Anderson, *Foucault and the Iranian Revolution: Gender and the Seduction of Islamism* (Chicago: University of Chicago Press, 2005).

44 Dabashi, *Theology of Discontent,* 103.

45 Abrahamian, 'Ali Shariati', 28.

46 Bayat, *Revolution without Revolutionaries,* 35.

47 Keddie, *Roots of Revolution,* 223.

48 Matin, 'Decoding political Islam', 121.

49 Byrd, 'Ali Shariati and critical theory', 122.

50 Keddie, *Roots of Revolution,* 23.

51 Abrahamian, 'Ali Shariati', 28.

52 Bayat, *Revolution without Revolutionaries,* 47.

53 H. Algar, 'Foreword'. In Shariati, A., *On the Sociology of Islam.* Translated by H. Algar (Berkeley: Mizan Press, 2017 [1979]), 4.

54 See S. Saffari, *Beyond Shariati* (Cambridge: Cambridge University Press, 2017).

55 Bayat, *Revolution without Revolutionaries*, 48.

56 G. Tavassoli, 'A Bibliographical Sketch'. In Shariati, A. *On the Sociology of Islam*. Translated by H. Algar (Berkeley: Mizan Press, 2017 [1979]), 32.

57 Algar, 'Foreword'.

58 A. Bayat (ed.), *Post-Islamism: The Many Faces of Political Islam* (New York: Oxford University Press, 2013); M. Mahdavi, 'Post-Islamist trends in Postrevolutionary Iran', *Comparative Studies of South Asia, Africa and the Middle East*, 31:1 (2011), 94–109; Y. Shahibzadeh, *Islamism and Post-Islamism in Iran: An Intellectual History* (New York: Palgrave, 2016).

59 See S. Fadaee, *Social Movements in Iran: Environmentalism and Civil Society* (London: Routledge, 2012).

60 Saffari, *Beyond Shariati*, 9.

61 *Ibid.*, 12.

62 A. Rahnema, 'Ali Shariati: teacher, preacher, rebel'. In Rahnema, A. (ed.), *Pioneers of Islamic Revival* (London: Zed Books, 2005), 208–250.

63 D. Byrd and S. J. Miri, 'Introduction'. In Byrd, D. and Miri, S. J. (eds), *Ali Shariati and the Future of Social Theory: Religion, Revolution and the Role of the Intellectual* (Leiden: Brill, 2018), 3.

64 Byrd, 'Ali Shariati and critical theory', 123.

Chapter 9. Subcomandante Marcos

1 N. Henck, *Subcomandante Marcos: Global Rebel Icon* (Montreal: Black Rose Books, 2019).

2 I am heavily indebted to the two biographies by Nick Henck: *Insurgent Marcos: The Political-Philosophical Formation of the Zapatista Subcommander* (Raleigh: University of North Carolina Press, 2016); and *Subcomandante Marcos*.

3 Subcomandante Marcos quoted in S. Marcos, G. G. Marquez and R. Pombo, 'Punch card and hourglass', *New Left Review*, 9 (2001), 78.

4 Henck, *Insurgent Marcos*, 56.

5 N. Klein, 'The unknown icon', *Guardian*, 3 March 2001. https://www.theguardian.com/books/2001/mar/03/politics (accessed March 2024).

6 B. Orr-Alvarez, 'Masking revolution: Subcomandante Marcos and the contemporary Zapatista movement'. In Santos. A. (ed.),

Performing Utopias in the Contemporary Utopias (New York: Palgrave Macmillan, 2017), 113.

7 Henck, *Insurgent Marcos*, 11–12.

8 D. O'Hearn, 'Foreword, forward!' In Lynd, S. and Grubačić, A. (eds), *Wobblies and Zapatistas: Conversations on Anarchism, Marxism, and Radical History* (Oakland: PM Press, 2008), xiii.

9 Orr-Alvarez, 'Masking revolution', 113–114.

10 A. Khasnabish, *Zapatistas: Rebellion from the Grassroots to the Global* (London: Zed Books, 2010), 71–72.

11 *Ibid.*

12 S. Marcos, *Our Word Is Our Weapon: Selected Writings* (New York: Seven Stories Press, 2002), 41.

13 *Ibid.*, 294.

14 S. Marcos, 'The Fourth World War has begun', *Nepantla: Views from the South*, 2 (2001), 559.

15 *Ibid.*, 559–560.

16 *Ibid.*, 562.

17 *Ibid.*, 569.

18 *Ibid.*, 570.

19 M. D. De Huerta and N. Higgins, 'An interview with Subcomandante Insurgente Marcos, spokesperson and military commander of the Zapatista National Liberation Army (EZLN)', *International Affairs*, 75:2 (1999), 269–279.

20 *Ibid.*, 271.

21 *Ibid.*

22 *Ibid.*, 272.

23 *Ibid.*

24 *Ibid.*

25 Marcos, *Our Word Is Our Weapon*, 540.

26 Henck, *Subcomandante Marcos*.

27 *Ibid.*, 50–51.

28 *Ibid.*, 75.

29 N. Henck, 'Subcomandante Marcos: the latest reader', *Latin Americanist*, 58:2 (2014), 49–73; Henck, *Subcomandante Marcos*.

30 Henck, *Subcomandante Marcos*, 82.

31 J. Holloway, 'Dignity's revolt'. In Holloway, J. and Pelaez, E. (eds), *Zapatista: Reinventing Revolution in Mexico* (London: Pluto Press, 1998), 159–160.

32 *Ibid.*, 160.

33 *Ibid.*, 165.

34 *Ibid.*, 159–198.

35 *Ibid.*, 165.

36 *Ibid.*, 170–171.

37 *Ibid.*, 167.
38 *Ibid.*
39 *Ibid.*, 167–168.
40 *Ibid.*, 180.
41 *Ibid.*
42 *Ibid.*, 182.
43 *Ibid.*, 183.
44 Marcos, *Our Word Is Our Weapon*, 44.
45 Khasnabish, *Zapatistas*.
46 L. Lorenzano, 'Zapatismo: recomposition of labour, radical democracy and revolutionary project'. In Holloway, J. and Pelaez, E. (eds), *Zapatista: Reinventing Revolution in Mexico* (London: Pluto Press, 1998), 154.
47 Khasnabish, *Zapatistas*, 199.
48 Henck, *Subcomandante Marcos*, 88.
49 Holloway, 'Dignity's revolt', 188.
50 *Ibid.*, 180.
51 Khasnabish, *Zapatistas*, 172.
52 L. Cox, 'Making other worlds possible: why the Zapatistas matter to us', English-language translation of the Spanish-language pamphlet 'Haciendo otros mundos posibles: por qué los Zapatistas nos importan' (Cooperative Editorial Retos, 2021).
53 Khasnabish, *Zapatistas*, 176.
54 J. Holloway and E. Pelaez (eds), *Zapatista: Reinventing Revolution in Mexico* (London: Pluto Press, 1998).
55 *Ibid.*, 17.
56 M. Mentinis, *Zapatistas: The Chiapas Revolt and What It Means for Radical Politics* (London: Pluto Press, 2006), 166.
57 R. Debray, 'A guerrilla with a difference', *New Left Review*, 128 (1996), 134.
58 Khasnabish, *Zapatistas*, 163.
59 *Ibid.*, 163.
60 J. Petras, 'Latin America: the resurgence of the left', *New Left Review*, 223 (1997), 37.
61 Quoted in Henck, *Subcomandante Marcos*, 84.
62 Khasnabish, *Zapatistas*.
63 Quoted in Henck, *Subcomandante Marcos*, 88.
64 *Ibid.*, 92.
65 Mentinis, *Zapatistas*, 136–137.
66 Henck, *Subcomandante Marcos*, 93.
67 Orr-Alvarez. 'Masking revolution', 117.
68 Henck, *Subcomandante Marcos*.
69 Khasnabish, *Zapatistas*, 16.

70 Henck, *Subcomandante Marcos*, 108.
71 Klein, 'The unknown icon'.

Conclusion

1 For an excellent discussion of the dictatorship of the proletariat see
   L. Ypi, 'Democratic dictatorship: political legitimacy in Marxist perspective', *European Journal of Philosophy*, 28:2 (2020), 277–291.

Bibliography

Abrahamian, E., 'Ali Shariati: ideologue of the Iranian Revolution', *Merip Reports*, 102 (1982), 24–28.

Afary, J. and Anderson, K. B., *Foucault and the Iranian Revolution: Gender and the Seduction of Islamism*. Chicago: University of Chicago Press, 2005.

Ahmad, A., *In Theory: Nations, Classes, Literatures*. London: Verso, 1992.

Ahmad, M., 'Movement texts as anti-colonial theory', *Sociology*, 57:1 (2023), 54–71.

Alatas, S. F. and Sinha, V., *Sociological Theory Beyond the Canon*. London: Palgrave Macmillan, 2017.

Algar, H., 'Foreword'. In Shariati, A., *On the Sociology of Islam*. Translated by H. Algar. Berkeley: Mizan Press, 2017 [1979].

Al-Saif, B. M., 'Musulman-e Marksisti: the Islamic modernism of Ali Shariati in *Religion vs. Religion*'. In Byrd, R. and Miri, S. J. (eds), *Ali Shariati and the Future of Social Theory: Religion, Revolution and the Role of the Intellectual*. Leiden: Brill, 2018, 271–276.

Amankwah-Amoah, J. and Osabutey, E. L., 'Newly independent nations and large engineering projects: the case of the Volta River Project', *Critical Perspectives on International Business*, 14:2–3 (2017), 154–169.

Anderson, J. L., *Che Guevara: A Revolutionary Life*. London: Bantam Books, 2010.

Anderson, K. B., 'Marx's late writings on non-western and precapitalist societies and gender', *Rethinking Marxism*, 14:4 (2002), 84–96.

Anderson, K. B., *Marx at the Margins: On Nationalism, Ethnicity and Non-Western Societies*. Chicago: University of Chicago Press, 2010.

Appadorai, A., 'Recent socialist thought in India', *Review of Politics*, 30:3 (1968), 349–362.

Arjana, S. R., 'The new Islamism: remembrance and liberation'. In Byrd,

D. and Miri, S. J. (eds), *Ali Shariati and the Future of Social Theory: Religion, Revolution and the Role of the Intellectual*. Leiden: Brill, 2018, 181–199.

Arjomand, S. A., *The Turban for the Crown: The Islamic Revolution in Iran*. New York: Oxford University Press, 1988.

Asia News Monitor, 'Vietnam: Vietnamese leaders celebrate legacy of Hồ Chí Minh', 4 September 2009. https://www.proquest.com/docview/1027266451 (accessed March 2024).

Asia News Monitor, 'Vietnam: Paris seminar spotlights Hồ Chí Minh's legacy', 23 September 2011. https://www.proquest.com/docview/893614154 (accessed March 2024).

Bardawil, F. A., *Revolution and Disenchantment*. Durham: Duke University Press, 2020.

Bayat, A., 'Shari'ati and Marx: a critique of an Islamic critique of Marxism', *Alif: Journal of Comparative Poetics* (1990), 19–41.

Bayat, A., *Revolution without Revolutionaries: Making Sense of the Arab Spring*. Stanford: Stanford University Press, 2017.

Bayat, A. (ed.), *Post-Islamism: The Many Faces of Political Islam*. New York: Oxford University Press, 2013.

Bayly, C. A., 'The ends of liberalism and the political thought of Nehru's India', *Modern Intellectual History*, 12:3 (2015), 605–626.

Bhambra, G. K., *Connected Sociologies*. London: Bloomsbury, 2014.

Bhambra, G. K. and Holmwood, J., *Colonialism and Modern Social Theory*. Cambridge: Polity Press, 2021.

Biney, A., 'The legacy of Kwame Nkrumah in retrospect', *Journal of Pan African Studies*, 2:3 (2008), 129–159.

Biney, A., *The Political and Social Thought of Kwame Nkrumah*. New York: Palgrave Macmillan, 2011.

Boateng, C. A., *The Political Legacy of Kwame Nkrumah of Ghana*. Lewiston: Edwin Mellen Press, 2003.

Bose, A., 'Frantz Fanon and the politicization of the Third World as a collective subject', *Interventions*, 21:5 (2019), 671–689.

Botwe-Asamoah, K., *Kwame Nkrumah's Politico-Cultural Thought and Policies: An African-Centered Paradigm for the Second Phase of the African Revolution*. New York: Routledge, 2005.

Brigham, R. K., 'Hồ Chí Minh, Confucianism, and Marxism'. In Anderson, D. L. and Ernst, J. (eds), *The War That Never Ends: New Perspectives on the Vietnam War*. Lexington: University Press of Kentucky, 2007, 105–120.

Brocheux, P., *Hồ Chí Minh: A Biography*. Cambridge: Cambridge University Press, 2007.

Brutens, K. N., *National Liberation Revolutions Today*. Moscow: Progress Publishers, 1977.

Burawoy, M., 'Marxism after communism', *Theory and Society*, 29:2 (2000), 151–174.

Burawoy, M., 'Decolonizing sociology: the significance of W. E. B. Du Bois', *Critical Sociology*, 47:4–5 (2021), 545–554.

Burawoy, M., 'Why is classical theory classical? Theorizing the canon and canonizing Du Bois', *Journal of Classical Sociology*, 21:3–4 (2021), 245–259.

Burawoy, M., 'Walking on two legs: Black Marxism and the sociological canon', *Critical Sociology*, 48:4–5 (2022), 571–586.

Byrd, D., 'Ali Shariati and critical theory: from Black affirmation to Red negation'. In Byrd, D. and Miri, S. J. (eds), *Ali Shariati and the Future of Social Theory: Religion, Revolution and the Role of the Intellectual*. Leiden: Brill, 2018, 98–127.

Byrd, D. and Miri, S. J., 'Introduction'. In Byrd, D. and Miri, S. J. (eds), *Ali Shariati and the Future of Social Theory: Religion, Revolution and the Role of the Intellectual*. Leiden: Brill, 2018, 1–8.

Cabral, A., *Unity and Struggle: Speeches and Writings*. New York: Monthly Review Press, 1979.

Cabral, A., *Unity and Struggle: Selected Speeches and Writings*. Pretoria: Unisa Press, 2012.

Cabral, A., *Resistance and Decolonisation*. London: Rowman and Littlefield, 2016.

Chabal, P., 'The social and political thought of Amílcar Cabral: a reassessment', *Journal of Modern African Studies*, 19:1 (1981), 31–56.

Chakrabarty, D., *Provincializing Europe: Postcolonial Thought and Historical Difference*. Princeton: Princeton University Press, 2008.

Chatterjee, P., *Nationalist Thought and the Colonial World: A Derivative Discourse?* London: Zed Books, 1986.

Chibber, V., *Postcolonial Theory and the Specter of Capital*. London: Verso, 2013.

Chilcote, R., 'The theory and practice of Amílcar Cabral: revolutionary implications for the Third World', *Latin American Perspectives*, 11:2 (1984), 3–14.

Connell, R., *Southern Theory: The Global Dynamics of Knowledge in Social Science*. London: Routledge, 2007.

Coulthard, G. S., *Red Skin, White Masks: Rejecting the Colonial Politics of Recognition*. Minneapolis: University of Minnesota Press, 2014.

Cox, L., 'Making other worlds possible: why the Zapatistas matter to us', English-language translation of the Spanish-language pamphlet 'Haciendo otros mundos posibles: por qué los Zapatistas nos importan'. Cooperative Editorial Retos, 2021.

Crowe, D., *Hemingway and Hô Chí Minh in Paris: The Art of Resistance*. Minneapolis: Fortress Press, 2020.

Dabashi, H., *Theology of Discontent: The Ideological Foundation of the Islamic Revolution in Iran*. New York: New York University Press, 1993.

Dabashi, H., *Brown Skin, White Masks*. London: Pluto Press, 2011.

Davidson, B., 'On revolutionary nationalism: the legacy of Cabral', *Latin American Perspectives*, 11:2 (1984), 15–42.

Davidson, B., *Black Star: A View of the Life and Times of Kwame Nkrumah*. Oxford: James Currey, 2019.

De Huerta, M. D. and Higgins, N., 'An interview with Subcomandante Insurgente Marcos, spokesperson and military commander of the Zapatista National Liberation Army (EZLN)', *International Affairs*, 75:2 (1999), 269–279.

Debray, R., 'A guerrilla with a difference', *New Left Review*, 128 (1996), 128–137.

DeCaro, P. A., *Rhetoric of Revolt: Hồ Chí Minh's Discourse for Revolution*. New York: Praeger, 2003.

Dirlik, A., 'The predicament of Marxist revolutionary consciousness: Mao Zedong, Antonio Gramsci, and the reformulation of Marxist revolutionary theory', *Modern China*, 9:2 (1983), 182–211.

Dirlik, A., 'The postcolonial aura: Third World criticism in the age of global capitalism', *Critical Inquiry*, 20:2 (1994), 328–356.

Dirlik, A., *Marxism in the Chinese Revolution*. Lanham: Rowman and Littlefield, 2005.

Dirlik, A., Healy, P. and Knight, N. (eds), *Critical Perspectives on Mao Zedong's Thought*. Atlantic Highlands: Humanities Press, 1997.

Dodoo, V., 'Kwame Nkrumah's mission and vision for Africa and the world', *Journal of Pan African Studies*, 4:10 (2012), 78–92.

Du Bois, W. E. B., *The World and Africa*. New York: Oxford University Press, 2007 [1947].

Duiker, W. J., 'What is to be done? Hồ Chí Minh's Road Kach Mei'. In Taylor, K. W. and Whitemore, J. K. (eds), *Essays into Vietnamese Pasts*. New York: Cornell University Press, 1995, 207–220.

Duiker, W. J., *Hồ Chí Minh: A Life*. New York: Hyperion, 2000.

Dutt, R. C., *The Socialism of Jawaharlal Nehru*. Delhi: Abhinav Publications, 1981.

Ekotto, F., 'Frantz Fanon in the era of Black Lives Matter'. In Kim, D. D. (ed.), *Reframing Postcolonial Studies*. London: Palgrave Macmillan, 2021, 249–259.

El Nabolsy, Z., 'Amílcar Cabral's modernist philosophy of culture and cultural liberation', *Journal of African Cultural Studies*, 32:2 (2020), 231–250.

Elam, J. D., 'Conscience and conscious in the global South: B. R. Ambedkar, Kwame Nkrumah, and anticolonial sociology', *Comparative Literature Studies*, 58:3 (2021), 604–622.

Emiljanowicz, P., 'Tensions, ambiguities, and connectivity in Kwame Nkrumah: rethinking the "national" in postcolonial nationalism', *Interventions*, 21:5 (2019), 615–634.

Emiljanowicz, P., 'From Karl Marx to Kwame Nkrumah: towards a decolonial political economy'. In Ndlovu-Gatsheni, S. and Ndlovu, M. (eds), *Marxism and Decolonisation in the 21st Century: Living Theories and True Ideas*. London: Routledge, 2021, 68–88.

Fadaee, S., *Social Movements in Iran: Environmentalism and Civil Society*. London: Routledge, 2012.

Fadaee, S., 'Bringing in the south: towards a global paradigm for social movement studies', *Interface: A Journal For and About Social Movements*, 9:2 (2017), 45–60.

Fadaee, S., 'Marxism, Islam and the Iranian revolution'. In Kirkpatrick, G., McMylor, P. and Fadaee, S. (eds), *Marxism, Religion and Emancipatory Politics*. London: Palgrave Macmillan, 2022.

Fanon, F., *A Dying Colonialism*. New York: Grove Press, 1994 [1964].

Fanon, F., *Toward the African Revolution*. New York: Grove Press, 1994 [1964].

Fanon, F., *Black Skin, White Masks*. London: Pluto Press, 2008 [1952].

Fanon, F., *The Wretched of the Earth*. New York: Grove Press, 2011 [1961].

Fanon, F., *Alienation and Freedom*. London: Bloomsbury Publishing, 2018.

Fanon Mendès-France, M. and Fhunsu, D., 'The contribution of Frantz Fanon to the process of the liberation of the people', *Black Scholar*, 42:3–4 (2012), 8–12.

Fenn, C., *Hồ Chí Minh: A Biographical Introduction*. London: Studio Vista, 1973.

Forsythe, D., 'Frantz Fanon – the Marx of the Third World', *Phylon*, 34:2 (1973), 160–170.

Foster, J. B., Clark, B. and Holleman, H., 'Marx and the indigenous', *Monthly Review*, 71:9 (2020), 1–19.

Freire, P., 'South African freedom fighter Amílcar Cabral: pedagogue of the revolution'. In Marcine, S. L. (ed.), *Critical Pedagogy in Uncertain Times: Hopes and Possibilities*. New York: Palgrave Macmillan, 2020, 159–181.

Friedman, J., *Shadow Cold War: The Sino–Soviet Competition for the Third World*. Chapel Hill: University of North Carolina Press, 2015.

Gao, M., *The Battle for China's Past: Mao and the Cultural Revolution*. London: Pluto Press, 2008.

Ghamari-Tabrizi, B., 'Contentious public religion: two conceptions of Islam in revolutionary Iran. Ali Shariati and Abdolkarim Soroush', *International Sociology*, 19:4 (2004), 504–523.

Gibson, N., 'Beyond Manicheanism: dialectics in the thought of Frantz Fanon', *Journal of Political Ideologies*, 4:3 (1999), 337–364.

Gibson, N., 'Fanon and Marx revisited', *Journal of the British Society for Phenomenology*, 51:4 (2020), 320–336.

Gokhale, B. G., 'Nehru and history', *History and Theory*, 17:3 (1978), 311–322.

Gopal, S., 'The formative ideology of Jawaharlal Nehru', *Economic and Political Weekly*, 11:21 (1976), 787–792.

Gopal, P., *Insurgent Empire: Anticolonial Resistance and British Dissent.* London: Verso, 2019.

Gopal, P., 'On decolonisation and the university', *Textual Practice*, 35:6 (2021), 873–899.

Guevara, E. C., *The Motorcycle Diaries: A Journey Around South America.* London: Verso, 1995.

Guevara, E. C., *Che Guevara Talks to Young People.* New York: Pathfinder, 2000.

Guevara, E. C., *Che Guevara Speaks.* New York: Pathfinder, 2000.

Guevara, E. C., *Socialism and Man in Cuba.* New York: Pathfinder, 2009 [1968].

Gupta, S. B., 'Growth of socialism in Congress and Nehru's role', *Indian Journal of Political Science*, 29:4 (1968), 359–368.

Hanley, D., 'Frantz Fanon – revolutionary nationalist?', *Political Studies*, 24:2 (1976), 120–131.

Hansen, W. W., 'Another side of Frantz Fanon: reflections on socialism and democracy', *New Political Science*, 19:3 (1997), 89–111.

Harper, T., *Underground Asia: Global Revolutionaries and the Assault on Empire.* London: Penguin, 2020.

Harris, R. L., 'Cuban internationalism, Che Guevara, and the survival of Cuba's socialist regime', *Latin American Perspectives*, 36:3 (2009), 27–42.

Harris, R. L., *Che Guevara: A Biography.* Santa Barbara: Greenwood Press, 2011.

Hazary, N., 'Democratic socialism and Jawaharlal Nehru', *Indian Journal of Political Science*, 26:4 (1965), 100–105.

Henck, N., 'Subcomandante Marcos: the latest reader', *Latin Americanist*, 58:2 (2014), 49–73.

Henck, N., *Insurgent Marcos: The Political-Philosophical Formation of the Zapatista Subcommander.* Raleigh: University of North Carolina Press, 2016.

Henck, N., *Subcomandante Marcos: Global Rebel Icon.* Montreal: Black Rose Books, 2019.

Herlinghaus, H., 'Subcomandante Marcos: narrative policy and epistemological project', *Journal of Latin American Cultural Studies*, 14:1 (2005), 53–74.

Hill, S., 'International solidarity: Cabral's legacy to the African-American community', *Latin American Perspectives*, 11:2 (1984), 67–80.

Hobsbawm, E., *The History of Marxism, Vol. 1*, London: Harvester Press, 1982.

Hodgkin, T., 'Nkrumah's radicalism', *Présence Africaine*, 85 (1973), 62–72.

Holloway, J., 'Dignity's revolt'. In Holloway, J. and Plaez, E. (eds), *Zapatista: Reinventing Revolution in Mexico*. London: Pluto Press, 1998, 159–198.

Holloway, J. and Pelaez, E. (eds), *Zapatista: Reinventing Revolution in Mexico*. London: Pluto Press, 1998.

Holubnychy, V., 'Mao Tse-tung's materialist dialectics', *China Quarterly*, 19 (1964), 3–37.

Hubbard, M., 'Culture and history in a revolutionary context: approaches to Amílcar Cabral', *Ufahamu: A Journal of African Studies*, 3:3 (1973), 69–86.

Hudis, P., *Frantz Fanon: Philosopher of the Barricades*. London: Pluto Press, 2015.

Hudis, P., 'Frantz Fanon's contribution to Hegelian Marxism', *Critical Sociology*, 43:6 (2017), 865–873.

Hughes, A., 'The appeal of Marxism to Africans', *Journal of Communist Studies and Transition Politics*, 8:2 (1992), 4–20.

James, C. L. R., *Nkrumah and the Ghana Revolution*. Durham: Duke University Press, 2022.

Keddie, N., *Roots of Revolution: An Interpretive History of Modern Iran*. New Haven: Yale University Press, 1981.

Khasnabish, A., *Zapatistas: Rebellion from the Grassroots to the Global*. London: Zed Books, 2010.

King, M. L. and West, C., *The Radical King*. Boston: Beacon Press, 2015.

Klein, N., 'The unknown icon', *Guardian*, 3 March 2001, https://www.theguardian.com/books/2001/mar/03/politics (accessed March 2024).

Knight, N., 'Soviet philosophy and Mao Zedong's "Sinification of Marxism"', *Journal of Contemporary Asia*, 20:1 (1990), 89–109.

Knight, N., 'Applying Marxism to Asian conditions: Mao Zedong, Hồ Chí Minh and the "universality" of Marxism'. In Glaser, D. and Walker, D. M. (eds), *Twentieth Century Marxism: A Global Introduction*. London: Routledge, 2007, 141–153.

Knight, N., *Rethinking Mao: Explorations in Mao Zedong's Thought*. Lanham: Lexington Books, 2007.

Koller, J. M., 'Philosophical aspects of Maoist thought', *Studies in Soviet Thought*, 14:1–2 (1974), 47–59.

Lenin, V. L., *Imperialism: The Highest Stage of Capitalism*. London: Penguin, 2010.

Lindner, K., *Marx, Marxism and the Question of Eurocentrism*. London: Palgrave Macmillan, 2022.

Llorente, R., *The Political Theory of Che Guevara*. Lanham: Rowman and Littlefield, 2018.

Loomba, A., *Colonialism/Postcolonialism*. London: Routledge, 2005.

Lopes, C. (ed.), *Africa's Contemporary Challenges: The Legacy of Amílcar Cabral*. London: Routledge, 2010.

Lorenzano, L., 'Zapatismo: recomposition of labour, radical democracy and revolutionary project'. In Holloway, J. and Plaez, E. (eds), *Zapatista: Reinventing Revolution in Mexico*. London: Pluto Press, 1998, 126–158.

Louro, M. L., *Comrades Against Imperialism: Nehru, India, and Interwar Internationalism*. Cambridge: Cambridge University Press, 2018.

Löwy, M., *The Marxism of Che Guevara: Philosophy, Economics, Revolutionary Warfare*. Lanham: Rowman and Littlefield, 2007.

Lugones, M., 'Heterosexualism and the colonial/modern gender system', *Hypatia*, 22:1 (2007), 186–209.

Lundy, B., 'The importance of cultural capital in rebuilding a successful education system in Guinea-Bissau'. In Manji, F. and Fletcher Jr, B. (eds), *Claim No Easy Victories: The Legacy of Amílcar Cabral*. Dakar: Codesria and Daraja Press, 2013, 365–378.

Macey, D., *Frantz Fanon: A Biography*. London: Verso Books, 2012.

Magubane, B., 'Amílcar Cabral: evolution of revolutionary thought', *Ufahamu: A Journal of African Studies*, 2:2 (1971), 71–87.

Magubane, B., 'Toward a sociology of national liberation from colonialism: Cabral's legacy', *Contemporary Marxism*, 7 (1983), 5–27.

Mahdavi, M., 'Post-Islamist trends in postrevolutionary Iran', *Comparative Studies of South Asia, Africa and the Middle East*, 31:1 (2011), 94–109.

Manji, F. and Fletcher Jr, B. (eds), *Claim No Easy Victories: The Legacy of Amílcar Cabral*. Dakar: Codesria and Daraja Press, 2013.

Mao, Z., *Selected Works of Mao Tse-tung, Vol. 1*. Peking: Foreign Languages Press, 1965.

Mao, Z., *Selected Works of Mao Tse-tung, Vol. 2*. Peking: Foreign Languages Press, 1965.

Marcos, S., 'The Fourth World War has begun', *Nepantla: Views from the South* (1997), 559–572.

Marcos, S., *Our Word Is Our Weapon: Selected Writings*. New York: Seven Stories Press, 2002.

Marcos, S., Marquez, G. G. and Pombo, R., 'Punch card and hourglass', *New Left Review*, 9 (2001), 69–79.

Marouda, M., 'The unending death of an immortal: the state commemoration of Hồ Chí Minh in contemporary Viet Nam', *South East Asia Research*, 21:2 (2013), 303–321.

Martin, T., 'Rescuing Fanon from the critics', *African Studies Review*, 13:3 (1970), 381–399.

Marx, K., *Capital, Vol. 1*. London: Penguin, 1976.

Marx, K. and Engels, F., *The Communist Manifesto*. London: Penguin, 2004.

Matin, K., 'Decoding political Islam: uneven and combined development and Ali Shariati's political thought'. In Shilliam, R. (ed.), *International Relations and Non-Western Thought: Imperialism, Colonialism and Investigations of Global Modernity*. London: Routledge, 2010, 124–140.

Mayer, A., *Naija Marxisms: Revolutionary Thought in Nigeria*. London: Pluto Press, 2016.

Mazrui, A., 'Nkrumah: the Leninist czar', *Transition*, 75–76 (1966), 106–126.

McCulloch, J., 'Amílcar Cabral: a theory of imperialism', *Journal of Modern African Studies*, 19:3 (1981), 503–511.

McCulloch, J., *In the Twilight of Revolution: The Political Theory of Amílcar Cabral*. London: Routledge, 2020.

McLaren, P., 'Revolutionary leadership and pedagogical praxis: revisiting the legacy of Che Guevara', *International Journal of Leadership in Education*, 2:3 (1999), 269–292.

McLaren, P., *Che Guevara, Paulo Freire, and the Pedagogy of Revolution*. Lanham: Rowman and Littlefield, 2000.

McLaren, P., 'Foreword', in Löwy, M., *The Marxism of Che Guevara: Philosophy, Economics, Revolutionary Warfare* (Lanham: Rowman and Littlefield, 2007).

Meghji, A., *Decolonizing Sociology: An Introduction*. Cambridge: Polity Press, 2020.

Meisenhelder, T., 'Amílcar Cabral's theory of class suicide and revolutionary socialism', *Monthly Review*, 45:6 (1993), 40–48.

Mendy, P. K., 'Amílcar Cabral and the liberation of Guinea-Bissau: context, challenges and lessons for effective African leadership', *African Identities*, 4:1 (2006), 7–21.

Mendy, P. K., *Amílcar Cabral: Nationalist and Pan-Africanist Revolutionary*. Athens: Ohio University Press, 2019.

Mentinis, M., *Zapatistas: The Chiapas Revolt and What It Means for Radical Politics*. London: Pluto Press, 2006.

Metz, S., 'In lieu of orthodoxy: the socialist theories of Nkrumah and Nyerere', *Journal of Modern African Studies*, 20:3 (1982), 377–392.

Mezzadra, S. and Samaddar, R., 'Colonialism'. In Musto, M. (ed.), *The*

Marx Revival: Key Concepts and New Interpretations. Cambridge: Cambridge University Press, 2020, 247–265.

Minh, H. C., *Hồ Chí Minh on Revolution: Selected Writings 1920–66*. New York: Praeger, 1967.

Mohan, J., 'Jawaharlal Nehru and his socialism', *India International Centre Quarterly*, 2:3 (1975), 183–192.

Moreno, J. A., 'Che Guevara on guerrilla warfare: doctrine, practice and evaluation', *Comparative Studies in Society and History*, 12:2 (1970), 114–133.

Mukandabantu, A. M., 'The political thought of Amílcar Cabral: a review article', *Review of African Political Economy*, 27–28 (1983), 207–2013.

Mukherjee, A., 'Nehru's legacy: inclusive democracy and people's empowerment', *Economic and Political Weekly*, 50:16 (2015), 38–45.

Musto, M. (ed.) *The Marx Revival: Key Concepts and New Interpretations*. Cambridge: Cambridge University Press, 2020.

Nanda, B. R., *Jawaharlal Nehru: Rebel and Statesman*. New Delhi: Oxford University Press, 1998.

Nayar, P. N., *Frantz Fanon*. London: Routledge, 2013.

Nehru, J., 'The basic approach', *AICC Economic Review: Fortnightly Journal of the Economic and Political Research Department of the All India Congress Committee*, 10:8–9 (1958).

Nehru, J., *An Autobiography*. New Delhi: Penguin Books, 2004.

Nizami, T. A., 'Marxism and the Communist Party of India', *Indian Journal of Political Science*, 29:2 (1968), 107–113.

Nkrumah, K., *The Autobiography of Kwame Nkrumah*. Edinburgh: Thomas Nelson and Sons, 1957.

Nkrumah, K., *Towards Colonial Freedom: Africa in the Struggle Against World Imperialism*. London: Heinemann, 1962.

Nkrumah, K., *Africa Must Unite*. New York: Praeger, 1964 [1963].

Nkrumah, K., *Neo-Colonialism: The Last Stage of Imperialism*. New York: International Publishers, 1965.

Nkrumah, K., *Handbook of Revolutionary Warfare: A Guide to the Armed Phase of the African Revolution*. New York: International Publishers, 1968.

Nkrumah, K., *Consciencism: Philosophy and ideology for De-colonization*. New York: Monthly Review Press, 1970 [1964].

Nkrumah, K., *Class Struggle in Africa*. New York: International Publishers, 1972 [1970].

Nkrumah, K., *Revolutionary Path*. London: Panaf, 1973.

Nursey-Bray, P., 'Marxism and existentialism in the thought of Frantz Fanon', *Political Studies*, 20:2 (1972), 152–168.

Nursey-Bray, P., 'Race and nation: ideology in the thought of Frantz Fanon', *Journal of Modern African Studies*, 18:1 (1980), 135–142.

Nzongola-Ntalaja, G., 'Amílcar Cabral and the theory of the national liberation struggle', *Latin American Perspectives*, 11:2 (1984), 43–54.

O'Hearn, D., 'Foreword, forward!' In Lynd, S. and Grubačić, A. (eds), *Wobblies and Zapatistas: Conversations on Anarchism, Marxism, and Radical History*. Oakland: PM Press, 2008, xi–xx.

Orr-Álvarez, B., 'Masking Revolution: Subcomandante Marcos and the contemporary Zapatista movement'. In Santos, A. (ed.), *Performing Utopias in the Contemporary Utopias*. New York: Palgrave Macmillan, 2017, 111–129.

Parris, L. T., 'Frantz Fanon: existentialist, dialectician, and revolutionary', *Journal of Pan African Studies*, 4:7 (2011), 4–23.

Parry, B., 'Directions and dead-ends in postcolonial studies'. In Goldberg, D. T. and Quayson, A. (eds), *Relocating Postcolonialism* (Wiley-Blackwell, 2002).

Parry, B., *Postcolonial Studies: A Materialist Critique*. London: Routledge, 2004.

Parry, B., 'Edward Said and Third-World Marxism', *College Literature*, 40:4 (2013), 105–126.

Patel, S. (ed.), *The ISA Handbook of Diverse Sociological Traditions*. London: Sage, 2009.

Petras, J., 'Latin America: the resurgence of the left', *New Left Review*, 223 (1997), 17–47.

Piketty, T., *Capital in the Twenty-First Century*. Cambridge: Harvard University Press, 2014.

Poe, D. Z., *Kwame Nkrumah's Contribution to Pan-Africanism: An Afrocentric Analysis*. New York: Routledge, 2003.

Power, P. F., 'Indian foreign policy: the age of Nehru', *Review of Politics*, 26:2 (1964), 257–286.

Pradella, L., 'Imperialism and capitalist development in Marx's *Capital*', *Historical Materialism*, 21:2 (2013), 117–147.

Pradella, L., *Globalisation and the Critique of Political Economy: New Insights from Marx's Writing*. London: Routledge, 2015.

Pradella, L., 'Marx and the global South: connecting history and value theory', *Sociology*, 51:1 (2017), 146–161.

Pradella, L., 'Postcolonial theory and the making of the world working class', *Critical Sociology*, 43:4–5 (2017), 573–586.

Prashad, V., *Red Star Over the Third World*. London: Pluto Press, 2017.

Purushotham, S., 'World history in the atomic age: past, present and future in the political thought of Jawaharlal Nehru', *Modern Intellectual History*, 14:3 (2017), 837–867.

Quijano, A., 'Coloniality and modernity/rationality', *Cultural Studies,* 21:2 (2007), 168–178.

Rabaka, R., *Africana Critical Theory: Reconstructing the Black Radical Tradition, from W. E. B. Du Bois and C. L. R. James to Frantz Fanon and Amílcar Cabral.* Lanham: Lexington Books, 2009.

Rabaka, R., *Forms of Fanonism: Frantz Fanon's Critical Theory and the Dialectics of Decolonization.* Lanham: Lexington Books, 2010.

Rabaka, R., 'Revolutionary Fanonism: on Frantz Fanon's modification of Marxism and decolonization of democratic socialism', *Socialism and Democracy,* 25:1 (2011), 126–145.

Rabaka, R., 'The weapon of critical theory: Amílcar Cabral, Cabralism, and Africana critical theory'. In Cabral, A., *Resistance and Decolonisation.* London: Rowman and Littlefield, 2016, 3–42.

Rahnema, A., *An Islamic Utopian: A Political Biography of Ali Shari'ati.* London: I. B. Tauris, 1998.

Rahnema, A., 'Ali Shariati: teacher, preacher, rebel'. In Rahnema, A. (ed.), *Pioneers of Islamic Revival.* London: Zed Books, 2005, 208–250.

Raj, K. N., 'Nehru, the Congress and class conflict', *Economic Weekly.* Special number (1964), 1231–1234.

Rao, V. V., 'Socialist thought of Jawaharlal Nehru', *Indian Journal of Political Science,* 48:2 (1987), 195–211.

Rathore, L. S., 'Political ideas of Jawaharlal Nehru: some reflections', *Indian Journal of Political Science,* 46:4 (1985), 451–473.

Rooney, D., *Kwame Nkrumah: Vision and Tragedy.* Accra: Sub-Saharan Publishers, 2007.

Rothwell, M., 'The road is tortuous: the Chinese revolution and the end of the global sixties', *Izquierdas,* 50 (2021). http://dx.doi.org/10.4067/s0718-50492021000100219 (accessed March 2024).

Saffari, S., *Beyond Shariati.* Cambridge: Cambridge University Press, 2017.

Said, E. W., *Orientalism.* New York: Pantheon Books, 1978.

Said, E. W., 'Traveling theory'. In Said, E. W. (ed.), *The World, the Text, and the Critic.* Cambridge: Harvard University Press, 1983, 226–247.

Santos, B. de Sousa, *Epistemologies of the South: Justice Against Epistemicide.* London: Routledge, 2014.

Santos, B. de Sousa, *The End of the Cognitive Empire: The Coming of Age of Epistemologies of the South.* Durham: Duke University Press, 2018.

Schram, S. R., 'Chinese and Leninist components in the personality of Mao Tse-tung', *Asian Survey,* 3:6 (1963), 259–273.

Schram, S. R., *The Political Thought of Mao Tse-tung.* Harmondsworth: Penguin Books, 1969.

Schram, S. R., *Mao Tse-tung.* Harmondsworth: Penguin Books, 1971 [1967].

Schram, S. R., 'Mao Tse-tung and the theory of the permanent revolution, 1958–69', *China Quarterly*, 46 (1971), 221–244.

Schram, S. R. (ed.), *Mao Tse-tung Unrehearsed: Talks and Letters, 1956–71*. Harmondsworth: Penguin Books, 1974.

Schram, S. R., 'Mao Tse-tung's thought from 1949 to 1976'. In MacFaquhar, R. and Fairbank, J. K. (eds), *The Cambridge History of China*. Cambridge: Cambridge University Press, 1991, 1–104.

Schram, S. R., 'Mao Zedong a hundred years on: the legacy of a ruler', *China Quarterly*, 137 (1994), 125–143.

Schwartz, B. L., *Chinese Communism and the Rise of Mao*. New York: Harper and Row, 1951.

Schwartz, B. L., 'The reign of virtue – some broad perspectives on leader and part in the cultural revolution', *China Quarterly*, 35 (1968), 1–17.

Schwarz, C., 'An agronomist before his time'. In Manji, F. and Fletcher, B. (eds), *Claim No Easy Victories: The Legacy of Amílcar Cabral*. Dakar: Codesria and Daraja Press, 213, 79–94.

Seth, S., 'Nehruvian socialism 1927–1937: nationalism, Marxism, and the pursuit of modernity', *Alternatives*, 18:4 (193), 453–473.

Shahibzadeh, Y., *Islamism and Post-Islamism in Iran: An Intellectual History*. New York: Palgrave, 2016.

Shariati, A., *Marxism and Other Western Fallacies*. Translated by R. Campbell. Berkeley: Mizan Press, 1980.

Shariati, A., *Man and Islam*. Translated by Hamid Algar. Berkeley: Mizan Press, 1981.

Shariati, A., *Religion vs. Religion*. Translated by Laleh Bakhtiar. Chicago: ABC International Group, 2010.

Shariati, A., *On the Sociology of Islam*. Translated by H. Algar. Berkeley: Mizan Press, 2017 [1979].

Sherlock, S., 'Berlin, Moscow and Bombay: the Marxism that India inherited', *South Asia: Journal of South Asian Studies*, 21:1 (1998), 63–76.

Singh, K., 'Jawaharlal Nehru as a humanist', *India International Centre Quarterly*, 6:2 (1979), 115–118.

Singh, S. K., 'Hồ Chí Minh and Vietnam's struggle for freedom', *Proceedings of the Indian History Congress, Indian History Congress*, 70 (2009), 795–801.

Smith, M. N., 'The limits of postcolonial critique of Marxism: a defence of radical universalism'. In Ndlovu-Gatsheni, S. and Ndlovu, M. (eds), *Marxism and Decolonisation in the 21st Century: Living Theories and True Ideas*. London: Routledge, 2021, 49–67.

Son, B. N., 'The Confucian foundations of Hồ Chí Minh's vision of government', *Journal of Oriental Studies*, 46:1 (2013), 35–59.

Sundar, N., *The Burning Forest: India's War Against the Maoists*. London: Verso, 2019.

Tavassoli, G., 'A bibliographical sketch'. In Shariati, A. (ed.), *On the Sociology of Islam*. Translated by H. Algar. Berkeley: Mizan Press, 2017 [1979].

Terrill, R., *Mao: A Biography*. Stanford: Stanford University Press, 1999.

Therborn, G., 'Dialectics of modernity: on critical theory and the legacy of twentieth-century Marxism', *New Left Review* (1996), 59–81.

Time Magazine, 'The legacy of Hồ Chí Minh', 12 September 1969. https://content.time.com/time/subscriber/article/0,33009,901394,00.html (accessed March 2024).

Tomás, A., *Amílcar Cabral: The Life of a Reluctant Nationalist*. London: Hurst and Company, 2021.

Traverso, E., *Revolution: An Intellectual History*. London: Verso, 2021.

Tuck, E. and Yang, K. W., 'Decolonization is not a metaphor', *Decolonization: Indigeneity, Education and Society* 1:1 (2012), 1–40.

Tunteng, P. K., 'Kwame Nkrumah and the African revolution', *Civilisations*, 23–24:3–4 (1973), 233–247.

Ude, D. M. C., 'Kwasi Wiredu's critique of Marxism: its philosophical application to the "African socialism" via Nkrumah, Nyerere and Touré', *Africology: The Journal of Pan African Studies*, 12:5 (2018), 181–207.

Viswanathaiah, K. V., 'Jawaharlal Nehru's concept of democratic socialism', *Indian Journal of Political Science*, 26:4 (1965), 91–99.

von Hatzfeldt, G., 'Agonistic democracy: the endurance of the Gandhi and Nehru legacy', *Contemporary South Asia*, 24:2 (2016), 149–163.

Wallerstein, I., 'Frantz Fanon: reason and violence', *Berkeley Journal of Sociology*, 15 (1970), 222–231.

Wei, C. X. G., 'Mao's legacy revisited: its lasting impact on China and post-Mao era reform', *Asian Politics and Policy*, 3:1 (2011), 3–27.

Wick, A., 'Manifestations of nationhood in the writings of Amílcar Cabral', *African Identities*, 4:1 (2006), 45–70.

Willmott, W. E., 'Thoughts on Hồ Chí Minh', *Pacific Affairs*, 44:4 (1971), 585–590.

Witzler, R., 'Ali Shariati: red Shiism and revolution in Iran', *Religious Studies Honors Projects*, paper 8 (2010).

Womack, B., *The Foundations of Mao Zedong's Political Thought, 1917–1935*. Honolulu: University Press of Hawaii, 1982.

Xiaorong, H., *Chinese Discourses on the Peasants, 1900–1949*. Albany: State University of New York Press, 2005.

Yaffe, H., *Che Guevara: The Economics of Revolution*. Basingstoke: Palgrave Macmillan, 2009.

Yaffe, H., 'Che Guevara's enduring legacy: not the *foco* but the theory of socialist construction', *Latin American Perspectives*, 36:2 (2009), 49–65.

Yaffe, H., 'Che Guevara and the Great Debate, past and present', *Science and Society*, 76:1 (2012), 11–40.

Yaffe, H., 'Che Guevara: cooperatives and the political economy of socialist transition'. In Piñeiro Harnecker, C. (ed.), *Cooperatives and Socialism: A View from Cuba*. Basingstoke: Palgrave Macmillan, 2013, 115–142.

Ypi, L., 'Democratic dictatorship: political legitimacy in Marxist perspective', *European Journal of Philosophy*, 28:2 (2020), 277–291.

Yu, G. T., 'Africa in Chinese foreign policy', *Asian Survey*, 28 (1988), 849–862.

Zak, T. F., 'Applying the weapon of theory: comparing the philosophy of Julius Kambarage Nyerere and Kwame Nkrumah', *Journal of African Cultural Studies*, 28:2 (2016), 147–160.

Acknowledgements

This book was born out of despair with the world we live in and hope for a better world that is yet to come. Researching and writing it has been a startling journey that opened up new horizons in my thinking and praxis. Thanks to Frank Welz and his Global Studies Programme, in my early twenties I studied in Germany, South Africa and India with a group of international students. This experience helped me put things into perspective at a rather young age. Growing up in post-revolutionary Iran, where hope turned to despair, and revolutionaries to prisoners, exposed me first-hand to the challenges of emancipatory struggles. Nevertheless, I soon learned the world was a more challenging place than I had thought. There was no other way but to learn from and contribute to other struggles in the years to come.

The journey I have gone through has been possible only because of the insights and support of many friends, colleagues and comrades around the world. They are too many to name here, but I owe my deepest gratitude to them all. My life would have been very different without Boike Rehbein. He was a great teacher, mentor and friend during my years in Germany and played an important role in my scholarly development as a global sociologist. His sudden death has left a huge gap among his friends, colleagues and students. He is dearly missed. The International Sociological Association (ISA) has been such a stimulating space for critical sociological debates beyond the common Eurocentrism of many academic associations. I have benefited from participation and great discussions at numerous ISA conferences and events around the world. One person who particularly stands out in this experience is Michael Burawoy and I am grateful to him.

In 2018, I joined the Sociology Department at the University of Manchester and have been there ever since. I have numerous caring and inspiring colleagues. I am so fortunate to be part of a department that is not detached from the most pressing issues of our times. I could not have had a better research group than movements@manchester. Our reading groups, events and the annual Alternative Futures and Popular Protests conference we organise have influenced the writing of this book in many ways. My students are so curious about the real issues of this world. Their curiosity teaches me a great deal. Living in Manchester, a city where Marx and Engels regularly met and worked, has been such a treat and inspiration. My favourite place remains Chetham's Library, where they undertook research for *The Communist Manifesto*. The city has kept its radical tradition and I feel lucky to be part of the community of comrades and friends who live there.

A number of colleagues and friends kindly read parts of the manuscript and provided valuable comments. I am indebted to Wenxing Cui, Zeyad El Nabolsy, Tom Gillespie, Peter Hudis, Graeme Kirkpatrick, Peter Mendy, Chris Moffat, Susann Pham Thi, Seth Schindler and Helen Yaffe. I alone am fully responsible for any mistakes the book may contain. Kim Walker of Manchester University Press showed much enthusiasm for this book. I appreciate her support and thank the team that has worked with me during the publication process. A huge thank you goes to my parents, Ashraf and Shareef, for all their unfailing care and encouragement. They raised me with values that were instrumental in writing this book. Seth's role has been enormous. We share the everyday, travel, meet people, read and discuss. He is the utmost source of intellectual curiosity and support. My greatest thanks are to him.

Index

Eurocentrism 3, 7, 272

Fanon, J. 135–136
Fanon Mendès-France, M. 152
Freire, P. 118, 128

Gadea, H. 156–158
Gandhi, I. 26
Gandhi, M. 26–27, 41, 64
Gramsci, A. 221
    see also organic intellectual
Great Debate 167–170
Great Leap Forward 78–79, 83

Hegel, G. W. F. 91, 135, 141
historical materialism 31, 94
Hobsbawm, E. 1, 22

internationalism 27, 55–56, 153,
    161, 173, 221
Iranian Revolution 175, 179,
    190–192

James, C. L. R. 18, 90, 106

Kautsky, K. 70, 220
King, M. L. 44, 215

land reform 42, 59, 61–62, 212
League against Imperialism and
    Colonial Oppression 27–28
Lenin, V. 8, 10–11, 36, 50–51,
    54–57, 59–60, 83, 91, 97–98,
    106, 110, 113, 139, 155, 165,
    198, 224
liberation theology 178, 191
Long March 72
Lumumba, P. 159
Luxemburg, R. 8

March, A. 158
Marxism-Leninism 54, 56–57, 97,
    201

May Fourth Movement 70
Mosaddegh, M. 177–178

NAFTA *see* North American Free
    Trade Agreement
nationalism 11, 16, 24–25, 27–29,
    32–33, 35–36, 41, 52, 55–56,
    59, 61–62, 90, 146, 219
Naxalite movement 2
    see also Naxalites
Naxalites 87
Négritude movement 113, 120,
    134–135
Nehru, K. 26
neo-colonialism 94, 96–100,
    102, 104–105, 107–108, 117,
    121–122, 165, 182
    see also anti-colonialism
neoliberalism 203–204, 211,
    213–214, 219
Non-Aligned Movement 44, 158
non-cooperation movement
    26–27
North American Free Trade
    Agreement (NAFTA) 195,
    199, 201–202, 206, 212, 220
Nyerere, J. 145, 171

October Revolution 2, 10, 28, 50,
    54, 69, 72, 74
organic intellectual 131, 221–222

Padmore, G. 91
Pan-African Congress 20, 91, 107
Pan-Africanism 12, 103, 105, 108,
    217
    see also Pan-African Congress
Paris Peace Conference 49
Peasant Movement Training
    Institute 52, 71
permanent revolution 12, 67,
    78–79, 83, 217
public sector 36, 42